Praise for

SOME NEW KIND OF TRAILER TRASH,
PART ONE

"In print, as in person, Brad Blanton is at ease in this first volume of his autobiography, *Some NEW Kind of Trailer Trash,* telling any tale about himself, including the most intimate, demonstrating the interior security and self-deprecating humor, which it would seem support his international reputation as a gestalt therapist, seminar leader, and writer published all over the world.

"He owns into his life in all its aspects, and finds in his weirdness his salvation, demonstrating the radical honesty he's made famous, and rooting his self-understanding, which is considerable, in his childhood. I love this model so much I'm thinking about stealing it. It's a great read. In the growing body of memoirs about the American upheavals commonly known as the 60s you won't find another to rival this one for a wild ride, an exemplary union of idiocy and brilliance, flat out truth telling about everything, irreverent rants, hard-earned self-discernment, and the existential creation of meaning and purpose. Read it and weep, as I did, for the cost and the promise of living into one's truth and finding there the one heart we all share.

"In the days to come, when we and our children face into the results of our political choices, Brad Blanton's work against artifice and subterfuge and in support of deep democracy in all situations will be widely read as a guide from the dark to the light."

> —*Casey Hayden, founding member of Students for a Democratic Society and the Student Nonviolent Coordinating Committee, and contributor to* Deep in Our Hearts: Nine White Women in the Freedom Movement, Being Bodies: Buddhist Women on the Paradox of Embodiment *and* Hands on the Freedom Plow: Personal Accounts by Women in SNCC

"*Some NEW Kind of Trailer Trash* speaks directly to the 'trailer trash' in each of us and serves as a living example of how we—each and every one of us—is challenged to find the balance between being an asshole and being a hero in life. And the way to uncork our courage to take a stand and consciously destroy the useless and barren ideals so we can create present moment beauty and open the gate for real transformation is to be with, express, and accept the particular kind of asshole that we are so that we don't, in trying to manage or control ourselves or others, lose, smother, or cripple the hero we could be and in fact are. There's an angel/asshole in each of us, and to love the asshole gives us a way to 'hire' that part of our nature to do good. That way we are less likely to blow up our own happiness and more likely to be contactful authentic beings consciously capable of co-creating life together. You may not find yourself willing (or even have that much desire) to as fully express anger or take risks as wild, or spend as much time (or as many ways) having sex as Brad describes in his book, yet I'd bet good money (and a chunk of your happiness) that the gods of change, desire, and creation within you are too often stopped by the old rules and the deference to external authority rather than being given freedom to take us more deeply and intimately into the wonderful, mystical, and sacred world hidden in plain sight behind the wall of belief and suppression that dulls our senses.

"This book takes what is taboo and restores it to realm of sacred, showing how, albeit imperfectly, the wounded healers and sacred tricksters throughout myth and history, often lived full and reckless lives yet inspired and assisted humanity along the way."

—*Raven Dana, author of* The Resurrection of the Mortician's Daughter

"Brad Blanton has managed to mix a lot of wisdom, charm, and truthtelling into a fun and joyous autobiography that is a pleasure to read. You learn more about America in his story than you will from dozens of years of watching the TV news or reading the newspapers or attending most colleges! Read and enjoy."

—*Rabbi Michael Lerner, editor of* Tikkun Magazine, *chair of the interfaith Network of Spiritual Progressives, and author of* Embracing Israel/Palestine

"Oh, my, we are in for it now! Brad Blanton, lifelong dispenser of crazy wisdom, blatant truth, and sidesplitting blather, has written an autobiography, and I for one couldn't be happier! I've been a big fan of Brad's writings from the get-go and have always wondered where a guy like that could've possibly come from. It turns out he comes from pretty much the same place I'm from and the same

place the rest of us can come from, too: a sincere dedication to telling the truth always and in all ways, even if you have to be obnoxious about it from time to time. Read this book, and find out how you, too, can become an enlightened hillbilly, spiritually evolved atheist, pure-truth bullshit artist who is focused night and day on waking himself and the rest of us up from the Big Trance."
     —Gay Hendricks, author of The Big Leap *and* Five Wishes, *and co-author of* Conscious Loving

"Brad's story is medicine for our time. I hope many people of my generation read this book, so that we can learn from the courage, struggles, mistakes, and realizations of his."
     —Charles Eisenstein, author of The Ascent of Humanity *and* Sacred Economics, *and other books and stuff. He writes about civilization, economics, consciousness, and the transition to a post-bullshit age*

"You can learn from Brad Blanton, his life, and his book. He is a radical and conservative all wrapped up into one human being. He wants to change things a lot for the better, so he is a radical. And he wants the things that are working today and have worked forever, to keep working, so he is a conservative. You can learn from Brad's courage and you can learn from what he wants to teach. Read and laugh and think and learn, and enjoy the journey. This book will really take you someplace, and it's a good place for sure."
     —Herb Rubenstein, founder and executive director of THE LEEEGH (Leadership in Education, Energy, Environment, Governance and Health), co-author of Leadership Development for Educators

"Brad Blanton changed my life. Everyone will benefit from hearing his story."
     —Mandy Stadtmiller, reporter New York Post

"I know Brad Blanton enough to flat out say that his is a life worth knowing, full of bold, adventurous and purposeful undertakings on behalf of himself and his friends and community. Brad's decision to go for radical honesty adds a unique dimension to the meaning of life and a powerful contrast to most autobiography."
     —John Breeding, author of The Wildest Colts Make the Best Horses

"I first read Dr. Brad Blanton's books on radical honesty many years ago. Then, I took some of his courses, which made a powerful, positive difference in my life and my business. He delivers the message that being radically honest, authentic, and direct is far more effective than other ways of being and communicating. I suggest that you read this book if you want to increase your enjoyment of life and your self-respect."

—*Jacques Werth, president,* High Probability Selling

"When I met Brad some years ago at a conference in Mexico and sat down to read *Radical Honesty,* by the end of the first few *paragraphs,* I thought, "Who IS this guy?! He writes as if he doesn't care what people think!" And that turns out to be the whole point. In fact, in *Some NEW Kind of Trailer Trash,* he shows us the awesome, life changing power of coming completely clean about everything—with everyone. The world would tell us that makes us vulnerable and therefore weak. Brad shows us that it gives us the only kind of strength that ultimately lasts. Oh, and it makes us absolutely unbeatable."

—John J. Scherer, author of *Work and the Human Spirit* and *Five Questions that Change Everything* and honored by Stephen Covey as one of America's Top 100 Thought Leaders in Personal Development (he is number 77, just to be radically honest about it...). International change consultant for leaders and their organizations since 1980.

Here are some more comments from Raven Dana—sent to me in emails before and after she wrote the blurb up above… I like to call them Raven's ravins'… They make me happy and they are kind of a sampler so I'm putting them in here.

"I am loving it… the beginning about the Scots-Irish especially spoke to me, of course since we share that background… and when you wrote: 'Lord, lord. Pride and shame. I am proud to have the chance to apologize for all this. This is the blessing and the curse. This is the hole out of which I am still climbing, and from which I claim to have gained some virtue.' I was reminded of something else I just read about the pagan inheritors of the Scots-Irish traditions, otherwise known as the Faery Tradition (not like little flitting beings, more like the tradition that bridges the communication gap between seen and unseen influences) in which it is said that our responsibility is to redeem our ancestors—not in the Christian sense but in the sense that since we carry their accumulated history in our DNA it is our task to become more conscious beings and thereby right some of the wrongs our ancestors perpetuated on others and on each other. I really like that idea." *(So do I.—Brad)*

"I love the flashbacks... and occasionally I read something and it sends me off into my own history and I have to stop a few minutes and let whatever got triggered play out... I'm having quite a ride... I so appreciate you for how you are writing this... I also enjoy the good guy/asshole reality of being human that comes through... examples...

"'My capacity for compassion was growing, as was my inner rigidity as a moralistic dictator and a self-righteous prick.'...

"'I am responsible for the cultures I have been in, as they live in me; and I am the one responsible for the violence I've perpetrated on the people I love. This has become less as I've become older, but I haven't set any God-damned speed records getting over myself.'"

"I had to go back and re-read my favorite parts and laugh and cry all over again...What I have taken away most from your life story (Part One), or at least the meaning I have made of it, is some way in which we all, while doing the best we can—which sometimes ain't so great—still have this enormous capacity to tip the scales towards love and kindness by getting over ourselves and accepting our-selves and each other, warts and all. This book has moments of unexpected beauty through sadness and anger as well as celebration. I find myself happier after read-ing this book to have had the life I had and more courageous to peel back the cur-tains and expose my own life with deeper honesty. So many times as I read I had to just stop and let my own memories wash over me, and then think about the similarities between your story and my own. I think that all our stories serve each other in the telling. We can remember what's important: that we survived the bad times, took away some real gifts from them, and perhaps because of them, learned to appreciate the good times, the simple pleasures, and the kindness of others."

"THESE PARAGRAPHS (made me sob, by the way)...

"'My therapist looked at me, and then she reached over and touched me, and said, 'It's okay if you do. Go ahead and feel sorry for yourself. You've had some pretty hard times in your life. It's okay if you feel sorry for yourself. Go ahead.'

"'All of a sudden I just started crying. Then I cried and cried and cried. No one had ever told me that before. I'd never told myself that before. I never even considered the option. I couldn't believe it was okay to feel sorry for myself, and when I did it a whole floodgate was opened. Grief flowed through me like a river. I cried until my bones ached. That little boy I was trying to take care of all the time wasn't just my younger brother and my baby brother, he was me. The people I helped in the community and in the group therapy groups and wanted to help as a therapist, and the people I was fighting for in the civil rights movement, were who they were, but they were not just who they were—they were me, too.

"'Up until that moment I could feel sorry for anyone else in the world but myself. And still it was me I was feeling sorry for when I did. Why not feel sorry for all of us, including me? Why not? It's okay. Go ahead. So I did. And I do. I am crying right now as I'm writing this. But I am not resisting it. I've never resisted it again like I did before that therapy session. When my sadness deepens and I let myself experience it, I feel better again: less angry, less depressed, and more willing to forgive even myself.

"'I still hate whiners, particularly when they compare themselves to other people and make themselves the greater victim and try to torture those around them with their indirect bitching and whining. But now I can work with them because I see they're disowning anger in themselves, just as I disowned, and still occasionally disown, my grief. We recognize each other after a while and quit lying about what it is we're really feeling, and it helps us move on to other stuck places instead of staying stuck in just one place, which is practically the whole point of therapy.

"'Therapy is feeling your way through, and not avoiding anything, and then moving on to the next place of resistance—until there's less resistance altogether and more willingness to be where and how you are.

"'I am grateful for those years of psychotherapy when I was in college and for the years of therapy, psychoanalysis, and training therapy I did for years during and after receiving my doctorate. The insights I got into what makes me tick were helpful, but not nearly as much as the opportunity to feel what I hadn't let myself feel. My listening improved and my capacity for empathy eventually sometimes included myself.…

"'My disdain for authority wasn't all bad. I think the civil rights movement was therapeutic for me and for a lot of my fellow protesters as well. We were a bunch of neurotic kids. We were doing battle the best we could with a bunch of neurotic so-called adults. But we knew that we'd learned a lot of things those people didn't have a glimmer about, and that they had no right to impose their ignorance on us or on anyone else. By God, we were going to see to it that they didn't. We learned not only from books and therapy, but also from drugs and honesty about our own and society's pretenses—things we knew the "authorities" didn't know shit about.

"'The same was true of the anti-Vietnam War movement: It was therapeutic. That whole total waste-of-life phony fucking war came and went, and all it did was keep the phony bureaucracy in place along with the phony capitalist-corporate-fascist dictatorship. The problem is, after all these years, that nothing of great substance has really changed. Period. The therapy hasn't worked for society. Most of us never grow up beyond the feelings of being jilted and abused as children, or being invested in denying it, partly because we are swimming in a culture of denial and ignorance in the first God-damned place.'"

"I especially liked the story in Chapter 36 (in the fog), and also the one that followed in Chapter 37 (in Greece) and that they followed each other... the play of scenery, mood emotion... just lovely and moving.

"I read those two chapters three times...

"Here are a few more quotes I especially liked:

"'I've said before, as have many others, that the only thing that can save us is love—for all of each other and with all of being. But now I think love will probably not save us. Most of the time, the love human beings experience is not wide enough. Love for a narrower, smaller family group brings about defense against, and violence toward other groups. In our evolutionary social experiment to get all the goodies or nothing, the limbic brain is failing to integrate with the prefrontal lobes soon enough. We cannot develop the capacity to care for all human beings, much less all beings, as our own. Humankind is coming to an end because of our failure to include all life as our own.'...

"'Love, and the loss of it, and the poison often mixed with it, is the very source of the sadness and the meanness in the world. People learn to live by what they've learned whether they learned the wrong things or not. Because of what I've learned and learned to live by, I know that the loss of love is inevitable. The consequences are always sad, painful, and infuriating...'

'I am good at "getting" what's really going on with people and it's a great way to avoid having to do work on myself. I needed a lot of therapy for any of it to soak in for me. I was slow to get it because I was so quick to get it...'

'Those of us who have been possessed by Holy Spirit, and are looking to be repossessed whenever we can, are the richest poor folks in the world.'...

'Hope for change is often a rationale for inaction, and this life history of mine of which I used to be proud, now, upon further reflection, is beginning to stink.'...

'My mind uses its valued method of survival to justify its existence and maintain a bloated view of itself. You could definitely say my mind has been a critical element in the story of my life (heh heh), though it's not always all that useful, come to think of it, if you don't mind. Mind fullness is not always mindfulness. In fact it never is, but never mind.'...

"I swear I had mystical experiences while I was reading it and even the few hours while I was sleeping!... there's another layer beyond the hero story and that's the story of sacred Initiation— the decent to the underworld— the stripping away of the ego and facing the truth of who/what we are only to fall in love with the god/dess of the underworld (the self that we see reflected in each other's eyes) and so return to the surface able to integrate and fully use the dark to support the Light in us."

Some NEW kind of trailer trash

The Story of an Outsider's Inside View
of the Revolution of Consciousness

an AutoBioGraphy
VOLUME ONE

Brad Blanton, Ph.D.
Author of *Radical Honesty*

Sparrowhawk Press
Stanley, Virginia

Cover design by Victoria Valentine
www.victoriavalentine.com

*I dedicate this book to my four bears
and my progeny:*

*To those teachers who granted me the kindness of
their caring attention*

*To Jack Bruno Buddha, Elijah, Carsie,
Amos, Ian, Shanti, and my unknown son:
You, my children, are by far the best gift of
the world to my life and the best gift of
my life to the world*

CONTENTS

Prelude   *What My Life Is about* ....*xv*

Introduction *The Story about Stories* ....*xii*

Chapter 1   My Heritage and Home Life 1

Chapter 2   Life in the Country 12

Chapter 3   The End of the Beginning 16

Chapter 4   School and Home 18

Chapter 5   Home Again, Home Again 21

Chapter 6   Good Will Hunting 33

Chapter 7   Texas 36

Chapter 8   A New Beginning 40

Chapter 9   Despair 47

Chapter 10   Another New Beginning 55

Chapter 11   The University of Texas (1959–1961) 59

Chapter 12   Catch 22 in 1962 64

Chapter 13   Married Life, Graduate School, and Drugs 68

Chapter 14   Texas Nonviolence 77

Chapter 15   Another God-damned Serious Rant about
             Civilization and Its Criminal Intents 84

Chapter 16   Therapy: Growing up 95

Chapter 17   Groan up 100

Chapter 18   A Man Fit for My Times 104

Chapter 19   Jim Bevel 112

Chapter 20   Peace? 116

Chapter 21   Summer 1967 119

Chapter 22   Sgt. Pepper's Lonely Hearts Club Band and the
             Murder of Our Leaders 123

Chapter 23   The Work of Stanley Milgram 134

Chapter 24   Shanti Is Born 142

Chapter 25   Experiments in Community 145

Chapter 26   Fritz Perls and Training in Gestalt Therapy 151

Chapter 27   1971 May Day Protests 157

Chapter 28   What Kind of Hero? 175

Chapter 29   When I was 31: My Personal, Political,
and Professional Life 178

Chapter 30   On the Road Again 181

Chapter 31   The Time of My Fucking Life! 183

Chapter 32   Psycho Therapy 196

Chapter 33   On the Road Again, Again (1973–74) 199

Chapter 34   American Express 204

Chapter 35   Song of Affirmation 206

Chapter 36   Sound of Fog Horn, Picture of Fog, Feel of Limbo 211

Chapter 37   From the Land of the Midnight Sun to a
Place of Peace in Greece 214

Chapter 38   Istanbul, Teheran, Kabul 222

Chapter 39   India 227

Chapter 40   Goa at Christmas 231

Chapter 41   End of Travelogue, End of Trail 234

Chapter 42   The Rest of 1974 and 1975: Home Again, Home Again . .237

Chapter 43   1976 and 1977 240

Chapter 44   What I Learned in My First 37 Years: 247
The Aesthetics of Presence

Acknowledgments 253

Coming up in Volume Two 261

Radical Honesty Resources 261

PRELUDE
What My Life Is about

This book tells a story about me, Brad Blanton, a not-so-lone ranger from the quaint, gross, violent, shit-upon antique American South. I've turned out to be a rough-cut but compassionate kind of Bubba Buddha. I am a poor kid from the hills of Virginia who overcame abuse, ignorance, and poverty to become a social activist, psychotherapist, best-selling author, pretty good father, bad guitar player, and a poor politician. It is a tale of how, for most of my life, I was often cheerfully alive, happy, and in love, and simultaneously extremely pissed off at a lot of dumb-assed people for a lot of horrible, stupid things they did to millions upon millions of other people. I give some details about that.

Basically, I've lived my life as a dung beetle in the shit pile known as the United States of America during the time when its corporate capitalists took the lead in destroying the world, without me ever killing a God-damned one of them. As it's turned out, though I thought I was brave I was a coward after all, and just as full of shit as everyone else of the social classes that I have lived in and with. And I have helped keep up this ignorant, powerful, and poisonous place in the world where I grew up.

I want this epithet for my epitaph:

> *"I am glad for what I did with my life except that I sincerely think
> I could have helped a hell of a lot more of humankind and the Earth
> if I had killed more God-damned rich people."*

What I think is admirable and worth striving for in this world turned deaf and dumb by blind belief is taking responsibility for honesty between and among people, which means to:

Have the capacity to lie, and not do it.
Have the ability to control others, and by choice not do it.
Confess deceits and promise not to deceive, despite knowing one can get by with it.

What value do these hold? This approach is the source of the greater intelligence, or *co-intelligence,* and of the greater heartedness, or *co-heartedness,* which are now the only keys to the survival of the human species. We must advance beyond the mere capacity to deceive or dominate or control each other, or be hoisted by our own retard. At least this is the myth I live by.

Out of that myth, for the last twenty or thirty years, I have designed my life consciously, according to the following vision that I came up with, based on the experiences of my life, but not determined in reaction to my life:

The purpose of my life is to use my perceptiveness, intelligence, love of children, love of people, love of life, and sense of humor by writing books, designing and conducting workshops, sharing honestly with friends, giving talks, making media appearances, being with my family, and helping raise children and grandchildren in such a way as *to create the possibility of a lifetime of play and service for every human being on the planet.*

Because of the way I have lived, which is partly a byproduct of my era in history (especially the 1960s and 1970s, when I came of age, left home, got married, had kids, became a psychotherapist, and took part in the civil rights and anti-Vietnam War movements), and also a byproduct of what has interested me, I have learned how to employ my mind in service to my *being,* which is who I am. My *being* identifies strongly with other beings.

Now that I know that who I am is not my ego anymore, I feel right proud of it! Oops! There I go again! . . . And that is what my life is like and has been like for a long time, which is what I intend to share with you.

Brad Blanton
Sparrowhawk Farm,
Stanley, Virginia

INTRODUCTION
The Story about Stories

I love stories. I love hearing them and telling them. And I think stories are just about the best way we have of learning things. I will tell you a short version of my story now, and then I will tell you a longer one with a little more detail and description. I hope you learn something useful and are entertained by this story of my life. At the time of this writing, I am seventy years old. I have a five year old boy, Jack Bruno Buddha Blanton, who had a shirt when he was a baby that said, "I suck. Therefore I am." I try to model myself after him.

For most of my life I have done psychotherapy, written books, and conducted personal growth workshops for a living. One of the things we do in my *Course in Honesty Eight-day Workshop*, which I have been conducting for the last twenty-plus years, is provide an opportunity for everyone in the workshop to tell the whole story of his or her life. We are each given one hour and prompted every fifteen minutes so we can know how much time we have left for the story we have left to tell. These stories are videotaped and given to the storytellers to keep. The workshop participants take their videos home from the workshop and show them to their parents, siblings, and others who were talked about in their story, and have them reject, confirm, be offended by, pleased by, or contradict the story. What happens when people start opening up about their lives like this is told about in *The Truthtellers: Stories of Success by Radically Honest People*, a book I edited that was mostly written by people who attended my workshops.

I have heard a lot of life stories and I have told my own life story many times. And those of us that have repeated the workshop numerous times have found that it actually takes a little less time to tell your story each time you retell it. In fact, as my ex-wife Amy has pointed out, after being in a bunch of these workshops, a number of us have got our stories down to about thirty seconds.

Here is our common theme: "I was born an exceptional child to obtuse and ignorant parents who neglected and abused me in many ways, yet, in spite of their ineptitude and insensitivity, and because of my individual virtue and courage, I overcame the rotten and unfair circumstances of my life to become the sterling individual standing before you now."

What follows here is just a more elaborate take on that one central plot. I like life stories, and I like telling the story of my life. And it is just a story. I know that stories can be dangerous in both good and bad ways. Stories can change our lives. Stories can ruin our lives. The danger comes from putting too much stock in stories and in believing that our stories are who we are.

Our life story is the core of our false identity of ourselves as our reputation and performance—the identity we lie a lot to maintain.

Attachment to the idea that who we are *is our reputation* is a damaging distraction from our identity as a present-tense, noticing being—a being in love with being and joyous in the face of uncertainty—which is our fundamental identity. We tend to attach to our stories as our identity when we are afraid to be vulnerable, present-tense beings. We are afraid of too much intensity as feeling beings, and protect ourselves from it by fighting to maintain an illusion of control. That is why we play as if we are and always have been in charge of our lives, when the truth is that "we" have actually seldom, if ever, been in charge.

"I" have been a reactive being all of my life, playing as if I was a rational being who knew what was going on, and consciously choosing how to deal with it. So have you. That is mere pretense. It's bullshit. My life story has mostly been a hard-earned, hand-built lie. Just like yours.

My friend, the theologian Gene Marshall, says there are three kinds of truth.

1. Objective knowledge
2. Personal experience
3. Rational overview

Objective knowledge is scientific: directly observing what occurs, describing it, having other witnesses to it and agreeing on what has happened.

Personal experience involves interior consciousness, or the ability to notice and record what is going on and to describe that. And a *rational overview* is a kind of collectively agreed upon perspective.

Drawing from the work of Fritz Perls, Werner Erhard, and Radical Honesty, we also say, analogous to Gene Marshall's formulation, that there are always three aspects of the truth in the world of events.

1. That which occurs
2. The story about what occurred
3. The meaning made out of the story of what occurred

This story I tell now has to do with all three of those perspectives. It is a story of my times and of the perspectives of my times, as well as of what happened to me and what I made of it.

So I want to start out by saying that this is a work of fiction. I don't say that because I am inventing fiction on purpose, like a novelist. I don't intend to tell any whoppers, or anything but what "really" happened to me as best as I can remember, and I won't invent stories out of whole cloth. But I think it is important to note here at the beginning of the book, that we can never know exactly what actually occurred in any life. All life stories are fictional. Because of selective memory, habitual lying, and a few other things, all we can ever get to, try as we might, is a story. Stories are wonderful things, but they are not replicas of reality.

In fact, when people have gone through my workshops and gone back home and taken care of unfinished business with their parents, ex-spouses, ex-lovers, siblings, and others, and then come back to another workshop and tell their life story again, it is not just the relationship to those people that has changed, the whole story of their life changes! And, indeed, since I am the listener the second time around who has also told his story (so the hearing of the story for the listener changes as well!) it becomes almost impossible to tell exactly how our stories change, but they are changing like hell all the time if we are growing in our capacity to remember, understand, and handle what has happened to us and as life keeps on happening, stories change in subtle but important ways.

You and I are about to have our own life-changing experience as I tell you and you read my current version of my "rags-to-riches" story. Remember, this is only my *current* story of what occurred; and the meaning it holds is *only that which you and I make of it.* As Malcolm Gladwell points out so well in his wonderful book *Outliers* (Little, Brown and Company, 2008), the whole rags-to-riches American myth is bullshit, because there is always a passel of people and of chances, forming a parade of support, influence, encouragement, and luck that exists behind every single hero story. And everyone has a story about every story. I try to be true to Malcolm's insight here and give credit for the luck of the times.

Here is the short and long of it, as I see, right now, from my own story. The best thing I've *learned* from my life is how to love and nurture children, and from that, and from them I've also learned how to love and nurture the childlike being of other human beings. The best thing I have *done* in my life has been to help raise children who knew they were loved and love life, and to love people who were damaged by life and help them into loving life again, and when I could, to help them suffer less and help them discover how to cause less suffering in others.

Here is the short story about how I think that learning happened. My father died when I was almost six years old. My brother, Jimmy, was four. My sister, Anno, was twelve. My mother remarried when I was seven to a shell-shocked man, Tommy, who was an alcoholic wife beater and child abuser. My half-brother, Mike, was born when I was nine. I helped raise him. My sister left home that year. Because of this luck, I became sensitized to subtle cues about human behavior, and I wanted to try to help people who were hurting. I also developed skills for dealing with my life circumstances, which required me to take care of my younger brothers because my mother and stepfather were often gone or too drunk to do so.

I learned to be wary, alert, and quick to respond to cues to predict mood and likely behavior changes in drunken adults, so I could keep them from killing each other or hurting one of the kids. I considered myself a smart kid and a hero, and I couldn't afford to admit to being scared and sorry for myself. As a psychologically reactive, homemade, individual humanoid, I ended up as an adult wanting to help people, take care of them, teach them how to take care of themselves, and show off my perceptiveness. I resented people if they didn't appreciate me a lot, or do what I said, behave the way I wanted, or turn out the way I'd thought they should.

I am a neurotic, twentieth-century, Judeo-Christian tradition-twisted American survivor designed by my life to be a helper who wants to keep those already hurt from being hurt more. I purchase allegiance by helping others. I generally charge this allegiance to the "helpee" in an inexplicit way, such that a vague sense of obligation binds them to me, protects me from them, and gets me praise. At essence, I am a manipulative, co-dependent, lying survivor (just like that low-life bastard Dick Cheney, who I fucking hate from top to bottom).

As a result of how I grew up and adapted to my circumstances, I now possess a hand-built, home-built set of neurotic survival techniques, my carried-around-with-me-at-all-times way of getting-along-feeling-protected-and-surviving set of tools. But along the way, in spite of myself, I also learned something else that turned my whole life around. . . and this is what makes this story worthwhile for you to read and for me to tell yet again.

I found out that by transforming my relationship to this Dick Cheney-like system of survival, instead of being victimized by it, criticizing it, and resisting it—or trying to "fix" it—I can choose how to use it of my own free will, much like the Greek mythical hero Sisyphus transformed hell into heaven.

Albert Camus, in his book *The Myth of Sisyphus* (1942), wrote that Sisyphus's condition of being in a special hell, condemned to roll a big boulder up a mountain and have it roll back down again for all eternity, was a perfect analogy for the human condition. *We are all condemned for life to engage in completely futile tasks that take everything we've got.*

Sisyphus, who used to be quite a man and a hero like Hercules and Pan all rolled up into one when he was on Earth, was thrown into this special hell forever just as we, who were once happy as children, have been thrown into the hell of the meaningless meaning-making machine of the mind, the obligations of adult life, and the delusional system of a corrupt culture based on rabid economic abuse of the poor by the rich.

If we are to discover the secret to happiness as human beings, said Camus, we must be able to imagine some way Sisyphus could come to be a happy man—even while living in that special hell! If we were to catch a glimpse of him just as he turns to walk back down that mountain to find his rock and push it up again, we would see a beaming smile on his face. How could that be?

Camus said there was only one way that man could be happy (and by implication, only one way any human could be happy), which was by *choosing to do what he had been condemned to do.*

Sisyphus was condemned to the hell of rolling that rock up the mountain and having it roll back down again, for all eternity, as his punishment. But he conquered hell by transforming his relationship to what he was condemned to do by *choosing* to do it. Sisyphus decided to choose to do what he was condemned to do. He owned his life when he said, "This is *my* job. This is what I do for a living. I am good at it because it is what I do. I roll *my* rock up *my* mountain and back down again. This is what I do and I'm doing it. I'm doin' my job!" And he was all smiles as he went about doing his chosen work.

I think Camus is right. Sisyphus could have been rolling that rock every day, saying, "Damn! I miss those parties with my friends. I wish I had a glass of wine. I haven't been laid in a looonnng time. Damn! I wish I could go back." Instead, he took on what his present life was by doing what he was condemned to do of his own volition. This is reminiscent of the movie *Groundhog Day:* When the lead character (played by Bill Murray) finally surrenders to having the same day happen over and over without resisting it, he gets so good at living it that it finally becomes a new day.

As the Renaissance philosopher Michel de Montaigne said, "A person is not hurt so much by what happens, as by his opinion of what happens" or, I think we could paraphrase, by "his resistance to what happens."

I can choose to serve people as a design for my life simply because it is a good choice given my design—with which I am condemned to live. I can escape the oppression of the historical personality that drives me even though I cannot escape the personality itself. In other words, the meaning made for me without any choice on my part from the life, times, family, and culture I was born into, and formed by, was not under my control. What *is* under my control now is:

1. The use of that personality as a creative instrument.
2. What I use it to create.

By using the equipment I have available to me, I can choose to serve people, envision how to do it, and make it happen.

So this is how I view my life: I learned to survive by taking care of some people and being wary, paranoid, and defending against other people. I will always operate from that mode, and I have no choice in the matter. Still, serving people *can be a choice* for me and can be very fulfilling and fun if I choose to use that model to create my life. If I consider myself to be this being in the moment who is typing now and my history to be something my present-tense self possesses, *I can use my memory, in the present, to design a future to live from.*

Rather than continue to react to the past, which designed—out of circumstance and reaction to circumstances—how I should live at about age eight or nine, I can transform my life by my own design, *by choosing to do what I have been condemned to do.* I can design the projects of my life, using my developed skills in surviving, to bring about the results I plan to bring about. I can use my personality to bring about my dreams for the future. Instead of trying to fix or change myself, I can simply *use* my "self" to create the future life I want and contribute to other people's lives in the way I want. This has been a valuable lesson for me.

In itself this autobiography is a project to contribute information to you and others that moves you and helps us all be moved—to move on—instead of dying from pretense. I want you to consider the possibility that we are *all* alike in the ways I've just described: We can either have an *unconscious, reactive life* or have a *conscious, creative life.* I have done the latter in the latter part of my life. And I think I can tell you how you can begin to, too, just by osmosis from reading this story.

Even Dick Cheney could become like Jeziz! Cheney's chains are rattled for Jeziz and he comes again! (I know there is more than one way to take that. Pick whichever one you like. Heh-heh.)

I am going to use this autobiography to describe my evolution to leading a conscious, creative life and show you how to do it, too, warts and all. Then I will design the remainder of my life (from seventy years of age to the end) as a model. Then I will design my next life, for when I get brought back to life after being frozen for a while. I have a cryogenics contract to be frozen in liquid nitrogen when I die, and be preserved until science advances enough to thaw me out and bring me back to life and make me young again. This probably won't work, but I'm giving it a shot anyway. If you have ever said, "If I only had my life to live over again . . . ," you probably didn't really think that was possible. Now it may be. If so, I am going to do it. (I am *not* going to write more than three autobiographies though, I'll tell you that right now!)

So this autobiography is two volumes (I apparently have a two-book-sized ego). Volume one covers the first thirty-seven years of my existence. Volume two is my life from 1977 to now and short plan for my next life. (First volume, *Cheney, the Dick!* Second volume, *Changing Cheney's Chains!*)

Headline: "Childhood is Hell!" Claims Former Child

Most of the ways of survival that work for us when we are children no longer serve us as adults, but we persist with them anyway. After we bang our heads against the wall of life long enough, either we become more conscious and join up with folks who help us keep conscious, or we join a group of permanent adolescents (as members of most organized religions and political parties and their ilk are) where we simply *work to keep from becoming more conscious.*

Now and then some of us transcend our childhoods and our groups of permanent adolescence called a "culture." This transcendence is usually temporary. Even after these moments of enlightenment, we become neurotic again and get wrapped up in bullshit beliefs just like we were before we last escaped the jail of the mind.

Most of the first thirty-seven years of my life was lived almost purely reactively, based on unfinished business from my childhood, with occasional interference from present-tense awareness. As I slowly shifted my identity from my reactive rationalizing pretending-to-be-in-charge self, to myself as a noticing being, I could then began to consciously *use* my past to design my future, rather than have my life be designed by reaction to my past. So Volume One of my autobiography is the story of that which led me to consciousness. Volume Two is about what I did with that new consciousness.

The best reason for *choosing to do what we are condemned to do,* like Sisyphus, is that what we know and have experienced from our past history is the very most useful thing we have for creating from the present toward a vision of the future. It actually gives you some power to make a life you imagine you'll love. When energy formerly spent on worrying becomes applied to envisioning and creating a future, the power to create, and the joy, is much greater. And the gift of our lives to other people is more generous and inspirational.

Unless we create some vision to hitch our wagon to, we automatically fall back into being controlled again by reactions and defensive mind-made moralism, which are based on formative experiences. As children we store ways to survive both in our unconscious minds and in our conscious minds: beliefs and standards of operation based largely on fear.

My most recent years have been lived from my vision of what I wanted to create and contribute, and have I've been successful in this to the degree that I have transcended the beginning story of my life and used it as an artist uses paints on a canvas. Most of what I have spent my energy on for the last thirty-five years has been consciously created, using my reactions to the past as instruments of creation. I will tell you more about that in the second volume of this work.

Each time we regress to operating on the basis of automatic survival and belief we have a chance to be delivered from it. Deliverance is always at hand when we acknowledge the truth of our experience in the moment to another person out loud and in the open. We can then assign our mind a job to do so it has something to chew on other than our own asses and something to do other than crow about itself. We can free ourselves from the relentless taboos and controls of our unconsciously built systems of survival in two ways: first through honesty, and second by employing what used to be our neurotic minds to accomplish projects that we design for the future. In this way, we can transform our life of obsessive preoccupation with survival and avoidance to a life of creating.

Our lives can become conscious works of art. And a life lived in a community of people who know and practice honesty and conscious creation is the life of an artist, artfully lived. That is the good fortune I now have.

Life as an artist is a choice that provides an alternative to the usual "civilized" and depressing way of living. To remain free of our culture, or civilization, means cultivating this ability to live outside of the mind in the world of noticing, and giving the mind some bone to chew on to keep it busy and out of our way. *We need to give our minds work to do, in obedience to our heart's desire, and continue to share with each other honestly about our goals and our "rackets," in order to create, and keep consciously creating, what we want in life.*

Making the choice to do what one is condemned to do is called "transformation." My own life is continuously transformed by my choice to serve people, because the purpose of my service is no longer merely to manipulate and control them to get what I want, but to contribute to them and affiliate with them in order to realize a common vision. I aim to be both a leader and a servant, usually at the same time, *so that we can enjoy and love our lives together.*

As a being that notices, a being that lives in the moment and is satisfied in the present, I already have everything I want. What I've got right now is enough. So it turns out, as a secondary effect of transformation, some healing of the wounds of the past does occur. We know this because the yearning for life to be different than it is, decreases. Also, I've given up the demand that other people make up for how I was deprived, so I can see that I got some neurotic demandingness fixed, as another side effect of transformation. Since I dropped the relentless demands based on unfinished business from the past I feel quite happy with the opportunity to face whatever the moment brings. The same is true for others who live this way.

As my grandmother used to say, *"I do declare!"* Being of unsound mind and using that to create a future, this is what I declare: *My life is to serve people.* (Not because I was psychologically built to be a caretaker, Jewish social worker, superman, savior, con man, and so forth, but *because I say so.*) Declarative speaking comes out of nowhere and what happens from it is because I say so, *using the accident of my upbringing rather than being used by it.*

Because of my decision to use a country boy, redneck, hillbilly trailer trash kind of history to create a life with rather than have that create my life, I have turned out to be a new kind of trailer trash (and the first, I hope, of a new trail of kinder trash). From this comes the title to this book (and the wonderful cover designed by my friend Vicki Valentine).

I hope this story is a contribution to you. It is a story that belongs to you as much as it does to me in the sense that in telling how I came to be who I am at this point in history I am talking quite a bit about your place in history, as you've been living it parallel to me, and about how you're handling it. I hope my life story will serve as an inspiration, providing a model of the artistic life, and as a warning. I hope it makes you laugh and cry and love your life . . . and live your life out loud!

Chapter 1

My Heritage and Home Life

My grandmother, Cynthia Anne Bruce, owned a ladies' hat store in Knoxville, Tennessee. She looked like a powder pigeon. She was buxom and compact, and walked with a strut much like a powder pigeon, puffed up chest forward, as if top heavy, but with a stride that seemed somehow stoic, albeit a little jerky. She was proud of her heritage of being of almost purebred Scottish descent. Her great-great-great-grandfather was Robert Bruce himself, the "only Scot who ever defeated the British," as she said.

My siblings and I were always taught by my grandmother never to kill a spider, but to take it up and remove it from the house and release it outdoors. This wasn't because she was ahead of her time in ecological consciousness. She was maintaining a family tradition that went all the way back to when Robert, The Bruce, was pursuing the British and came to a fork in the road, and he couldn't decide which route the fleeing British troops had taken. When he stopped, dismounted his horse, and looked around carefully, he found a spider web across one route, so took the other. Thus he found, attacked, and defeated the British troops. So spiders were treated with great respect in my grandmother's family.

In addition to bragging about that, she always told us, "We are direct descendants of Robert Burns, the great Scottish poet." And though everyone from the Old Country apparently claimed this, for us it appears to be true. Later on, when I was in college, I did a little research on our genealogy and it seems that, indeed, we are descendants of Bobbie Burns through one of his bastard children, born out of wedlock while he was married to another woman. Apparently the woman who bore his child (and she was not alone) was proud of being the mistress of Burns and the mother of his child, and she didn't care who knew it.

I told my grandmother this, along with the interesting historical fact that his fame was as much from his bawdy songs and fairly un-Calvinist, un-Presbyterian, unholy, and more than occasionally alcohol-inspired life, as it did from writing "Auld Lang Syne" and compassionate poems and songs about wee mousies.

"Bradley! You should never have told me such a thing!" she exclaimed.

I think she really was hurt that I would do such a thing, and I felt ashamed. But since I was also a little proud of my heritage in the way she wanted me to be, she at least laughed when she overheard what I told my cousin I'd said to a few people at various times, including a cop attempting to detain me in a demonstration: "Don't mess with me. I come from a long line of bastards!"

My grandfather, Warren Rutherford, was skimming along the same line of second- or third-generation immigrant survivor upper-lower class, trying to scramble into the middle class and get a piece of the pie that comes from asserting oneself by oppressing others in socially approved ways to get on top. He was short. He smoked big cigars and drove a Buick. And he bragged and talked tough and could shoot straight, and he had a lot of guns that he kept in good condition.

Before becoming my grandfather, he'd had an adventuresome younger life, including being a photographer right after the turn of the century. He'd spent a lot of time traveling with the circus before he eventually settled into frequent travel for the purpose of organizing for the Kiwanis Club, the Lions Club, the Moose Lodge, and various other social organizations for men. It is likely that all this travel came to be a way of being free to drink, smoke, and escape the oppression of the in-house moralist, my grandmother. (Like his frequent two-month-long visits to my mother and father's place to visit his grandchildren before my Daddy died.) He loved his grandchildren, and he loved hunting and going for long walks in the woods carrying his rifle, and shooting a few squirrels for breakfast the next day. Eventually, as he grew older and settled down, he helped with the establishment of a few business schools, and enrolled a few of our family members in them.

His son, my uncle Marvin, made it. He got a business education and became an established administrator, higher up than most in the food chain, working for a paper mill in rural Tennessee. He had a cabin in the Great Smoky Mountains. The place where he worked polluted the skies and stunk up the whole valley, but his family had a good life. They were established as good, middle-class Americans in the Land of the Fee. Like his father, he was a great hunter and fisherman and loved "going to the cabin" way up in the Smokies. Me, my brother Jimmy, and my sister Anno got to go there now and then, too, and we had great fun with our cousins.

We were protected and nurtured, oblivious to the bloodshed and shame of our cruel and murderous heritage. Though we heard stories about forbears who were "revenuers" and "bootleggers," we never got told the real story about what it *really* meant to be an American. Nobody did back then.

When my grandmother and grandfather grew old together they became kinder to each other. Grandpa gave up smoking and drinking and treated Grandma sweetly, his days as a rebellious provocateur apparently forgotten. He died first, then after a few years she followed, as did my uncle and aunt. I haven't seen my cousins for forty years.

My friend and fellow redneck intellectual, the late Joe Bageant, reminded me again of the importance, both good and bad, of our Scots-Irish heritage in his book *Deer Hunting with Jesus* (Broadway Books, 2008). During his life, he and I were almost entirely on the opposite side of the cultural war raging now between the "believers" and the "anti-believers," coming from our heritage. But we were both more or less appalled at the real history of ourselves as quintessential Americans. When people in Europe these days think of Americans, they think mostly of the checkered Scots-Irish heritage that greatly influenced, for better or for worse, who we came to be.

On my father's side, the first Blanton came to North Carolina from the Northern Hills of England about 1740 or so. He and his brother were the only Blantons who came. His brother moved to New England, where that line died out after a generation or so. The one in North Carolina had seven children. Now there are a little over 40,000 Blantons in America. They all came from that one man. Of course, that is just the ones who kept the Blanton name because they were male offspring. So the real number is about 80,000-plus souls from that one Northern Hills British fellow and his Scots-Irish wife.

Blanton's offspring fought in the American Revolution. They fought on both sides in the War Between the States. They spawned generations of rednecks, leading to the current catastrophe described further here by Joe Bageant, another of this long line of bastards, in a passage from his book.

"Since arriving in America during the first seventy-five years of the eighteenth century . . . Calvinist Ulster Scots have constituted a parallel culture to that of enlightened Yankee liberals. Scots-Irish Calvinist values all but guarantee anger and desire for vengeance against what is perceived as elite authority: college-educated secular people who run the schools, the media, and the courts and don't seem to mind if their preacher is a queer. One Calvinist premise has always dominated: The word of God supersedes any and all government authority. Period. That same flaming brand of Calvinism brought here by the Ulster Scots launched American Christian Fundamentalism. Now it threatens to breach separation of church and state. Worse yet, its most vehement elements push for a nuclear holy war. Yes, push for a nuclear holy war. You may not meet them among your circle of friends, but there are millions of Americans who fiercely believe we should nuke North Korea and Iran, seize the Middle East's oil (KICK THEIR ASS AND TAKE THEIR GAS reads one bumper sticker). They believe the United States will conquer the entire world and convert it to American notions of democracy and fundamentalist Christian religion . . .

"To understand how such ominous political ideations reveal themselves in this century, we must look back 450 years to a group of Celtic cattle thieves killing one another in the mud along Hadrian's wall—the Borderers. Fanatically religious and war loving, the Scottish Protestants made their way first to Ireland as the 'Ulster Scots,' then to American shores during the early eighteenth century. These Scots-Irish Borderers brought cultural values that govern the political emotions of millions of Americans to this day. We have King James I of England to thank for this sordid state of affairs. My online friend Billmon (Billmon.com) who has made a study of the subject, says that more than any other person it was that sawed-off little Scot James who created the cultural psychosis that would Spawn Jerry Falwell, Ian Paisley, George W. Bush, the Oklahoma bombings, and the red state-blue state electoral map.

"'That's a lot to pin on one head, even if it did wear a crown,'" Billmon admits. 'But it's true,' he insists. 'Much of what made America America—and a lot of what the rest of the world has come to detest about us—can be traced back to this runty little Scotsman. There's enough irony there for a couple of Tom Stoppard plays, because King

James, whose name became the brand for fundamentalist Christianity, also happened to be a notorious homosexual—one of the most enthusiastic practitioners in the long, proud history of British Aristocratic buggery.'"

That is funny as shit! Politics makes queer bedfellows! He goes on:

"Like so many other English monarchs and prime ministers since his time, poor James was faced with trying to calm down some of the rioting and eye gouging at Ulster, Ireland, that ever festering boil on the rump of British Protestantism. James's solution was to settle pockets of loyal Protestant Scots in the middle of Ulster's native Catholic population. The results were predictably nasty. Later, Ulster Scot Protestant loyalty was transferred to William of Orange, creating the Orangemen, the Irish equivalent of America's redneck fundamentalists—both troublesome to a free and orderly republic and useful to the most malignant political elements.

"Ultimately, a program of high prices, ruinous taxes, and destruction of employment drove the Ulster Scots to the more promising shores of the New World. Given the New World's primitive conditions and general lawlessness, they chose to revert back into the murderous Picts the British crown had come to know and love along Hadrian's Wall. Blessed with an abundance of guns, Indians for target practice, bountiful corn for homemade whiskey, and a hated government that insisted on taxing that whiskey, they forged a new and indelible element in American Society: white trash, crackers, rednecks. People who had little use for government intrusions into such domestic aspects of live as moonshining, cockfighting, poaching, squatting on other people's land, and family feuds. These same people who had little use for an Injun and even less for a slave (their small homesteads in the hills were not conducive to the slave-based cotton and tobacco agriculture of their lowland 'betters' living in the Tidewater plain of Virginia and the Deep South) set their seed to the winds. Their offspring spread westward, melding West and South together in a place called Texas. The violent frontier life suited them just fine, thank you. And thus we find them today, still armed and suspicious of government but also enraged about Sept. 11—the best excuse to use firepower since the Alamo. Hell, since the Battle of Killiecrankie!

"Only a year before September 11 they had come streaming out of every corner of the red states to crown George W. Bush as their own smirking William Wallace, leader of the 1297 rebellion against the English. Of the thirty Bush red states, twenty-three were among the top thirty of the Scots-Irish states. Of the top ten Scots-Irish states, Bush won all but one with an average vote share of more than 55 percent. Conversely, Bush won only two of the ten states with the lowest Scots-Irish population: North and South Dakota. Spiritually, philosophically, and politically, Borderer cultural influence still runs deep in America. So much so that, as David Hackett Fischer points out in his masterful synthesis of British-American folkways, Albion's Seed, Germans, Italians, Poles, and many other ethnic groups, adopted the Scots-Irish values as quintessentially American. Scots-Irish political culture in America holds and always has held many things that draw in other ethnic groups and contribute to the spreading of its ethos. It is populist and inclusive. The Scots Irish do not envy wealth in general and measure leaders by what they see as their personal strength, which usually comes down to whether they will fight for what they believe in, physically if necessary. And they are Christian, as were the majority of the Ellis Island wave of immigrants.

"Another reason Borderer influence on America runs so deep is the Borderer affinity for nearly every kind of breedable human speciman: about one-third of Americans have a Borderer in their family. Yet until recently Scots-Irish culture has gone largely unexamined, maybe because it's so pervasive we take it for granted. The Scots Irish themselves know almost nothing of their own culture. We are too busy living it and do not even identify ourselves as Scots-Irish, which helps keep us invisible."

Lord, lord. Pride and shame. I am proud to have the chance to apologize for all this. This is the blessing and the curse. This is the hole out of which I am still climbing, and from which I claim to have gained some virtue. So now here's more of my story.

Back before I was born, when Aileen and Howard Blanton had been a small family with one baby girl named Eleanor (aka Anno), they had been happy and productive and in love and starting a new life in a new place on their own. They had met in high school in Norton, Virginia. They were both poets and romantics, and had worked on the yearbook together their senior year. They got married and had their baby girl after high school. This was around 1932.

My dad got a job working for the telephone company up north in Augusta County, and they had driven the eight-hour trip from Norton up to Staunton, Virginia, in order for them to start their new life together. They came in a little Plymouth Sedan, with little Eleanor, less than a year old, sleeping in a dresser drawer in the "jump seat" in the back. That trip was a big deal back then, leaving a hometown and getting away from family to start out on one's own. They were having the adventure of having a child together, and the adventure of taking off and trying it on their own at the same time.

My father worked as a lineman for the phone company, putting up telephone poles and stringing lines all over Middle Virginia. My mother pursued her interest in poetry and for a few years had a radio show where she read her own poetry and that of others. She also wrote songs and had several of them published. Both of my parents played the piano, and owning a piano and playing and singing together was a point of pride.

About a year before I was born my mother left my father. She went to Texas with her father and her seven-year old daughter because she had found out about my father having had sex with another woman and then lying to her about it. She took my sister with her (Anno was about six at the time), and she and my grandfather went to Galveston, Texas. They were there for about three months.

After lots of long distance calls and letters back and forth with my father (and possibly, after she got even on the sexual score), she finally came back to him and they reconfirmed their marriage by making a new commitment to live together, love each other, and have another child. That's where I came from. I was born nine months later, in Staunton, Virginia, on September 8, 1940, right at the beginning of World War Two. I was the confirmation of their recommitment after the seven-year itch that nearly split them apart for good.

I don't remember much about the war. But I remember learning at an early age that my father "didn't have to go" because he was a lineman for the phone company and they needed him at home to put in phone lines. Plus, he was over thirty and had a wife and two kids: my eight-year old sister and me. Anyone able to go to war was supposed to go, so when an able-bodied man didn't go he often explained why. I remember hearing that explanation and knowing at a very young age that somehow it was important, just like "having lived through the Depression" was important.

Fifteen months later, in January 1942, my brother Jimmy was born. We were now a family of five, and we were happy. Not long after my brother was born, when I was about two, my parents bought a house and a thirty-two-acre apple orchard, Lonesome Pine Orchard, on a dirt road, Morris Mill Road, about seven miles outside of Staunton, and we moved out to the country. Looking for a new place to settle on your own is typical of the poor, white, Scots-Irish, redneck tradition in America. While it's certainly not the only thing that defines us, or me, it is part of the history of our country. It has to do with a search for new beginnings. Here is another piece by Joe Bageant, entitled "American Literature Has Abandoned Poor Whites," that explains why it is relevant. It's his exchange with a reader, which he published on September 20, 2009 on his blog, JoeBageant.com.

"Dear Joe,

"First of all, please, I apologize for my poor English. I'm writing to you from Spain where we have a very deficient education system and a natural tendency to fail on learning foreign languages.

"Now, after being intentionally modest, I have to say that I'm an avid reader of your work and that your Deer Hunting with Jesus has been an inspiration for my end of graduate essay, a kind of a small thesis. The subject of my essay is the relation between literature (and also popular culture in general) and America's white underclass. The main idea is to see which image of the white low classes is being exported from the U.S. and how, for example, Europeans like me receive it.

"On literature I found out that during the first half of the twentieth century, American authors used to talk about the poor whites, especially the most representative novelist of that era (Faulkner, Steinbeck, Dos Passos, Caldwell). So, there was a quite general interest on portraying that reality from the canonic literature. But, after the '40s, this interest seems to vanish (at least as a major theme.)

"As I said before, this is about the foreign reception of American literature). So, my essay took a new turn and now I'm trying to find the reasons of the loss of interest in the poor whites. Is it because is something that is wanted to be ignored? What happened that make the Joads from John Steinbeck's novel The Grapes of Wrath (being an epic image of endurance in front of social injustice) turn into Cletus from The Simpsons (a mere caricature, the image of a "loser")?

"Well, I just thought that maybe you can give some clues or just your opinion about that, from your inner view as an American and as a journalist. (I don't know, maybe I'm completely wrong, this is all bullshit, and I'll have to rewrite my whole essay.) Anyway, thanks a lot for just reading this email and please, keep writing on your blog, we're following it from far away.

"Yours sincerely,

"Pol

"Pol,

"I have wondered about that very thing myself since the middle 1970s. As far as I can tell, there is any number of factors at work. Here are some thoughts, a sort of chronology:

"The Dust Bowl made the plight of displaced and poor rural whites unavoidable. They rose in the public consciousness during the Great Depression, thanks to sensitive writers, artists, etc. and in no small part due to the Roosevelt administration's funding of writers and artists to document American society and the times. Making work for the arts benefited us all. Back then, everything that made it into the media, be it print or other, did not have to turn a corporate profit to be produced or published.

"World War Two created boom times for urban America. Some of the white rural poor moved toward the cities and the jobs.

"After the war, 22 million rural Americans were pushed off farms by government and corporate planning so they could work in industry. They did not rush happily toward the new American lifestyle, as portrayed in the official national storyline. Nearly all white rural soldiers surveyed in 1945 said they wanted to return to their family farms or rural homes. Neither corporate America nor the administration wanted to see the wartime prosperity (profits) end. The best way to accomplish that was to put rural Americans into the industrial work force. Once they were migrated to the cities and towns and working in industrial production, they provided two things: cheap labor and a market for industrial products. Before the war 45 percent of Americans lived on small farms. Ten years after the war less than 10 percent lived on farms.

"*However, rural Americans were poorly educated. The U.S. government census considered a fourth-grade education to be literate at the time. More than a quarter of the rural migrants did not even meet that standard. They suffered from poor education because the oligarchies at the local, regional, and state level did not want to pay taxes for schools, particularly in the South. The cities had long ago embraced public education.*

"*These uneducated rural whites became the foundation of our permanent white underclass. Their children and grandchildren have added to the numbers of this underclass, probably in the neighborhood of 50 or 60 million people now. They outnumber all other poor and working poor groups, black, Hispanics, immigrants.*

"*Because they are not concentrated in given neighborhoods, they are pretty much invisible as a group in America. But because they are nevertheless encountered individually in society, we get representations of them as the hillbilly or white trash next door. Or the redneck stereotype as the butt of humor—the people whose social skills do not resemble what is supposed to be the white Anglo norm. And in truth, they do not conform to the middle class behavior models presented by the media and the Corporate States of America as examples for approved societal behavior. They are not obsessed with their credit scores, they are always in the informal mode, they are rule breakers, and, in short, they do not behave like property of the state. So they are useful as a bad example. Usually they are portrayed as having a Southern accent, which for good reason is associated with a lack of education and sophistication.*

"*However, because they cannot be encountered in aggregated numbers, they cannot be seen by the rest of America as a distinct culture. Only as nonconforming individuals as an object of ridicule. And in a sense, fear. Because what is left of the middle class is afraid of falling into that white underclass.*

"*This brings us back to the subject of the poor white underclass not being represented in America literature. What literature? All I see these days is shallow crap. Real literature helps us understand the world and the human condition. Obviously, that is no longer America's cup of tea.*

"I could write much more on the topic, but it's complex. So this is the best distillation I can do in an email.

"In art and labor,

"Joe"

***

I loved Joe Bageant and I am so sorry he just died as I was writing this book. Like him, I was the first person in the history of my family to ever go to college. I think small pieces of this book are literature from, and about, the invisible underclass of which Joe spoke. (Tom Robbins, Cormack McCarthy, and Kurt Vonnegut for a sampling of the candidates for writers of great literature, though brilliant cynical literary poetic articulate men and fine examples of the best of America, are from the middle class.) We Borderers who have become literary stand out because our spirits don't like domination, while at the same time we constantly look for excuses to prove we won't stand for it, because that is "just what we do."

CHAPTER 2
Life in the Country

My family was even happier when we moved out there to the apple orchard. Every spring we lived in a perfumed and beautiful white and pink world of apple blossoms, and every fall we had apples and cider. We had a big garden that we all worked in. My daddy had friends that he worked with who would come out from work or on the weekend, for barbeques, and stand around at the barbeque pit and drink beer, and sometimes a little moonshine, and laugh a lot. We went to the river on Sundays to swim and have picnics. We kids all got to play outside quite a bit, and all of us working and playing together was a lot of fun.

I particularly liked my sister, Anno. That became her name because that's what came out when I tried to say, "Eleanor," when I was learning to talk. She loved me and my brother a whole lot because she'd been loved well by my father and mother. She loved us as much as they did. I am so happy to be telling this story now to honor this wonderful, loving family. (And saying that, I have a sense of dread coming on . . . like the setup for a horror show is happening.)

My granddaddy, my mother's father, was also very loving and kind to us. He used to come in the summers and live out in the "smokehouse" and take us hunting. He'd already taught Anno to shoot years earlier, and he taught my brother and me to shoot a .22 when we were three and four years old. We'd go visit him and Grandma and our cousins in Knoxville now and then, but what I remember most is back at the orchard in Virginia, and those shootin' matches we'd set up. He would bet money on us boys and we would shoot pennies from a hundred feet away and keep the nicked pennies to show off what good shots we were.

There were some occasional shocks and scares in our life at home, but mostly I feel like the luck of my birth was really good luck, and the start I had in life was truly wonderful. I had a really good beginning, though it contrasted quite a bit with the next six or seven years.

The following is a flashback that happened on an acid trip when I was twenty-three, when I was remembering back to between one and two years of age. It's a replay of a moment of total recall, like you get now and then on LSD.

I am sitting on the kitchen floor. I hear the sound of my mother's bedroom slippers sliding step by step across the floor, as she comes into the kitchen. Now I hear the sound of water when she turns the tap on at the sink. Now I hear the click when she turns on the electric stove to heat the pan of water she put on top of it. I hear the slop bucket handle flip over and bang against the side of the bucket and the splash sound when she throws something in the slop. I am completely content.

Now, in the moment of the flashback, I try to "say" these sounds. I am completely flabbergasted that I cannot say these sounds. I know where I am. I know what these things are, but I cannot say them! I cannot speak what I know! I do not know why I can't speak these familiar things I know, and I am shocked to discover that I can't speak them. Then I realize that my adult verbal mode of operation does not apply to the mode of operation I had as a twelve- to eighteen-month old. I understood the world then, and had it categorized in terms of familiar sights and sounds, and was oriented by it, but I had no verbal system with which to label it. I could be in it, know where I was, and be comfortable in it, but I couldn't talk it, or talk about it.

I think we all continue to live in a world we can't talk about and the more in contact with it we remain, the better off we are . . . but I'll say more about that later.

My mama worked. She helped run the apple orchard and scandalized the country folks around there by wearing pants and bossing the older male workers who knew more about what they were doing than she did. But they kind of liked showing her what she needed to know in order to tell them what to do.

My mama and daddy played the piano and sang songs together and my mother wrote songs and they sang them. Life was good. I was pretty happy. I think we all were. Even the minor traumas that occurred now and then seemed less than traumatic after they were over. For instance, I can recall a time when my brother Jimmy fell out of the car on our country road.

We are driving to pick up Daddy from work. Mama is in a hurry. We are driving fast. Jimmy and I are in the front seat with her. Jimmy is playing with the door handle. All of a sudden the door flies open and Jimmy falls out on the gravel road. Mama slams on the brakes. She jumps out of the car and is running back on the gravel road and dust is all around. Jimmy is sitting up. There is blood running down the side of his head and some skin or something is hanging down.

Jimmy starts crying, and says, "I got dirt in my mouth." Mama jumps in the car with him and holds him while she drives to Mrs. Britt's house. She runs in and gets a towel, and wets it and wraps it around Jimmy's head, and then comes running back out still holding him. We drive into town and take him to the hospital where he "gets sewed up." Later we pick up Daddy from work. Jimmy comes home with his head bandaged up with Mama and Daddy and me after it is dark.

Then, all of a sudden, my daddy died.

My mother told me that the morning of the day my father died, when they were lying in bed together, he'd said how glad he was that they had "moved to this place and done what they'd done." She said that he said he was happy about his life and the choices they'd made. He died at about a quarter to two in the afternoon on the second Sunday in August 1946—of a massive heart attack—just before we were supposed to go down to the river for a picnic. He was thirty-seven years old. I was almost six.

I'd been riding around piggyback on my father's shoulders that morning. He was complaining of having acid stomach, and took some Bromo-Seltzer. After he had given my little brother a piggyback ride as well, he went inside the house. My sister and I were out on the front porch steps, putting flowers we'd picked in the orchard into a vase when we heard a thud from something hitting the floor in the house. I don't know how I knew it, but I knew immediately that it was my father, that he had fallen down, and that he was dead.

We ran inside and saw my mother take out Daddy's pocket watch and put her finger on his wrist to try to get a pulse. Then she slapped him in the face and tried to get him to wake up. Then she was frantically massaging his legs and arms and talking to him in a high pitched voice. "Howard.

Howard! Howard, wake up!"

A phone call was made. Some other people came. My sister took us up the road to a neighbor's house, and then she went back home. My little brother played happily at the other house, but I stayed inside and cried. I felt like I knew what had happened and that it was serious. I thought I would now have to help take care of things because my daddy was dead, including helping take care of Jimmy who was too little to know what was happening.

Knowing the gravity of the situation, and resolving to be brave and help were my first ways of showing I was responsible and would be a big help in a way my daddy would be proud of. I decided right then that when I grew up I was going to be just like him. I was going to live just like he'd lived. And I was going to die at just the same age he did, the same way he did. I was going to be just like him.

After I made that resolve when I was at Mrs. Hevener's house, up the road from where we lived, on that day Daddy died, I was sure up until I was thirty-eight that it would come true. I knew that by thirty-seven I'd be dead, so I lived like I was going to die young. I always felt like my father was watching me from somewhere and knew what I was doing and what was happening at home. I was surprised to still be here when I hit thirty-eight, and I felt like I'd been given a whole new life.

CHAPTER 3
The End of the Beginning

In a couple of days a lot of relatives showed up. My uncles, who were my father's brothers, took Jimmy and me out to a car and explained to us that our daddy "had gone away to a better place" and he'd wait there until we came to him some day.

I thought, *What in the hell are these guys trying to put over on us?* But I didn't say anything because I didn't want to make them feel bad. I figured anyone dumb enough to believe such nonsense needed my protection. I made another resolve right then, to watch out for what adults said about things because they had a lot of bullshit you had to sort out if you really wanted to know what was going on.

I kept all of this a secret, of course, not just because I didn't want them to feel bad, but because it let me know that I was big enough to take care of myself and not as dumb as they were. I didn't want to buy their soft sales pitch. Somehow they were trying to say that what had happened to my daddy and me had not really happened.

We traveled to Norton, Virginia, about six hours drive south, where we buried my father. On the way back we had a head-on collision on the highway that pretty much totaled the car. My sister was singing the song, "I'm a Big Girl Now," which was popular at the time, and as we topped a hill there was another car right there coming toward us in our lane. We crashed right into it and my sister's head hit the windshield. My brother and I got thrown off the seat. We all got by with just a couple of bloody noses and some cuts on the forehead. No big injuries.

Looking back now at that day, it was an obvious turning point in my life. But I feel fortunate because I was well loved in my early childhood. Recently I was reading a book, *The Science of Evil,* by Simon Baron-Cohen (Basic Books, 2011), who says:

> *"John Bowlby [is] a psychoanalyst and child psychiatrist at the Tavistock Clinic in London. It was here that he developed his remarkable attachment theory, which explored (on the negative side) the consequences of parental rejection and (on the positive side) the consequences of parental affection. I say remarkable because the theory made predictions that have been amply proved and are extremely important socially.*
>
> *"According to Bowlby, the infant uses the caregiver as a 'secure base' from which to explore the world, feeling that when they move away from their parent they can also return to him or her for 'emotional refueling.' (The caregiver is often, but not necessarily, the child's mother or father.) By giving praise, reassurance, and a feeling of safety, the caregiver's affection helps the child manage his or her anxiety, develop self-confidence, and trust in the security of the relationship.*
>
> *"My paraphrase of Bowlby's theory is this: What the caregiver gives their child in those first few critical years is like an internal pot of gold. The idea—which builds on Freud's insight—is that what a parent can give his or her child by way of filling the child up with positive emotions is a gift more precious than anything material. That internal pot of gold is something the child can carry inside him or her throughout their life, even if they become a penniless refuge or are beset by other challenges. This internal pot of gold is what gives the individual the strength to deal with challenges, the ability to bounce back from setbacks, and the ability to show affection and enjoy intimacy with others, in other relationships."*

I had my pot of internal gold.

The end of that year was full of surprises. Daddy died and then Mama wrecked the car and almost killed the rest of us. We survived both events, but my mom immediately began to fall apart. She started disappearing every so often, and coming back in a day or so drunk or hung over. My sister took care of us when Mama was away, sometimes for days at a time. School started then, on September 8, 1946, the day I turned six. Here came life . . . ready or not.

CHAPTER 4

School and Home

My first grade teacher, Miss Maude, was wonderful. I was her pet. She told my mom when she visited the school once that year that I was a "very good boy" and that when I had burped during "quiet time" in class I said, "Excuse me." That was for her a model of politeness for all the other kids, and she was proud of me as a good boy who was smart and polite. I loved school. I was good at it. I was finding out I was smart and I liked being there. I was the teacher's pet and I liked it.

I also loved the radio programs after school. After the forty-five-minute ride home on the school bus I would do my chores quickly so I could listen to *The Lone Ranger* on the radio at five o'clock every weekday. At recess every day my buddy Donnie Hevener and I would play like we were the Lone Ranger and Tonto. Every single recess through the first and second grade, I think, we played this game. Most of the time, I was the Lone Ranger.

When my mother would disappear now and then for her drinking binges, she'd sometimes come home with her panties in her purse. My sister covered for her, but not very well. Mama tried to act cheerful sometimes, but she was sad and desperate and lost, and looking for comfort anywhere she could find it. Unfortunately, help was on the way.

The war was just over in the Pacific and people were coming home from the service. Tommy Hevener, the son of Sally Hevener, the woman up the road (the same lady who had taken care of us the day my father died), came home from the Pacific. He was shell shocked. He was a hellion. He was charming. He was an alcoholic. He was a hell of a good distraction. Mamma married him when I was seven.

Tommy was a machinist. He got drunk a lot. He got and lost a lot of jobs, and continued to do so all the rest of his life. People hired him because they knew he was good at what he did, even if he couldn't always be relied on to be there to do it. With a little effort though, he almost always managed to get fired, even though now and then a former employer would hire him for "a job" or "by the job" when he was down and out. He beat my mother up a lot when he was drinking. He had terrors and dreams and memories of firing a "five-inch gun" from a ship at targets too far away to see, and then for days on end floating among swollen and rotting bodies surrounding the ship in the sea for "as far as you could see."

He screamed sometimes when he was almost falling asleep, and sometimes when he was drunk, and sometimes in his sleep. For a while, when he was sober, Tommy would take a swipe at being a daddy for us, but when he realized he couldn't he pretty much gave it up and stopped pretending.

We moved to Bristol, Tennessee, when I was in the second grade. It was one state and 300 miles away from his mother and, for my mother, a chance to escape the memories she had of my father living with her in the same house she now lived in with Tommy. They had drunk up the social security checks that came for us kids and hadn't made the house payments with them for several months in a row, so they decided to move to Bristol, put the place up for sale, and become bootleggers for additional income. After six months, however, they moved back to the house in the orchard on Morris Mill Road, renegotiated the house loan, and decided to try to live there again.

Mom and Tommy had not done good at the bootleg business. Their idea (like other bootleggers in Virginia) had been to sell booze at double the price when the ABC liquor store was closed on the weekends. But because they drank up most of what they bought during the week to sell on the weekends before the weekends came around, they never could quite figure out the profit-and-loss statements until after they were sober, which was a little late for them to do that kind of reckoning, I reckon.

So we came back home. The same house. The same orchard. The same outdoor John, same garden, same cistern. The same dirt road in front. The same neighbors. The same memories. The same mother-in-law and step-grandmother up the road. The same father-in-law and father to my stepfather ("Pappy" Hevener) and fellow drunk and dirty old man up the road. And, unfortunately, the same way of living as before: everybody but the kids drunk on the weekend; hung over and broke on Monday.

Money, and sometimes food, was thin Tuesday through Thursday, but if the social security checks didn't come that week (meaning, Mama and Tommy couldn't get drunk again), I'd have some worry-free days. Normally they'd be getting groceries and getting drunk on Friday night. Drunk on Saturday. Drunk on Sunday, if there was anything left to drink. Back at work on Monday . . . most of the time.

This situation was tolerable until my next little brother got born.

CHAPTER 5

Home Again, Home Again

When we moved back to Staunton from Bristol, Tennessee, things at home got a lot worse. Mama had a couple of miscarriages from beatings. She and Tommy drank every weekend or whenever payday came for either one of them. The first week after the social security checks came usually meant Tommy not going to work, or both of them not going to work, until there was no more money. They'd buy groceries then, too, but the groceries often ran out before the alcohol did. Peanut butter and mayonnaise sandwiches, school lunches, and some milk from up the road for the baby would get us by until the next money showed up.

School made up for a lot of the scariness, lonesomeness, and hurt of my home. I fell completely in love with my third grade teacher. I was always slow doing the morning class work, even though I tried to do well. I'd have to stay over at recess to finish my work; this meant I could be closer to her without so many other kids around. Being at school and listening to *The Lone Ranger* when I got home were still the highlights of my life.

My older sister was still at home then, and though her interests as a teenager competed with her substitute mothering for us, she always loved me and my brother; she was with us most of the time when Mama and Tommy were gone.

When my mother had another baby, Mike, I was nine. He came early, also because of a beating, but he survived. My sister left home pretty soon after the baby arrived because my stepfather started making a lot of passes at her. Anno graduated from high school, met a sailor, got married, and moved to Texas.

All of a sudden my sister was gone. All of a sudden there was the new baby in the house. Nothing major changed about my folks' drinking or general lifestyle after the baby came, so it ended up being me who became the main caretaker of my little brother Mike, and a poor substitute for a parent for my brother Jimmy, who was just fifteen months younger than me.

During those years between nine and thirteen, I went through a gradual transformation from being a nice, polite kid to being a different kind of kid. When I came home from school I often had to take care of the baby, cut wood for the fire, fix the food, clean the house, wash the diapers (or just hang them up to dry so they could be used again), and try to get my brother Jimmy to help out so little Mike could survive.

I did the best I could, but when he was not quite three years old, Mike got rheumatic fever. He was very sick for a while and it damaged his heart. This scared me. It made me come to a serious, grounding realization: I was twelve and my little brother was three, and he had rheumatic fever and it had damaged his heart, and I was the only one in the house who was really paying attention. The doctor said Mike had to have rest and that he needed quiet if he was to have a chance of healing. I became then not only his caretaker, but also his protector from the chaos of our family. I worried about that a lot and I loved him a lot, and I tried to take care of him well. But I became a tougher individual with everyone else in the world other than him, and I was gradually becoming a meaner person. Here is another flashback.

I am almost eleven-years old. My little brother, Mike, is sick and there is nobody here but me to take care of him. I am worried. I check on him constantly, walk him around when he is crying, lay down with him to put him to sleep, feed him bottles, and feed him some baby food. I am doing everything I can, but I don't know if it is good enough. I am always a little bit afraid. I am always a little bit mad. I check on my little brother, and then, when my younger brother Jimmy gets home from school, I try to browbeat him to help me by going out to get some more wood for the fire or staying with the baby and walking him around while I go get wood.

I don't know how to do this. I pray a lot. I ask God to take care of my little brother. I ask God not to let Tommy kill my mother. I ask God to make them run out of whiskey quick. I ask God to make things okay. I am not sure God is there, but I keep saying I will be good if He will just help me, in case he is there.

I am always alert. I am always a little bit tense. I wish my sister was here again. I wake up quickly when my brother stirs, when my folks come home, when my stepfather or his father come into the house, when other people come over and come in. I try to tell what level of drunk they are. I am not scared of most of them except for Tommy, and I am not scared of him for myself, but on behalf of others, and I am scared that any of them will make a ruckus and wake the baby.

When Tommy is drinking, I watch him carefully to see which kind of being drunk he is in: the mean kind or the harmless and helpless kind. I watch to see if my mother is going to be okay to take care of Mike before I go to school in the morning. If she is I go get on the bus. If she isn't, I act like I am going to the bus, put my brother Jimmy on it, and return to the house. I want to go to school if I think I can, though, because there I can relax a little bit.

My stepfather kept drinking. He kept beating up my mother and any of the rest of us he could reach or catch. And the bums that were their usual cohorts kept coming over to the house for binges, making noise, and getting in the way. I was being as good as I could to make it so everything would be okay. I had to be good and be alert and manage things. But more and more it seemed to me like I would have to do something other than just be good and polite, and quick on my feet, or else my brother's chance of healing his damaged heart—and maybe even his chance to live—was going to continue to be taken away. Prayer didn't seem to work.

The baby was going to keep on getting scared and being woken up and having a hard time resting. So, as I got more worried and angrier, I changed. I became an increasingly active, meaner, and more aggressive protector. What happened to my mother, my little brother Mike, and (sometimes because of me being mean to him) my brother Jimmy, started to change. And what happened to Tommy, because of me, began to change pretty quickly. Ultimately I saw that I couldn't manage my little brother being able to rest, or heal, or not be scared, unless I did something to end the conditions that blocked that. Tommy, it seemed to me was at the heart of those conditions—and I didn't like the sonofabitch, anyway—so what I did next seemed like the best way to handle him.

When I first started crisis interventions, they were of the "run in and run out" kind. I ran in and hit my stepfather over the head with something several different times when he was beating on Mama, or about to, or had just knocked her down or was choking her. One time I hit him with a plate, which broke and cut his head. I also ran in and hit him with various other objects. Once I hit him hard over the head with a ketchup bottle, and when the glass bottle broke on his head, it cut his head open, and there was some blood, but there was also a hell of a lot of red ketchup that just blew all over the place. It scared the shit out of him! It also made me happy as hell! I laughed so hard and hysterically that he almost caught me that time. It felt really great to scare the shit out of him for a change!

After that, whenever I'd run in and bust Tommy with something, I'd run like hell. He'd almost always get winded before he could catch me, and even if he did catch me, he was too winded to hold onto me. I'd slip out of his grasp. Sometimes the noise would wake the baby, so I'd circle back and get the baby, and then run away again. I'd take little Mike to his grandmother's house up the road, or to the barn for a while, or to the chicken house. Or we'd just go out in the orchard until things blew over or Tommy got drunker, or got patched up and was no longer a menace.

After the baby went to sleep or was at his grandma's house, Tommy would ask me to fix him a sandwich, which I would do, if there was bread and anything to make one with. The battle would be over until the next episode. I spent a lot of time on the following flashback in therapy but I am still not quite over it.

I am eleven years old. It is morning. I am standing in the kitchen. Tommy has just slapped me hard across the face. I stand right there and say, "Fuck you, you sonofabitch!" He backhands me as hard as he can and knocks me down. I get up.

"Fuck you, you God-damned cock-sucking bastard!" He slaps me again, knocks me down again. I get up. My nose is bleeding. "Fuck you! You God-damned piece of shit. Kiss my fucking ass, you cock-sucking bastard!" Backhand again. Didn't knock me down. "Fuck you!"

Slap!

"You can kill me, you cock-sucking bastard, but I will never fucking shut up! Kiss my God-damned ass, you God-damned, stupid motherfucker!"

Tommy walks out. I yell after him, "Fuck you, you chicken shit sonofabitch!" I wash my face in cold water. The water's all red. I think, Fuck him. *If I am willing to die and he is not willing to kill me, I win. Fuck him.*

My grandfather who had taught me and Jimmy to shoot a .22 rifle as little kids used to put us up in target shooting matches against other local country boys who were teenagers or older, wanted us both to have .22 rifles. After Tommy came on the scene, my grandfather gave my brother and me each another rifle every Christmas. He did it each year for three years in a row because we wouldn't have one anymore by the time the next Christmas rolled around again. By February or March every year, Tommy would destroy the rifles we'd just got for Christmas by beating them on the edge of the concrete back porch in some paranoid fit. We'd tell Granddad that Tommy had ruined our guns, and the next year he would give us two more.

The third time it happened, I took a hacksaw to the bent barrel left over from Tommy's attempted demolishment and taped up the busted stock, and had me a sawed-off .22. It didn't look like much, but made a hell of a lot of noise when it was fired. I kept it hidden out in the woodshed, or up at the barn or in the orchard, and I began to use it to run off various bums who came out to the house to hang out with Tommy and my mother. I would pull my sawed-off .22 on them when they came up the steps to the porch and threaten to shoot them if they didn't get the hell out of there. I also started telling them they needed to stay the hell away or I'd destroy either them or their cars.

One guy came back more than once. I busted out the front windshield of his car with a big rock, which the owner found to be so convincing that he didn't come back again. I myself found it convincing that this behavior on my part worked so I elaborated on it.

If Tommy was passed out, when I ran people off by meeting them at the front door with my sawed-off gun they'd threaten to beat the shit out of me. But eventually they'd always leave, even when I was holding an obviously damaged gun and several times when I had no ammunition and was, in fact, completely bluffing!

"If you walk through that fuckin' door I will shoot you in the gut."

"Put that gun away kid, or I'll take it and beat the shit out of you."

"Go ahead," I'd say. "All you've gotta do is come through that door to reach me. Come on!"

I cussed like a sailor, having learned how from my stepfather, who was a sailor for six years in the Pacific, and his cronies, some of whom came from the war as well. As a twelve- and thirteen-year-old, I did have a hell of a presentation and a good bluff; I tended to communicate with a fair amount of forcefulness and graphic images from years of listening to *The Lone Ranger,* and my other homeschooling. And I had some degree of clarity about exactly what was required on the part of the person I was addressing, and what was going to happen if they didn't do what I requested, a skill and fault that has remained with me until this very day. I became a cocky little sonofabitch. And the only part I have grown out of completely is the "little" part.

I definitely was learning something. Mostly what I learned was that your bluff works if you're completely willing to have it not be a bluff and communicate that fact clearly. When I actually had bullets, I was willing to shoot them, and I was kind of eager for the chance to see what would happen. Though this is a two-edged sword, one that has sometimes cut me, it is still a sword.

Later on in life when I struggled to remain non-violent in the '60s, I recalled these confrontations from earlier in my life. In civil rights confrontations, and when I spoke in opposition to racists, warmongers, right-wingers, and moralists of all kinds, I seemed to be able to get their attention and scare the shit out of them fairly well even while apparently advocating nonviolence. I have a presentation, and it is fairly accurate, of being just about to lose control. Of course, in a way, I am just as scared as they are about what I might do. That helps, too.

Over those years of the civil rights and anti-Vietnam War movement, and more recently when I raised hell about Bush, Cheney, and the rest of the God-damned, ignorant, shit-for-brains, self-righteous, dumb-assed pricks that surrounded them in Washington, D.C., everyone in range had no doubt what the fuck I was talking about. I have my stepfather to thank for that. He set up the model and the conditions of practice for that important part of my education, and I am grateful for it.

I've never really been taken up on my bluff in any fights since becoming an adult. Standing there shaking and being completely willing to die with tears running down my cheeks and cussing like a sonofabitch with my voice barely making it seems to show a pretty good offense, making defense pretty much unnecessary. Likewise, whenever I have faced anyone who looked just like me in that state I've had enough sense to back off and leave them the hell alone. That has saved me from getting my ass kicked a few times, and possibly saved my life.

I do know where the line is between threat and mayhem, and this has helped me help people as a psychotherapist many times, because anger doesn't scare me. I know it well. I know when to press and when to let up. I usually win because I know where the edge is about losing control with a slightly finer distinction than whomever I am up against.

After my thirteenth birthday in September 1953, things at home got even worse and I got even madder. Leading up to Christmas, Mama and Tommy drank up the money from the social security checks, including the portion that was usually used to make the house payment. They bought liquor and didn't get hardly any groceries. We lived off of the end of the garden harvest, me killing groundhogs, and us getting milk from the neighbors, hog meat from the late-October butchering, and handouts from Mrs. Hevener up the road. Then, my brother Jimmy and I got nothing for Christmas that year but one God-damned pair of blue jeans each.

That really pissed me off.

My little brother had a lot of colds and was still not being cared for enough to help him heal the damage to his heart, and he couldn't rest on weekends much for all the racket and trouble. That pissed me off more than ever. And right around the first of the year, I remember finally consciously deciding, "No more Mr. Nice Guy!" I decided that this shit was coming to an end. There were two main episodes that seemed to emerge from that decision that changed our family history.

One night Tommy came storming in, about two or three good drinks into the bottle (his meanest time). He was pissed off and hollering and mean as hell, and he went to beat up on Mama again. Jimmy and I were standing next to the stove. The baby was asleep in the bedroom. We looked at each other, and without speaking, both of us reached for a stick of firewood. Together we turned on Tommy and started hitting him. We hit him hard with those chunks of wood, with all of the fury of years of pent-up hatred and hurt for abuses received, and for all of the times we'd watched helplessly and done nothing when he was beating Mama. We suddenly became no longer weak, and we absolutely beat the living shit out of him.

We sliced half of Tommy's scalp off his head, fractured his skull, and broke three of his ribs. When he was struggling to get back up from the floor, I dipped a towel in the slop bucket and then, menacing him with my bloody piece of firewood in one hand, made him mop up the blood splattered on the floor and the spilled slop. Afterwards I told him to get his fucking ass out the backdoor or die. He took off, but on his way around the house he threw a rock through the kitchen window.

I went running outside with my bloody stick of wood still in my hand and when he ran for his life from me I knew something had changed for good. I ran his ass down the road. And I liked it. I wasn't bluffing anymore. I decided to make it policy.

The next day when Tommy returned from being taped up and sewed up, we had a conversation that was mostly me talking and him listening, with him still not feeling too good, but stone-cold sober. I got right in front of his face and I explained to him how he couldn't continue as he had, drunk or sober, without consequences, and that I would personally, God-damned guarantee the fucking consequences would be worse than anything he'd seen so far in his miserable, fucking life if he ever laid a hand on anyone in our house again.

It was only a few nights later that the next chance for change occurred. After the social security checks arrived and they'd cashed them, my mother came into my room where I'd laid down with my little brother to help him fall asleep. She said, "Bradley, this is the money for the house payment. I am leaving it with you. We're going out and I don't want to spend it, so you take care of it for me."

I said, "Okay," and they left.

The next morning they hadn't returned and I didn't get on the school bus when my brother Jimmy did. I put that $93 in my pocket. I took my little brother, Mike, up the road to his grandma's house and asked her to take care of him for a day. Then I went down to the road and caught a ride into town. I went to the hardware store in downtown Staunton. I bought a twelve-gauge shotgun for me and a sixteen-gauge shotgun for my brother, along with a case of shells for each of us. I bought a basketball hoop and a basketball, and a rod and reel. I took a cab home and gave the driver all that was left of the money for a tip. I'd spent every cent of it.

I went into the woodshed, assembled both guns, and loaded them. It was about 11:30 in the morning. My brother had gone to school and wouldn't get home until 4:00. Mama and Tommy had come home late that morning while I was gone, and they were asleep. My little brother Mike was still at his grandma's. I walked into the house with a shotgun under each arm, rousted my mom and stepfather out of the bed, and told them to get the hell up and clean the fucking house right now or else I was going to kill them. And they cleaned the hell out of it! I didn't even have to shoot a hole in the wall to prove I was serious, as I had planned.

When my brother Jimmy got home from school I met him right after he got off the bus and gave him his shotgun. He was really happy. We walked around and shot everything we could find to shoot at out in the orchard. Then, a little later, he shot my new basketball, thinking it was the old one. I got mad at him and we started hiding behind trees and shooting at each other. Luckily we were far enough apart that the bird shot missed. But later, I took his gun away from him and hid both of them out in the orchard.

That night, our folks disappeared again. The next morning they came home and we had a serious conversation. I told my stepfather again that I wanted him to understand, while he was cold sober, that the next time he laid a hand on anybody I was going to kill him. Now I was better armed for the job, having two shotguns and nearly two cases of shells. My mother said this was very serious, that they wanted me to give the guns back so that they could be returned and the house payment made, because we were already three payments behind and would lose the house if a payment wasn't made.

I wasn't about to give those guns up. But I decided we needed some kind of help from outside. I called my grandmother and grandfather in Knoxville, Tennessee, and asked them to come because I was sure something bad was going to happen if they didn't. They came. It was pretty clear to everyone, once the truth got told about all the shit that had been going on, that our family couldn't stay together as it was without someone getting killed—and it sure as shit wasn't going to be me or one of my brothers I told them with the absolute self-righteous arrogance of a thirteen-year-old looking for a chance to be the Lone Ranger.

Eventually I negotiated, meaning I relented and dictated the changes other than murder that I would accept. I told them what conditions needed to be met in order for me to give up the guns, and they did as I said. My little brother, Mike, was to move in and live permanently with his grandma who lived up the road. He could stay with Mother and Tommy now and then, but he *lived* with Mrs. Hevener now. He'd get on the school bus from there. He'd stay overnight there every night except now and then on weekends if she said so. I'd be kept informed of how that agreement was maintained by Mike's grandma. They understood that if anything changed I'd be returning to set things right. My brother, Jimmy, would go to live with our uncle and aunt and his two cousins in Etowah, Tennessee. I would go live with my sister and brother-in-law in College Station, Texas. They all, including Grandma, agreed. When they agreed to, and did everything I said, I gave them the guns and the fishing pole and the rest of the shells back.

They got the money back from the hardware store for the guns and the basketball hoop, and the rod and reel, and a third of the ammunition, and they made another house payment. My grandmother and grandfather paid my bus fare to Texas and gave Jimmy a ride to Tennessee. And the social security checks from the government were changed to go directly to our caretakers.

Since the social security checks for me and Jimmy were no longer coming to Mother and Tommy, and were being sent per my original instructions (as dictator of the deal) to our real caretakers until such time as we might move back to Virginia, they had more of a task than they could handle making the monthly house payment themselves instead of drinking it up.

Within a couple of months, they missed another house payment, and the place was repossessed by the bank.

Tommy and Mother moved into a trailer up on the hill at Tommy's parents' place. When the trailer burned from Tommy passing out while he was smoking a cigarette, all the last remnants and pictures from our whole family past went up in flames. Just about the only record of those times is now this book. After that happened, about a year after her kids left home, my mother left Tommy and moved in with her mother and dad in Knoxville, Tennessee. Tommy moved in with his mother and father and his younger brother, Joe, and my little brother, Mike, who was then about six years old.

After I moved to Texas, I wrote my little brother several times a week. I missed him and loved hearing from him. The Heveners had no telephone, so we never talked. He and his grandma sent me a lot of printed letters with stories of how he was doing starting school and riding the bus and living with Grandma, and some school pictures. I made plans with them to come back to visit for the summer after I'd been away in Texas for about fifteen months, from March 1954 until June 1955.

When I came back to Virginia, I was fifteen years old and bigger than when I left. I'd grown a lot. I had worked three months full time, hoeing crops in the Brazos River Bottom in Texas the summer before. I had "gone out" for basketball and played on the B-team in the fall season. I also had been learning a lot. When I got to Virginia, I got a job eight hours a day thinning apples in the orchards. I lived there with Mrs. Hevener for almost three months.

In the early summer, about a month after I got there, when I was coming home one evening from work, as I approached the house I heard Mrs. Hevener and Mike screaming. Instantly I knew that Tommy was mean-drunk again and beating his mother. I could hear her hollering and the familiar sound of fists hitting flesh. I became like the Hulk. I ran full speed up the driveway for the house and came the wrong way through the kitchen screen door, splitting it in half and knocking the molding completely from the door frame.

When I hit Tommy in the mouth on the first punch I swear to God I knocked him ten feet into the air and entirely across the dining room into a doorjamb on the other side. He landed on all fours before he finished sliding down to the floor. Two of his teeth were showing, sticking out on the front side of his lip, and blood was squirting down over the front of his tee-shirt, which I ripped to pieces when I fell on him and began pummeling the shit out of him. Then I heard my little brother yelling and begging me to stop, and I did. He'd been terrified already that his daddy would kill his grandma, and now he was terrified that I would kill his daddy.

I stood up and said to Mike, "Okay, okay, I won't hit him anymore," to try to calm him.

His grandma took Mike with her, while I helped Tommy up by his arm and pulled him into the living room and seated him on the couch. One more time I got right in front of him. I was still breathing hard. I looked in his eyes and said, "You can do two things now for the next half hour. You can sit very still and you can bleed. That's it. Or you can say another fucking word, or move in any way, and I will kill you." I was shaking and crying, and he didn't move a fucking inch.

Then I left the house and took my little brother outside. We walked around through the fields and up to the woods and talked. I told him that everything would be better now, and that when his daddy got mean he wouldn't hurt his grandma anymore, not ever again, and that I wouldn't hurt his daddy anymore because I wouldn't have to. And I didn't. I never hit Tommy again.

After that, whenever I'd go back to Virginia to visit my brother, Mike, drunk or sober Tommy was always very well behaved. We talked some as I got a little older. He introduced me as his stepson to people and said he was proud of me. We got drunk together a couple of times, but we never fought. I began to forgive him. I began to feel a little sorry for him about how he had been fucked up by the war and how he had fucked up his life since he came back.

During one drunken conversation when I was about seventeen, Tommy asked me a favor. He said that after he died he wanted me to visit his grave, bring a bottle of whiskey, take a drink, pour the rest on the head of his grave, and then piss on the foot of it. A few years later, in my early thirties, I did that: I went out to his grave with a girlfriend of mine and we took a few swigs. But when the time came, instead of pouring the whiskey on his head and pissing at his feet, I pissed on his headstone and poured the whiskey at his feet.

I still had a little completion work to do.

Tommy died at the age of forty-nine. When Tommy started asking for it again, his brother Joe, who also lived in the Hevener household, had kicked him so hard in the leg that he broke it. The next week a blood clot separated from his injured leg and went to his brain. He died of a stroke at work, just a day before payday. It was a kind of pitiful, but fitting, end to that sad life.

I inherited from Tommy his "Jap" rifle, which he'd brought home from the Pacific. Years later some junkie in Washington, D.C., stole it and probably hocked it for money for a fix. Shit happens. Shit just keeps on happening.

Tommy Hevener's life was futile. He did the best he could. This will be the only biography he'll ever have. Yet his contribution to humanity through me and Mike, and my brother James, and my sister, Eleanor, is still going on, and is hard to estimate. Not just because of what he contributed to us, but because of all the lives he touched and all the lives touched by us, and on and on. Like six degrees of separation over a long span, from Tommy Hevener to Kevin Bacon, onwards to the end of time, the reverberations in the field of the body politic, like the wisdom of God, cannot be calculated and can't be known. But I am grateful for his life and for mine, and for that of my little brother Mike who is sixty-one years old at the time of this writing. Our contributions to the world, for better or for worse, are out there reverberating as we speak. The tock from our tick may be what saves humankind from itself.

Like George Bush creating the chance for Barack Obama to remake America and the world (though Barack apparently doesn't have the balls to do it), Tommy Hevener did his damage and his part in creating a future some of us may still have the chance to be present to and joyful about . . . if we have the balls to do it.

CHAPTER 6

Good Will Hunting

Before we leave that life on the farm and in the apple orchard, I want to say that I really loved a lot of things about my life back then, even though there was often a lot of trouble with the people who were in charge and I felt powerless to do much about it until I was twelve or thirteen. When I look back, what stands out for me emotionally were the moments of fear and pain and hurt and anger I experienced, and I tend to select those more dramatic memories from out of all the memories I have of my childhood home. But in terms of quantity, the truth is that I really had many more ongoing pleasant experiences than negative ones.

My grandpa, for instance, taught me how to hunt when I was very young, and I hunted squirrels, groundhogs, and rabbits for years. I skinned and cleaned them, and the family ate everything I killed. I also trapped or killed some animals, including skunks, and sold their hides. The skunks were sold to the junkyard in town. Tommy would take them in for me and my brother. Our friend Joe Cook sometimes hunted skunks at night with us. We got 25 cents for a number four skunk (almost all-white), 50 cents for a number three, 75 cents for a number two, and a full dollar for a number one (almost all-black), and we didn't even have to skin 'em ourselves!

We hulled walnuts each fall by collecting them and putting them in the driveway so they could be driven over to separate the hulls from the shells. Tommy took these to town when he went to work. He sold the dried-out, uncracked walnuts at the junkyard for us, too. I really loved hunting and providing food for the family, and skinning and tanning the hides of animals. I even liked feeding the chickens and collecting their eggs, feeding the hogs and helping butcher them in the fall, riding on the horse, and cutting wood with the Model-T circular saw, and then going in the truck to the mountains to get slab wood. We had a pretty good life for ourselves except for the drinkin' and fightin'.

I liked building fence, too. One of the only times where I felt like Tommy and I related was when we built fence together. I can remember starting to have muscles that stood out from digging post holes when I was about eleven. I liked working in the sun, getting a tan, and becoming muscular, and also being able to show progress in the work as the posts lined out and we got the fence stretched tight.

I liked helping bring in the apples in the fall, both helping load them to take them to the press and bringing back the barrels of cider to drink some while it was sweet—and also waiting for it to get to be hard cider when it had fermented. Before getting on the school bus in the morning to go to school, sometimes I liked going down to the basement to get a little drunk on cider.

On Sundays, if I could leave Mike with relatively sober parents or with his grandma, Jimmy, me, and our friend Joe Cook would walk seven miles through the woods to the store "up at the 'pike." There we'd buy a candy bar and a cold drink and then walk all the way back. When we were about ten or so we started stealing a little whiskey from my stepfather or wine from his old man, who often came to get drunk with his son and daughter-in-law. He used to feel Mama up now and then when his son was asleep. We stole some cigarettes from Tommy, along with the whiskey, and then we'd smoke and take a drink in the woods. On occasion we'd buy chewing tobacco at the store for ourselves to augment the experience. We felt like we were really getting away with something, and it was a delicious secret—a mark of us growing up.

Living out in the country in the Shenandoah Valley was a blessing of wondrous proportions. Every day I was surrounded by beautiful, protective mountains in the distance and hills close at hand. The apple orchard bloomed in the spring, at which time the whole world was beautiful and smelled especially sweet. There was a garden we worked all the time, and we had chickens and ate eggs and milk and hog meat. Basically, we lived in the land of plenty in the boom time of the 1950s. We had a cistern with running water and built a new outhouse every five or six years (or at least dug a new hole to put the old one over). We had a barn and a smokehouse and a woodshed and hog pens and a packing shed. It was a good place to grow up.

These days, I live in the Shenandoah Valley for the most of each year again. I am only about fifty miles from that place where I spent my first thirteen years. I came back to the Valley after many years of living elsewhere and wandering the world, and I still love it here. It is like living in a great big, snuggling, nurturing meditation. I feel very lucky to have been born here and to live here now.

Most of my many years of personal psychotherapy focused on unresolved anger and hurt, denial of fear, and memories of aggression on my part where I won or lost, outfoxing stupid adults or getting caught. Moments of joy or commonplace happiness take a back seat in most therapists' minds, and in most clients' minds, because of how we all think about psychotherapy as trying to make up for, or fix, what went wrong. I've found that when I am able to allow myself to recall the memories of what went right as well as what went wrong, and experience them in my body, it frees me up to be open to new moments without prejudice or defensiveness. The bitterness recedes and forgiveness happens, and then gratitude emerges. It does . . . really . . . I swear. Not just because I think it should, but because it seems to be a natural outcome of facing the truth of experience, and being willing to have things be "as they were" and "as they are."

Please forgive the commercial here for body-oriented psychotherapy, but I can't resist—and don't really want to. I think part of my ability to do this kind of embodied recall myself, and my skill in leading clients through it, is due to an advantaged childhood. I had to face a lot of intense experiences and not run away from them, because I couldn't run away if I still wanted to take care of my little brother and protect our youngest brother.

From my work with other adult children of alcoholics I've discovered that there are advantages to having alcoholic parents. It is good training in terms of getting ready for life and for psychotherapy as a vocation. Being comfortable with unpredictable circumstances is a must for that profession, as is being watchful and being able to discern changing moods regardless of what people are saying. I think the background support of country living and experiencing a wide-ranging emotional and physical territory helped me cultivate this latter ability, probably as much as, and perhaps more than most of the professional training I received in the course of becoming a clinical psychologist.

Sometimes truisms are true. It's never too late to have a happy childhood. Pig's ears make the best purses. Shit grows good veggies. Been down so long it looks like up to me. Thank God, I'm a country boy . . . and on and on. All true!

CHAPTER 7
Texas

When I was in the middle of my thirteenth year, relocating to College Station, Texas, I moved into the old World War Two army barracks converted to married student housing at Texas A & M University where Anno and her husband lived. My brother-in-law, Joe, was going to school on the G.I. Bill to become an electrical engineer. He'd left the Navy, married my sister, and started college a few years before. My sister was working as a secretary at the Air Force Base.

I was grateful for them letting me stay there and happy they could start getting my social security check to help take care of me. I looked for a chance to contribute back to them and found out that there were garden plots for each couple in the housing project, located in a field behind the buildings. Here I planted a garden, filling all the space they let me have. I raised so many tomatoes and so much corn, green beans, lettuce, carrots, and radishes that I ended up supplying a lot more folks than just us with fresh vegetables. I was proud of that garden and happy so many people appreciated me for what I could provide. I felt like I could contribute and not just be the one being taken care of.

My new school was quite different than the little country school I'd come from. A&M Consolidated High School was a teacher training school for Texas A & M, and everyone in my class was ahead of me in what they knew. It was March when I arrived, and since I'd been a freshman in high school back home they made me a freshman there. I continued the path I'd begun. Only, the administrators didn't know that I'd gone from seventh grade to freshman in high school in Virginia mainly because there was no eighth grade. I was used to being the smartest one in my class back in Virginia, but now that wasn't true anymore.

Everything was all new, even the school building. It had modern classrooms and a big assembly hall. The subjects I took (Chemistry, English, History, and so forth) were taught by different teachers in each period. That was a new thing. I learned a new concept called "studying." I hadn't really "studied" anything before. Sure, I'd liked reading and writing and cutting up in school, but now it looked like there was a whole new way to be in school. My brother-in-law studied his ass off and griped all the time from being tired. He carried a slide rule and books around with him, and worried about passing tests and making grades. It was a brand-new world for me. I liked it. But it was different as hell.

Not long after arriving in Texas, I joined the Boy Scouts. I was a "Tenderfoot" scout. I went to a Jamboree. At the Jamboree you could earn "merit badges" for doing certain things. I couldn't believe what they gave merit badges for: Chopping wood! Hell, I'd been chopping wood all my life. I cut a sapling down and they gave me a badge. "Cut that log in two with that ax." Okay, I cut it. They gave me a badge. *God-damn!* "Split some wood." I split it. Another badge! *Damn. This life here is easy!*

Want me to slop the hogs? Kill and pluck and gut and cut up a chicken? Ride a horse? Run a wood saw? Feed the chickens? Drive? Hunt? Tan a hide? Shuck corn? Pick apples? Build Fence? Put up hay? Plow and plant and weed and grow and harvest a garden? Shit, I'll have merit badges out the ass in this place! And sure enough when I got badges for cross-cut sawing, shooting a target, sharpening a knife, and picking up a snake, I thought: *Shit, I didn't know how meritorious I'd been all my life!*

I first heard about Elvis Presley by attending an assembly at the school where one of the seniors did an imitation of Elvis singing "Heartbreak Hotel." Every kid in the whole place stood up, sang along, and danced, hollered and clapped, and went crazy. I thought, *By God, I have arrived!* It was fun being there. I was living high!

I went out for basketball in the fall. I made the B-team and only got to play in four or five games—usually playing at the end when the game was already lost. But I really worked hard at it. I truly believed that if I just practiced enough I could be a great basketball player. I went to every team practice and also practiced on my own. I took a basketball with me everywhere I went. I dribbled my way to classes and to and from school. At the end of the season in which I scored a total of four points, I dribbled my basketball up into the bleachers where the coach was sitting. I said, "Coach, I want to ask you a question."

He said, "All right."

I said, "I came to every practice and practiced on my own and worked hard at the game and dribbled this ball all over the place. You only played me in a few B-team games all year for only a few minutes usually at the end." Then I asked, "How come you didn't play me more?"

He replied, "Well, you're not a very good basketball player."

It was a shock to me. I knew it was probably true and that he was being straight with me. But I really had thought, until that very moment, that if I was dedicated enough and practiced hard enough I'd get to be as good as anybody could be. Apparently not. This was an important modification of the American Dream for me.

In recalling those days of new beginning, I think probably that this period of my life, which is usually marked as emotionally significant for adolescents, was particularly significant for me because of all the geographic, emotional atmosphere, and class changes happening all at once. One day I was a country boy in rural Virginia on the brink of committing murder and refusing to be bossed by adult idiots anymore. Then the next day I was thirteen and a half in a small city in Texas, living calmly in the married student housing project with my loving relations. They took me into their lifestyle of living on the G.I. Bill and my social security check and working extra on the side, and I joined in gratefully. But, by God, it was different.

I really missed my little brother Mike. And I missed my brother Jimmy, too! Nevertheless I thought living with Anno and Joe in Texas was just wonderful. So many new and pleasant things happened to me. Joe taught me how to play golf, and before long I joined the golf team at school. We went on trips as well as playing matches at home. I bought a used motor scooter to go back and forth to school, and soon learned my way around College Station. I was mobile . . . suddenly, middle class! And there were girls! And some of them thought I was cute!

I went to the Methodist Youth Fellowship (MYF) to meet girls. It was like what had happened when I had joined the Boy Scouts! They liked the ways I talked and acted. At MYF I learned to talk to girls, to flirt, and how to dress up and act civilized. I read and wrote things I liked, and I watched and listened to Elvis Presley, and I learned to dance and make friends, and be out there in the world and live in town, and *not have to worry all the time*. I had a real sense of coming into my own in a positive way. And I liked it.

Here was another time of grace and welcome. Who would've thought it? How lucky could one boy get?

My sister was very sweet to me. That first summer she was pregnant and I helped her out while my brother-in-law was away during the week working elsewhere in Texas. She was working as a secretary and I was working full time in the castor bean fields at the Agricultural Extension Experimental Farm on the Brazos River. I was a hoer. I hoed beans from morning 'til night, and stayed out to watch over the irrigation pumps all night sometimes as well. By the end of the summer I was one of the chief hoers. We were working and helping each other, and we had a baby on the way. A family was happening again, and I was a part of it.

When my niece, little Tina, was born, I helped some with her (being that I was an experienced parent), but I had some conflict with my brother-in-law about how he treated her when he was stressed. He spanked her once for crying when she was just a little baby. I jumped in and cussed him and he knocked me down. That was when I was headed for Virginia on a visit anyway, so I said I was leaving for good then and that I wasn't coming back, that I'd put up with shit like that before in my life, and I didn't ever intend to again.

Joe and my sister talked, and then he came and apologized to me before I left, promising never to do it again. I thanked him for that. Even with some troubles, all in all we were feeling then like we were creating a life and a home that was basically working pretty well.

CHAPTER 8

A New Beginning

When I returned from a three-month visit to Virginia at fifteen, Anno and Joe had already moved to Arlington, Texas. Joe had graduated and gone to work for Chance Vaught Aircraft Company, located near Dallas, as an electrical engineer. Thus I started my senior year at Arlington High School. I turned sixteen a week after school started. My brother Jimmy soon came from Tennessee to join our household. He'd been having a harder time getting along with my uncle and aunt and his cousins than I'd had with my sister and her husband, so when he asked to come to Texas they took him in. Nonetheless, he still had a pretty hard time in Texas.

I can't remember much about my brother Jimmy that particular year. My life as a senior and his as a sophomore were so separate. We had different classes and ways of getting to school, as well as different friends. When I got my driver's license Joe let me use his car now and then, and I started taking girls out on dates. As I write, I feel guilty now about not helping Jimmy feel welcomed or helping him adapt better. He had some hard times with Joe and Anno, and they didn't like the kinds of kids he hung out with, so there was a lot of secretiveness. We never really had an open discussion of how they were comparing what he did with what I'd done when I came to live with them. But it was clear they were disappointed because he was more troubled and rebellious against them than I had been.

I was preoccupied with my own things and didn't do much to help. We went on a few trips together. Once I went back to College Station in Joe's car and Jimmy came along. I treated him mean and drove one-hundred-miles-an-hour for a long stretch because I got angry at him for reading the map wrong and causing us to go a long way in the wrong direction. I don't think I was a very good brother to him; that is one of the places where, if I had my life to do over again, I'd do differently.

I always thought Jimmy got hurt more by our stepfather Tommy than I did because he was almost a year and a half younger than I was when Tommy came into our lives. He was very mechanical and so was Tommy, thus he identified with his stepfather more and, I think, was more hurt by Tommy's meanness than I was. I had a longer time with our daddy and I could remember more about him. Jimmy still needed a daddy more than me, and he needed Tommy to step up to the plate. Tommy used to like to tease and criticize us. Some of it was joking, but most of it was a little harsh and I think Jimmy took it to heart.

For example, Jimmy used to take apart nearly everything he could get his hands on, and sometimes he had a hard time putting things back together. Tommy used to say to him, "What you can't tear up, you'll shit on." To other people, Tommy would say, "What that boy can't take apart, he'll shit on . . ." It was supposed to be funny, and yet it was critical and hurt Jimmy's feelings.

We had a Model-T wood saw: a circular saw hooked up to an old Ford truck with a pulley and a flat belt to turn the big, three-foot-diameter circular saw blade. My brother got a wrench and worked away for quite some time trying to take the nut loose to see if he could remove the saw. You could tell because he made a bunch of scratch marks in the rusty middle of the blade next to the rusted-on nut, but he couldn't get it off.

A few mornings after Jimmy's valiant try at dismantling that machine, I saw Tommy walk by the Model-T on his way to take a dump up at the packing shed next to the hog pen, which he did every day he had a hangover and at least once every weekend. When he got to the saw Tommy stopped and looked it over, and then looked up at the hood of the old truck and laughed. After he left for work, I went and looked closer myself. On the hood of the old truck a little turd stood straight up next to the monkey wrench that had scratched up the circular saw. As far as I know this was never mentioned by anyone, including me. But the lesson had been taken, and it had been confirmed and acknowledged. What Jimmy couldn't take apart he shit on, just like Tommy told him to do.

My brother was a mechanic all of his life before he got too old and injured. To this day, he still does mechanical work and works with computer hardware, and enjoys telling his kids how to fix things.

Tommy used to call me "Perfessor!" all the time, jeeringly, and I became one. Jimmy took a lot of things apart and put them back together again. And he shit on a lot of things that didn't turn out right, too, come to think of it. It's one of them things that makes sense, but is hard to understand because you don't want to.

Anyway, fuck Tommy Hevener! I want to get back to my story.

When I was sixteen, during my senior year in Arlington, I had sex for the first time in the front seat of my brother-in-law's Packard. It was wonderful! So wonderful! Judy Workman. She said she didn't want to have sex with me if it was my first time because she didn't want to be the cause of me losing my virginity. Though she didn't say it, we both knew having sex was supposed to be a bad thing, a sin.

I lied. I told her it was not the first time for me and so she let me fuck her. Of course, she wanted to anyway. It was so good. I had dreamed of this, jacking off every day, usually several times a day, since I was ten or eleven, imagining what it would be like. Five or six years! Despite what one would expect after developing such a large number of expectations from so many imaginings, it was even better than I had anticipated! It felt so hot and good to actually have my prick inside her, moving it back and forth. And it felt good because she liked it, too. The goodness was not just from coming, but from *almost* coming. Moaning and getting wet, and her coming were so much more exciting than what I had imagined. I could not only look at her breasts and see her breasts; I also could feel her breasts and suck on her breasts. And she liked it and it made her hot for me to do it. Touching her made her want to be touched more! Who could have imagined such a thing?

After we came, we rested a little bit and did it all over again! I couldn't believe how good it felt and how good it made me feel.

We fucked like rabbits lots of times and in lots of places after that. I was sold. We did it standing up, from behind, with her on my lap facing either way, at her house, outside in the yard, outside in the woods, in the front of the car, *on* the front of the car, in the back of the car, on the rug, and I am sure, in places I've forgotten. I was sold! That was one of the most fun things I'd ever done in my life. Still is.

In that last year at high school I made new friends, became Homeroom President, joined the high school choir, went to dances, talked a lot about big ideas, and worked several jobs. One of my jobs was working at a drug store soda fountain and being a drug store delivery boy. I wrecked the delivery car once trying to make up time for having fallen behind in deliveries by stopping off to have sex with Judy.

I graduated from high school in June. I was sixteen years old, a year or two ahead of most of my peers, and full of beans. I left my sister's house and moved out on my own and started college at Arlington State College in summer school, a few days after graduation. I'd broken up with Judy Workman and was dating other girls. It was the spring of 1957. Life was good.

Several of the girls I went out with had been given '57 Chevrolets for graduation. I had the time of my life driving around to every drive-in restaurant and drive-in movie theater in the Dallas-Fort Worth area with a pretty girl snuggled up next to me, listening to the radio, and showing off by "burning out" of parking lots and drag racing at stop lights. We were free! And kissing and dancing and humping and necking and fucking—being on my own was just wonderful! I was "choppin' in tall cotton," as they said then in Texas.

So much happened in that year and the next that I could hardly keep up. When I recall it now, I don't know how I did so many things and got in so much trouble, and had such a pile of good and bad luck.

I am a senior at Arlington High School and it is fifth period, about two o'-clock in the afternoon. I have Library Period for this hour. I decide I'm going to sit down at a library table and think. I'm going to decide what to do with my life. I actually reflect on my life and try to figure out what I am cut out for.

Before that hour is over, I've decided that what I want to do is to help people. In particular, I want to help people who are suffering or unhappy or miserable or oppressed. I want to help them become happy and free, to become nurturing to others, and to contribute to the world more than they take from it. I decide then and there to become a psychotherapist. I feel fine having made up my mind.

From that point on, I have never deviated from that original intent. I never took a course that didn't apply to the degrees I needed to reach this goal. I never saw anything I did to earn money to pay my way to get there as anything other than something that needed doing for the accomplishment of that intention.

At the end of the school year, when I moved out, I left Jimmy there alone with Anno and Joe. I feel like even though I wasn't much help being there, I abandoned him. My sister and brother-in-law told me I could have all of my social security check until I was eighteen, and that I could still come over when I liked. They told me they would help me along, if they could, as I went to college. But they never had to give me any money. Still they were kind enough to offer. I was the first member of my family who'd ever gone to college and Joe and Anno were proud of me. Jimmy pretty much stayed with his friends then, kids I hardly ever saw. He stayed pretty separate from Joe and Anno, as well.

I moved into a little cottage behind the United Christian Fellowship House, where I became the janitor in exchange for free rent. The UCF was the on-campus ministry for the Christian Church and the Methodist Church combined, on that relatively small junior college campus. I lived in that very small house with a guy named Chanmyung Kong, from Korea, who could not speak much English. He was a Christian and could sing and was cheerful.

The director of that place, newly graduated from seminary at Perkins School of Theology in Dallas, was a Methodist preacher named Phil Philbrook, who became my father substitute and mentor. He and his wife, Margie, kept an eye on me out of kindness and as a favor to my sister, who had befriended them and asked them to. I kept working at the drug store as a short-order cook, fountain manager, and delivery boy, as well as working for Phil. I bought myself an old car, took three courses in summer school, and got my new independent life going. I got an F in French. I made a D and a C in my other two courses, and I continued on in the fall, starting my first full semester in college already on scholastic probation.

At the end of that first summer school session I hitchhiked to Tennessee to see my mother. On the way there, I got picked up by a man who said he was homosexual and asked me if I'd ever had a blow job. I said no. He explained that most of the male population had experimented with homosexuality and said he thought it might be an interesting experience for me. If I would let him give me a blow job, he would take me an extra 150 miles down the road.

I said yes. We went to his place nearby and he took me to bed. I came in his mouth, and he and I both enjoyed it. After that, he gave me a ride further down the road and at the end asked me if he could blow me again in the car. I said yes, and he did. That was my first real homosexual experience that seemed like full-blown sex, so to speak. Before then, I'd played around some with touching genitals with my stepfather's brother Joe a few times before I left Virginia, and I'd had a circle masturbation competition with four guys once down along the river to see who could come the quickest.

What I concluded from this experience was that sex with boys was fun, but not as much fun for me as it was with girls. I was kind of glad that I liked girls better because it looked like a happier and easier life to me to have more conventional preferences. I was happy to have had the courage to experiment, and I thought I was pretty hot shit to survive on the road all back and forth across America, open to anything, and willing to learn, and getting by with it.

At the beginning of that trip to Knoxville something very strange happened. I'd started the trip by going with my friend Larry Gatchel to what had been his hometown in Missouri when he was a boy. We camped out and went fishing on a creek there for a couple of days. When it came time for me to take off hitchhiking for Tennessee he gave me a ride into town to let me out on the highway. On the way there, we stopped at a Dairy Queen so I could use the pay phone to call my mother and let her know I was on the way. When she answered the phone, she could hardly talk. She sounded like she was in shock. I told her I was heading out toward her, hitchhiking, and would be there in a couple of days. She said, "Okay, honey. I'll see you then," but when we hung up I still felt something was kind of strange about her reaction to my call.

When I got to her house, my mother told me why she'd sounded so strange. My call came on the anniversary of my father's death at exactly the moment of her realizing that he had died eleven years earlier. This time in Knoxville was also on a Sunday, the first Sunday to fall on that date since the day of his death. She said she'd been lying on the couch crying most of that morning. She had just prayed to God to give her some sign that "Howard (my father) knew how I was doing and how my life has gone since he died." The phone rang. When she got up to answer it she glanced at the clock on the wall above the phone. It showed the time to be about 1:45 P.M. The second hand was coming past the six at the bottom and moving toward the twelve at the top, an image that had frozen in her mind when she took my father's pocket watch out and was trying to find a pulse the day he fell down on the floor with a heart attack, *exactly* eleven years earlier to the second.

When I spoke to her on the telephone, my voice had sounded just like my father's. For a moment, she'd thought that God had answered her prayer and my father was calling her up to let her know he'd been watching her!

I had no idea it was the anniversary of my father's death, in any conscious way at least, but there it was: either a perfect coincidence or something we just aren't able to understand yet.

In the fall, when I went back to college, I kept my job at the pharmacy downtown and enrolled in the reserve officer training corps (ROTC) in preparation for becoming a lieutenant in the army if, or when, I graduated. I started going out with Marilyn Sue Miller, whose father had given her a '57 Chevy for graduation. (I wrecked that car once, and her dad's insurance paid to fix it.) We had sex absolutely everywhere, including her parent's bedroom, the living room floor at their house, on the stairs, in the woods, in my little cottage, front seat, back seat, hood, and side of her car, on a train, in a hotel, at a drive-in movie, and, like I said before about doing it with Judy, in a few places and ways I know I forget. She was pretty. She looked like Elizabeth Taylor. We loved sex. I was lovin' life.

I was on my own and feeling my oats, going to college and fucking like a bunny. I was also experimenting with lots of ways of being and lots of imaginary roles. Paul Lemming, the guy who owned the pharmacy and was the chief pharmacist, trusted me because I was pretty straight with him and he admired me for taking care of myself at my young age. Not long after I turned seventeen, the pharmacy went into bankruptcy and the doors were locked. Paul was banned from the premises until an inventory was taken, as the foreclosure people suspected he had been taking from the till a little bit, and possibly was using some drugs and might take more drugs from the pharmacy, knowing he was on the way out.

Paul lived upstairs above the store, and wanted to steal back for himself some of what had been taken from him in the foreclosure. He and I both knew where the laser light beams of the alarm protecting the doors to the pharmacy and pharmaceutical area were. He asked me if I would go down there and get some things for him, saying that while I was there I could take anything I wanted as well. When I snuck down the stairs from up in Paul's place, broke in, and rolled under the electronic surveillance system, I was wearing my ROTC uniform. I thought if I got caught they might be easier on me for being a loyal American about to go and risk my life in the Army. But, as it turned out, I didn't get caught. I didn't trigger the alarm, and I got by with my thievery. I stole pipes and tobacco, electric razors, deodorants and lotions, candy, and pocket knives, and everything else I could stuff into the pockets of my fatigue coat and pants, and into a big shopping bag. I gave it all away that Christmas, and my family and friends thought I was being really generous for a kid starting out on his own.

Life was an adventure. I loved it. I couldn't get enough of it.

CHAPTER 9

Despair

At Arlington State College I decided to be a cheerleader. We got to practice with the high school cheerleaders and they with us. I liked football, but I'd only gone out for football once at A&M Consolidated High School, the only season I was qualified to try out. Rules about changing schools got in the way; having gone to three high schools I didn't meet the residency requirements that were put in place to keep coaches from stealing each other's players. It didn't matter much because I wasn't that good at it and wasn't big enough. But I'd been a rabid football fan ever since I'd gone to see the Texas Aggies play the University of Texas, and then to a lot of other Aggie games. At the ROTC at my school, when we were in uniform, we tried to act like we were Aggies or the corps at The Citadel at our Arlington State football games. I got to wear a uniform, march, and ride on the train looking like a soldier.

My first real date with Marilyn Miller had been to go on a train to a football game with a train full of fans and the band and the ROTC guys in uniform so we could march at half time. She and I had sex for the first time on that trip and the whole thing was a great time. She was so beautiful and so hot. We were in lust together.

In spring 1958, after us being exclusively together for four or five months, I broke up with Marilyn Miller. I can't remember all the reasons my mind came up with for breaking up with her, but the feeling I had was that we had wonderful sex and it was fun, and yet something was still missing. I didn't feel like I loved her, or that we cared about each other enough, or that we were ready to settle down.

I started dating a cheerleader who was a senior at Arlington High School. Her name was Golden Keyes. We fell completely in love. She was a

Baptist and a virgin, and intended to stay that way until she got married. We didn't fuck because she wouldn't do it. But we had the best, most passionate, wonderful sex together, humping until we both came, touching, rubbing, kissing so deeply and so hotly that we sometimes came from just kissing. And we talked. We talked and talked about everything. She was planning on going to Arlington State College in the fall. I was in love. It was like recalling having been loved before, way back when I was a baby.

I think I had only been in love a couple of times before: once with my third grade teacher, and once when I was about eight years old. Mother and Tommy were hauling us kids around to visit some of Tommy's friends in Churchville, and a young girl my age, who years later I found out was Tommy's illegitimate child from high school, gave me a tablespoonful of Pepto-Bismol when I was sick to my stomach. She was very kind to me and, in the sweetest voice, said, "Take this. It will make you feel better." I looked into her eyes as I swallowed the spoonful of sweet, pink liquid and I no longer felt like I had to throw up. I felt pure gratitude. I remember loving her with all my heart.

Being in love with Golden Keyes was like that. I was really happy and, had not fate intervened, I would have probably married her, been a Christian, had a lot of babies with her, and stayed with her for life, come hell or high water. But fate did intervene and I was saved and damned or blessed to live in a different way.

I had to learn about despair again.

A couple of months after we had broken up, Sue Miller called me and said she needed to tell me something. We met and she told me she was pregnant. I was upset and shocked, and disturbed and worried, and, stupidly enough, surprised. I went and talked to Phil Philbrook about it (the minister at the United Christian Fellowship House where I worked as live-in janitor.). Then Phil and I met together with Sue and talked. We discussed having an abortion. Although abortions were illegal in Texas at the time, they were reliably attainable illegally. Sue and I left that session without deciding what to do, but we knew it was pretty important to make up our minds soon and that I was in favor of getting the abortion.

Early the next week, Sue called. She then brought to me a note from her doctor, saying she was not pregnant after all. She'd missed her period for a little over a month, but apparently was not pregnant. I was relieved and happy to hear the news. I told Golden Keyes about all of it and we were happy to be able to dodge this bullet together.

Three or four weeks later, Sue called again. She said that she was, in fact, pregnant, and had been pregnant all along; and she told me that the letter from her doctor had been a lie to keep me from pushing the decision that she needed an abortion. Now she was over three months pregnant and it was too late for an abortion. She wanted to know, what was I going to do now?

I can barely imagine what it must have been like for Sue during those first months of pregnancy. I don't think she told anyone in the beginning and I imagine she must have been desperate during that time of lying about not being pregnant. When she told me how she had lied to me I didn't get mad. I got real serious and felt like I now had to grow on up and take responsibility for what I had done.

Well, to make a short story long, I decided to do the honorable thing: I broke up with Golden Keyes, and married Marilyn Sue Miller the day after my eighteenth birthday. We had a big wedding in the First Methodist Church in Fort Worth. My sister and brother-in-law, and her parents were there, and we were resolved to make a go of it.

I dropped out of college and we moved to Dallas, where I continued there what had been my summer job as a door-to-door salesman of crystal, china, and stainless steel and sterling silver tableware. We holed up in a small apartment. I worked during days and evenings. We talked very little. We fucked a lot. We tried very hard to love each other and make things work out. We tried our best. But we were in despair. Neither of us wanted to be where we were.

Several evenings a week I would go out to Beatnik coffee shops, where I'd smoke cigarettes and drink strong coffee, and listen to Beat poets rant about the despair and futility of life and the way we are all being abused and killed by the "system." I identified quite a bit with what I was hearing, my only consolation being that I was not alone in my futile life. I knew from the poets and participants in the coffee house that I was not the only one who knew about futility, and not the only one living in it. Existentialists understood. I was in complete despair, though cheerfully not alone. Sue, however, wasn't having any of it, and we worked away at trying to overcome the blues. Nothing really worked.

After a couple of months of trying as hard as we could, I went back to see Phil Philbrook again, alone. When I came into his office we barely spoke before I cried and cried and I said I didn't think I could take it. I felt trapped, helpless, alienated, alone, and powerless to make things work for either me or Sue. I was lonesome and unhappy, and missed everything about my former life. He eventually suggested that he and I, along with Sue and Sue's parents, get together and have a talk. We went over to her parents' house in Arlington from his office and called Sue, and she came over from Dallas and we all talked. We talked about everything that hadn't been talked about while we tried to make the best of a situation none of us liked.

Sue's parents eventually said they would like for me to go away and never come back again, and that pretty much they'd felt that way all along. They wanted Sue to come back to live with them and they agreed they would help her raise the child, but they wanted me to agree not to interfere in any way. Eventually, that is what we did. I made the agreement not to interfere and I left. Later I learned that they immediately got the marriage annulled, and then arranged for Sue to go to a home for unwed mothers in Florida to have the baby and give the child up for adoption. Sue agreed and that is what happened.

When I left that meeting I felt even worse than I had before. I went back and lived alone in my apartment in Dallas. I'd dropped out of college. I'd gotten Sue pregnant, and I hadn't lived up to my responsibility for the child. I'd been weak and dishonorable. I wasn't strong enough to be a decent person. In about a month, I left that apartment and moved to Fort Worth where I lived with my mother for a while.

I didn't contact Golden Keyes for a long time. When I did, she said it was too late. I thought then, as I had before, that I might as well kill myself. I nursed that thought and drank black coffee and smoked cigarettes and listened to beat poetry and read existentialism, and felt like a miserable failure in an absurd world.

On top of all that I was still being a salesman. I was still working in Dallas selling stainless steel silverware, china, and crystal to airline stewardesses and telephone operators. Then my friend Dan, who had flunked out of college after his first year at Arlington State College, started coming over from Arlington to visit me and talk about life. He was depressed and in existential despair as well. We talked and explored the depths of futility together, and came up with a plan. We cooked up a plot to either get rich or die.

We decided to go north to Canada and ride the rapids during the spring flood for 150 miles on the Peace River in Alberta Province until we reached a place near an old, abandoned gold mine that was a known prospecting area on the river. There, if we made it, we would pan for gold for two months during the summer until the weather started closing in again, ride the whitewater out for another 150 miles further north. (The Peace River is one of the few in North America that flows north for many, many miles.) We would escape with our gold and hitchhike back down the Alcan Highway to home, if we made it. We would be rich and happy. If we didn't make it, our problems would be solved anyway. We would have to survive the whitewater trip in and out, and the two months there. If we did, we would have (we figgered) about $8,000 dollars each, which was real money in those days. What made the risk entirely worth it was that we both clearly understood that if we didn't make it our problems would be solved anyway. It was a win/win kind of deal.

We needed to buy some supplies and a canoe, and more money for travel—we thought we needed about $2,000—so we ran an advertisement in *The Dallas Morning News* (for decades and decades the worst newspaper in the world, and the very heart of misinformation in Middle America). It said something like: "Solid investment in the future of two adventurous young men. Call 555-5555."

We got a couple of calls and did an interview with one prospective funder. We made an agreement with a fellow whose name was Brad Bradley (I haven't forgotten his name). He was a Bible salesman and supervisor of young Bible salesmen. He said he wanted us to sell Bibles with him for just two weeks and he would then loan us the money for our trip, or at least the difference between what we'd made working for him and what we needed. The next week we left for Houston and ended up walking door to door selling a very expensive family Bible that cost, just by chance, the same amount as a retired person's one-month social security check, which was $36 back then.

My friend Dan lasted only two weeks, and then left for home in Illinois. I kept on selling Bibles for a few more weeks than Dan because I was making some money at it. Brad Bradley extended, but didn't come through with his agreement. I was pretty much alone in a strange place. My friend had left me and my plans were wrecked. I had now not only ruined what had seemed to be a wonderful life, I'd fucked up my plan to escape my failure. I was such a failure! I couldn't even pull off an attempt at either suicide or escape by becoming a gold digger in Canada. And I was in Houston. And it was getting to be summertime. And it was hot. And I was working outdoors, walking door to door selling a family Bible I didn't believe in.

I was flirting with middle-aged housewives like I had with the airline stewardesses and telephone operators, and giving a little credit on the down payment for occasional illicit (but not penetrating) sex play, where it wasn't clear who was getting the advantage and who might owe the other. Were it not for my growing understanding and fellowship with existentialists in despair and rebellion, and the reading I did at night, and were I not so young, deluded, and hopeful in spite of the mess I felt I was making with my life, I might have succumbed to the depressing state of affairs I considered myself to be living in. But I plodded on.

I was living at the YMCA, getting picked up each morning by Brad Bradley or another salesman, and being put out in some sprawling, moderately poor suburban neighborhood with my sales kit. I was picked up again around 1 P.M. for lunch, put out again in the afternoon, and picked up again at around 5 P.M. to be taken back to the Y.

What I now know to be a *reaction*, I then considered to be "making a decision." I "decided" to go on another kind of adventure that I had dreamed about before. I was still reading existentialism and Beat poems, but I had a particular memory that kept recurring and haunting me and it gave me some hope. It was this . . .

It is late at night and I have to mop, wax, and buff the floors in the United Christian Fellowship House at Arlington State College in preparation for a new semester. I look in Phil's office for an audiotape to listen to while I am working running the floor polisher. I find a tape of a sermon by someone named Joseph Wesley Mathews. I put the big reel on the tape recorder and hook up the tape to the take-up reel and turn it on. I start work, but am soon stunned into stopping altogether, and just stop the floor polisher and sit down to listen because I can't believe what I am hearing. This man is preaching in the First United Methodist Church of Dallas—at least that's what it says on the label— and he is shouting and cussing!

He picks up a book and pounds it on the lectern and, very loudly, he says, "People say this book is holy! There is nothing holy about this damned book!" I can hear him tearing out the pages, and wadding them up and throwing them into the middle of the aisle! He says, "I'll tell you what is holy! It is not an answer! It is a question! And it is the only damned question worth asking! And that question is 'What is life all about?' And I don't mean the namby-pamby little polite kind of asking you usually hear in church. I mean, 'What in the HELL is life all about?!'"

Now, sitting alone in the Y in Houston I kept thinking of that sermon. I had never heard a preacher be so daring and so loud. Never before in my life! To cuss like that and to say that question in so challenging and demanding a way and be really serious about it! And to tear up a Bible right in front of church people! In the First United Methodist Church of Dallas! I knew now, from the time I was selling them in Houston, that it cost $36 to replace that sonofabitch! So I decided I was going to go find Joe Mathews, wherever the hell he was, and talk to him.

This was, I think, the first time I made a choice like that, to go see someone I had read, or heard, or heard of, or read about, and see what the person was about, and ask for help. And because of the way it turned out the first time, I've made that same kind of choice over again at what seemed like critical times in my life.

Since all of the folks I ever contacted in this way were male, it may be that I was looking for my missing father, looking for some man to show me how to be a man: to protect and care for me, and be strong, and show me how it is done. I think that is probably true. I consider that reactivity to my past to be lucky, too—lucky early programming by the way life happened. It turned out lucky because the people I sought out were all very good people and kind to me, and, in fact, akin to me in a very deep way. Had I not found that out, my life could have been very, very different.

It turned out that the father substitutes I sought out in reaction to my past actually took on the task of fathering me. Helping me out was part and parcel of their commitment to renew the church. As both Joe Mathews and Phil Philbrook used to say of their role as ministers in a church that was almost totally failing (yet again) at being even minimally relevant in changing times, "The church is a whore . . . but she's my mother." These fathers, who held onto the lapels of the church so they could have a grip to kick her in the shins, were involved in the same kind of existential dilemma I was. How do you be committed to, and love such an ignorant bitch of a church and life and culture and country . . . and how could you live without her?

The theology within the church that mothered both them and me (as expressed by Paul Tillich, Rudolf Bultman, and many, many others) was formed for caretakers who needed caring for. They understood my dilemma as completely as I could have ever hoped. They were in a love/hate relationship with life itself, and they were being honest about it. And they'd chosen to affirm that life and call it good, and make it so, by affirming the great good luck of being here in spite of the suffering.

I found out that Joe Mathews was in Austin, Texas, at a place called The Christian Faith and Life Community, only two hours away from Houston.

I decided to go there and see him. I'd met the assistant director of the Y. He was gay. I let him give me a blow job, and he gave me a ride to Austin. I employed my wisdom from the road. Blow job. Ride. Ride. Blow job.

One Saturday, I got turned out in front of The Christian Faith and Life Community. My friend went straight back to Houston.

Chapter 10

Another New Beginning

Joe Mathews heard my whole story. He listened. He decided he wanted me there. And we proceeded in a businesslike fashion to deal with my future from that moment forward. This was one of the most important moments of my life because he became one of the most important mentors of my life. I even thought so then, right as the conversation happened.

To me it seemed like Joe Mathews listened to me and appreciated me for my persistence in pursuing what was real regardless of all the mistakes I felt I'd made. When I bragged or was ashamed, he listened. When I cried, he let me have my grief and didn't try to fix it or talk me out of it. I liked him and felt like he was a man I could depend on to honor what was so, rather than just to pretend that things were okay and try to make the pretending win out.

I told him I'd heard his sermon "What in the Hell Is Life All About?!" and that I was interested in this question more than any other I could think of. He said that the Christian Faith and Life Community was designed to deal with that question, so it was exactly where I needed to be and he wanted me there. His presence, his *way of being*, was attentive and kind. What he said was something like, "Okay, I see where you've been and what you've done, and how you feel about it. I get it. This is a good place for you and we'd like to have you here. You're a good candidate for us, as we are for you. Let's get started."

Maybe he just needed people to fill the rooms of the men's residence for the fall quarter, and that's why he invited me to come and live there immediately after we talked. Maybe he was flattered that his tape had made such an impression. For whatever reason, he invited me to come live there and study with him and his faculty of renegade preachers. He invited me to come right away for the summer session at the University of Texas. Because I'd been on probation when I quit attending Arlington State College in order to get married the year before, I would have to make passing grades in summer school in order to gain admittance to the University in the fall.

I wanted to move to Austin as soon as I could, so I went back to Houston and sold a bunch of Bibles in the next two weeks and then used the money to move and settle into my new home, and, I think, try to be with my father again. I sensed Mathews, like a good father, would be attentive and firm, and care about how I lived, what I did, and what I learned.

I got a job working (typing, filing, and copying) in the office of the Christian Faith and Life Community right away to pay for part of the cost of living there, and I took up residence in the men's dorm. I took Speech and English classes, and passed with good grades, qualifying to become a full-time student at the University of Texas. All this seemed easy. I was back in a place I wanted to be and knew something about how to handle being there. I'd also been chastened and taught a lesson or two about my arrogance.

Once again, my life changed dramatically. It would be years and years before I discerned the reenactment of my childhood in the comings and goings in my life, and the patterns of my reactive life. The pattern is a sequence of occurrences, and the whole sequence itself recurs: security, trouble, loss, and abandonment, then moving on bravely and making a new beginning, a new home, and a repeat again of the pattern.

I recreated this pattern because it was something I knew how to handle from having done so in the past. Acknowledging that I was the source of *all of this* was much later in coming. I spent most of my life in the "victor or victim" game, thinking that compensating for being a victim and becoming a victor was what life was all about, as it fit so well my pattern of survival from childhood. Once a victor though, I had to become victim again. This ongoing, unconscious creation was my ongoing recreation albeit in blissful ignorance and painful unawareness for forty to fifty years of my life. The time I spent at The Christian Faith and Life Community (CFLC) was the early beginning of the dawning of the light.

The layout of the CFLC looked like this: the men's residence, dining room, seminar rooms, chapel, and office were in one central location; the women's residence was about a block and a half away. We men had our meals with the women in the shared dining hall, went to chapel on a daily basis, and spent about ten hours a week reading and then participating in seminars about what we were reading from Paul Tillich, Rudolf Bultman, Dietrich Bonhoeffer, Frederick Nietzsche, Søren Kierkegaard, Richard Niebuhr, and Reinhold Niebuhr, Jean-Paul Sartre, Albert Camus, and other existentialist theologians, writers, and philosophers, including Joe Mathews and the staff of nine ministers who led our seminars.

Our teachers were misfits in Protestant churches of various brands who wanted very much to be able to be Christians, which to them at the time meant passing on the "Word" to current and future generations. And the word was that there was no word: There is no ultimate solution to the problems of life. There is no rescuer from above. The real Christian message, all along, they said, was that the declaration out of nowhere that "life is good" no matter what happens—an affirmation of all of life—is a possible courageous choice, out of which compassionate attention to others and action in the world proceeds. The spirit of Christ, and the meaning of being a Christian, was to dare to affirm that choice to respond with welcome to whatever life brings; through celebrating our capacity to do that together, then to work in the fields of the Lord toward making love and affirmation of life itself the primary organizing principle for human beings.

This short paragraph I've written is, of course, a reductionist rephrasing of hundreds of talks and pages and hours of participation to which I can't begin to do justice in this book. However, I hope you get that the picture of the affirmation of all of life is not in any way, shape or form related to the "power of positive thinking" that we all considered drivel and a bastardization of the Christian word, but represents the courage to be facing forward consciously into whatever life brings.

The transcendent affirmation we valued was more like Job at the end of his story, after the Lord let the Devil take away from him all he loved and cherished, when he said, "The Lord gave. And the Lord took it away. Blessed be the name of the Lord." He chose to affirm the gift of his whole life. This was a transcendent choice instead of a reaction. It is a possible choice for any of us. It is, in fact, the choice I have made and remake for this biography itself. I guess I am still a Christian. Shit. All that work to escape . . . for nothing.

I was in the CFLC for three years. I spent a good part of the first year rebelling and resisting a lot, of course. The second year I was a senior fellow, helping lead some of the teachings I'd spent most of the previous year resisting. And the third year I was a participant in the first attempt by Joe Mathews and the staff to forge a way of learning that could provide, in a short time, the essence of an educated global humanitarian perspective.

This eventually became "A College Education in Thirteen Weeks," a program conducted to educate people in the ghettoes of Chicago by the Ecumenical Institute, the research and development wing of the World Council of Churches. That is where Joe and his friends ended up in the next couple of years, and remained for many years thereafter.

Back to fall 1959, when I was just barely embarking on my trek toward the future establishment of the religion of Futilitarianism (my current claimed religion) and becoming the Pope of No Hope. I became a full-time student at the University of Texas, majoring in psychology, minoring in philosophy and anthropology, and participating in the extracurricular study program of the CFLC.

CHAPTER 11

The University of Texas
(1959-1961)

I dated a fair number of girls from the CFLC, and I had sex with many, including the woman in charge of the women's dorm. Religion and sex have always been intertwined. That has certainly been true in my life. Thank God, so to speak.

I loved sex. I suppose I was a sex addict. I am pretty sure I was also guilty of what today is called "date rape." We didn't have any concept of what those things were then, but I seldom let up when a woman said no. I kept trying until she said yes or just gave in and did it with me, or made me come in some way so I'd leave her alone for a little while. Sometimes we would kiss and feel and hump without fucking, and we would like both the trying and the holding back. Sometimes I'd come from the excitement of almost doing it. Sometimes we both would. Then, after that happened and we both knew it, and sometimes talked about it, the next time around we'd go ahead and fuck. Since we were making each other come anyway, we might as well enjoy it a little more.

I loved sex no matter how it happened, and was generally pleased and eternally grateful for anything any woman would do with me, on me, for me, in front of me, or around me. I was selfish and not a very good lover until after getting what I wanted, which was to come. I'd often come first, and then I would keep on playing with the woman and touching or licking or kissing her to make her more excited. When she got really hot, I'd be hot to go again and would fuck her longer before I came again. I was persistent and fascinated, and the second time around (and sometimes the third time around), I was a little bit better lover, though always a little frenetic. I could never be sure my date would keep on letting me do it. I was eternally grateful when she did. I loved it so much. And most of the women loved pleasing me so much; some even loved sex as much as I did.

For a couple of years I worked as an attendant on the 11 P.M. to 7 A.M. shift at Austin State Hospital. It was a good job because it gave me a chance to study at work most nights. I needed that because, in addition to my course work and extracurricular study in the CFLC, I became an active member of the civil rights movement and "stood in" at theatres three or four evenings a week in Austin to force the theatres to integrate. For the cause, we'd stand in line to buy a ticket to see the movie. When we got to the teller we'd ask, "Do you let people of all races come into this theatre?" The teller would say no. We'd say, "Okay, I'm not going to buy any ticket then." And we would go to the back of the line.

When we came up to the front again, we'd say, "Have you changed your mind yet about letting everyone in here?" Getting the same answer as before, we'd move to the back of the line again. In the interim, we talked to people who actually came to see the movie and ask them to join us in boycotting the theatre until it changed its racist policies. If they didn't join us and went to the movie, we asked them to consider what they were doing. Sufficient people wanted to avoid that kind of trouble and embarrassment that the ticket sales dropped to practically nothing during the months we were standing out there in those ticket lines.

Here is one flashback about an occasion that was important to speeding up our victory.

It's about seven o'clock in the evening. We are gathered at the Y for another planning meeting for times to stand in at the theatres and to strategize, and to get information updates and have a discussion of what else we will do over the next week or two to sustain the stand-in movement. We have been in both The Austin Statesman *and the university newspaper recently, and things are looking pretty good. I am chairing the meeting tonight. The chairperson for meetings varies according to who is there, but usually it is one from among the same three or four of us. I have to go to work at eleven and I haven't slept much today. I am kind of hoping we might finish early enough for me to get a nap before I have to go to work. We are sitting in folding chairs next to the middle part of the room.*

All of a sudden there is a very loud BOOM! The windows on the other side of the room shatter and hundreds of pieces of glass fly into the room. Some of us run outside and look to see if there is anyone running away from the building, but there isn't. We go back inside and examine the windowsills and frames, the ceiling, and each other. There are little pieces of lead stuck in the window frames and the ceiling, and in everything surrounding the windows, but none is stuck in any people. It was a lead pipe bomb.

The cops come. We talk to them. Then I go to work at 11 P.M. to start my shift. I didn't get my nap. I didn't even get to sleep at work later because I got calls from a reporter after I was at work at the mental hospital. The people at the hospital don't like that worth a shit, but not knowing what else to do they let me talk to the caller on the phone to keep the reporter from coming out to the hospital during the shift.

When I speak to the reporter I am very reasonable and calm and say it was probably just a college kid—not the Klan or local anti-segregation people. As it turns out, I am right. The student responsible is caught and kicked out of the University and has to do a little time. In the end, no one is hurt and it is very good publicity for our movement. And I get to appear very reasonable and a good leader in a movement that is justified and participated in by reasonable people who are opposed by irrational, dangerous, careless types. It is a little scary and very exciting and it helps us out a lot.

A few days after the bombing at the Y, I got a call at home. A man's very gravelly voice said, "You nigger lovin' motherfucker, I'm going to string you up and cut your balls off."

After a slight pause, I said, "Well, if you do it in that order, it won't be so bad."

He hung up.

I loved being in the University and I loved being in the Christian Faith and Life Community and I loved being in the civil rights movement. I was happy to be learning so much and doing so much that was valuable and important. I hardly ever got to sleep because I was livin' so large. All of us seemed to sense something really big was about to happen with regard to social change and that we were vital participants.

My first date with Judy Schleyer was to go see John Kennedy and Lyndon Johnson on the steps of the Capitol Building in Austin when they were campaigning to become President and Vice-President of the United States. We loved Kennedy, and Johnson seemed to tune-in to all of us. He expressed a seminal idea of our whole movement that was just being born. He took the mike from Kennedy, turned to the immense crowd, and said, "Ahh luuuvve *all* of ya!" and we cheered our hearts out. We were all in love with a possible future then, and thought it was just around the corner. That was a hell of a first date for Judy and me, and the beginning of us falling in love with each other.

She was living in one of the women's dormitories on campus. I think it was our second or third date that we both knew at the same time that we'd fallen in love. I walked her back to her dorm that night and all the lights turned on in both of us when we kissed goodnight, and then curfew was up and she rushed into the dorm. She told me later that she threw up as soon as she got inside. I was walking on air and smiling all the way back to my room at the community. The next semester she moved to live in the women's dorm of the CFLC. We started having sex and became a couple. In those days when that happened you started thinking about marriage.

We were being constantly challenged in the CFLC, partly because that's just the way existentialists are. They like raising questions to make sure they are not avoiding any. I had a lot of doubts about everything, and though I wasn't at all miserable I thought about suicide now and then, considering it a possible option. After all, I was an existentialist. But the truth is I did often feel hopeless, in the sense of not being able to be clear about the choices I faced. Fortunately, I was among friends who could hear that, and I'm glad I was.

Here are some excerpts from a journal I kept at intervals during those years that kind of speak to that ambiguity. They were periodic entries, usually, I can see now, when I was sad—made in a ledger book I stole from the Austin State Hospital where I was working.

10/02/61: Kierkegaard said that no man could know whether he was worshipping God or the Devil even though he conscientiously tried to worship God. Some philosopher (Hegel?) said that all bad came about as the result of seeking some good. Freud said that sickness comes about as the result of inappropriate attempts by the poor human psyche to be healthy.

What is it we seek? Perhaps there is a biological answer to the metaphysical question that can only be expressed in mythical or metaphysical language. We seek a state of being as individuals that is a heaven, a psychological utopia, a perfectly satisfying equilibrium of dynamic thrust which is impossible . . .

I'm stupid and need to learn more. Or maybe I can never learn enough. Maybe I had better accept life or die right now . . .

***

10/18/61: The Christian man acts on the basis of a primary decision to accept all of life as good, and a secondary decision to be responsible, or in other words, to use all of his rationality. This means that sometimes he must say no to some of the yes things in life and yes to some of the no things in life according to his feelings. But which ones?

Courage is necessary in order to live. How can you get it? . . . I feel I am a coward because I cannot dare to act on my feelings. I distrust my feelings because of my idealism.

I have only the present to go on. Say no to Judy.

***

01/27/62: Judy and I got married. . . . Can one say yes to one of the yes things in life and still say yes to some of the no things?"

How was that for reversing a decision? Those last two entries were one right after the other. I seemed to have a lot of uncertainty come up fairly often but still act anyway, in one direction or the other, and clearly sometimes the opposite of what I had apparently decided—and then see what happened. Impulsive, convulsive, high-risk, compulsive, sometimes revulsive-obsessive-depressive, yet still aggressive. I think I was a mess then, but a fairly happy and creative mess. That was how I was, but I liked it okay and I still do when I reflect on it now. I like it better than pissing away my life trying to conform.

CHAPTER 12

Catch 22 in 1962

Judy's father had been sheriff in New Braunfels, Texas, which was a mostly second-, third-, and fourth-generation German immigrant town, and a very conservative community, located between Austin and San Antonio. The town, as were most towns in Texas then, was completely racially segregated. When Judy and I got serious enough for me to meet the parents, I had her have her father and mother come pick me up from the stand-in line in front of the theater on the Drag, the main street in front of the university, to let them know who I was and what I was about. They didn't like me much and didn't much like what I was doing, but she was their only child, so they put up with me. Her father's brother was the judge in New Braunfels and a leading political figure—gentlemanly, Republican, racist, but kindly toward Negras and Mexicans, and so on. Her folks were good people. The way people were supposed to be good people in those days.

When we decided to get married in January 1962, Judy's aunt and uncle, mother and father made plans for a big wedding in their home church with a big reception in the main hotel in town. As the wedding date neared, we told them that we wouldn't get married in New Braunfels unless the church, the hotel, and the whole town were no longer segregated.

In the stalemate and ensuing negotiation I refused to budge, and Judy did, too. She stuck with her new man instead of her Old Man. Our values were different than those of her father and most of the rest of the family. The closest thing to compromise was when we discussed having our real wedding at the chapel of The Christian Faith and Life Community in Austin first, with our friends of all races attending, and then we'd come for a second ceremony in New Braunfels for the family there, at which time we would announce that we were already married in a non-segregated ceremony in Austin and had come to New Braunfels for a second ceremony for the family that lived in a segregated town.

About a week before the wedding, they decided that the embarrassment of the announcement at the second wedding was worse than desegregating the town, and they came around and agreed to our terms for the wedding in New Braunfels. A black woman who was a friend of ours sang at our wedding and came to the reception at the hotel along with a few other of our black friends. Thus, we integrated the church, the hotel, and the city of New Braunfels. We made a good beginning. And we did pretty good as we continued.

Judy and I had an adventuresome life together over the next ten years. I'm forever grateful for the years we slept together snuggling, making love, and lying entangled in each other's arms and legs. She was kind to me. She cuddled me and healed me of some of my childhood wounds. Those eternal hours of simply touching, holding, and sleeping together somehow restored my balance. She was a voracious reader, and all of the things we read, shared, and talked about, and all of the friends we took acid with, got stoned with, and ventured into the unknown with together, and all of the hours of therapy and training I did with her backing me up, and all of our travels together all over creation helped me become more whole and a little more decent human being.

Over the course of time, we stopped being in love the way we started out—as almost all couples do—but I'm forever grateful for her kindness to me, and for putting up with my wildness and bullshit, lying, self-righteousness, and violence, and for us having our daughter Shanti together and raising her. Shanti was, and has been, our greatest gift to each other.

I have no regrets about the choice I made to marry Judy. If I had it to do over again I'd make the same choice. If I'd known then what I know now I might be less deceitful, mean, violent, controlling, gullible, chauvinistic, arrogant, and stupid, but I would still choose to marry her and be with her through those times, and also for us to have Shanti together when we did.

When our divorce was final, Judy said, "Well, seven years of marital bliss is not bad."

I said, "We were married ten years."

"Yeah, I know," she said. "Seven out of ten is not bad."

Our daughter, Shanti, is a wonderful, talented, and loving person, whose whole life is a contribution to humanity and the planet. In her forties now, she's happily married and has two fine little boys who will benefit from the love she passes on from Judy and me to the future of life.

Well, there I did it again: another deviation from my linear story. These sidetracks and rants apparently must come where they come and go when they go. Here comes a whole section now of flashbacks and flash-forwards triggered by what I just told you.

Flashes of Light

So much happened during the five-year period between the summer of 1959 and the summer of 1964—and not just for me. When I look back on the period, for the life of me I cannot figure out how any of us who were alive then ever had time to do all that we did. The period of years when I was nineteen to twenty-four years old were one of the most incredible times to be alive in all of history, and, by God, I didn't sleep through much of it! In fact, I hardly slept the whole damned time.

In addition to being in the Christian Faith and Life Community and enrolled at the University of Texas, I worked at numerous part-time and full-time jobs in restaurants, grocery stores, doing day labor, moving, construction, typing, general office work, and being a mental hospital attendant on the graveyard shift for almost two years. Besides working, I carried almost a full load of coursework year-round.

We started the civil rights movement in Texas. As a result, I got arrested, detained, lead pipe-bombed, and variously mildly abused by the police, and we integrated the movie theaters in the entire South from our little spot in Austin. After that, our movement eventually integrated restaurants, service station rest rooms, department stores, and the football team at the University.

I married Judy, finished my undergraduate degree, and John F. Kennedy was elected. I moved into married student housing (again!), started graduate school, started experimenting with peyote, LSD, pot, mushrooms, speed, Ritalin, hashish, and various other mind-altering substances, and had sex with many women both before and after getting married. I also became a licensed preacher in the Methodist Church with a circuit of three churches. Then I got fired as a preacher, started designing my education in graduate school, worked as a research assistant, managed apartments, cleaned pools, did more day labor on weekends for extra money, and on and on and on.

During the time after Kennedy was killed, LBJ took over, and then he got elected, the civil rights bills were passed, we started the anti-Vietnam War movement, and we hippies started the beginning of our short, but wonderful parade in the process of taking over the country for a little while from Haight-Ashbury to Woodstock. We did it right under the noses of Richard Nixon and the dumb-assed Republicans, who were way too stupid to have any fucking idea of what was really going on.

We were busy. I slept very little during those years because I didn't have time to waste in sleeping. I was in so many new adventures at once that my capacity for dealing with ambivalence and uncertainty, and my willingness to do so expanded out of necessity. You can't drop acid fifty or sixty times over the course of a few years without wrestling with God and learning to surrender, to mention only one thing at the top of the list. At the same time, my tendency to be a caretaker of those who are hurt or afraid, and my enthusiasm for overthrowing the external established order was expanding. My capacity for compassion was growing, as was my inner rigidity as a moralistic dictator and a self-righteous prick. Everything was expanding. It was a very exciting time. It was a very heartbreaking time. It was a very liberating time. To say it was educational is the understatement of all time.

It broke so many of our hearts at the same time when Kennedy was killed. I don't think any of us ever really totally recovered from it. We were so disillusioned when LBJ turned up the stupid, fucking, useless war in Vietnam instead of stopping it, and when that dumb fuck Hubert Humphrey was defeated by Nixon, because we, the hippies and Yippies from Chicago to Washington, D.C., to San Francisco, so clearly demonstrated that we would not only fail to support chicken shit, weak-willed Democrats, but we'd oppose them, boycott them, and bring them down so that everyone could see the true assholes who were running the country for the fascist motherfuckers they were.

There was no way to disguise a fucking Republican. However, we understood finally that an obvious Republican asshole like Nixon in power was better than a lying asshole Caspar Milquetoast pharmacist Democrat like Hubert Humphrey in power. We did not cause that to happen consciously, but this is why Nixon won. Hippies elected him by not voting for Humphrey and by scaring the shit out of all the careful people. Obviously, some of us are not entirely over that yet either. Okay, I got a little ahead of myself there. I will whoa back and be linear again.

CHAPTER 13

Married Life, Graduate School, and Drugs

I started using mind-altering substances other than alcohol when I was twenty. I was and still am afraid at the beginning of every trip on big drugs. In those first times, particularly with LSD, I never knew for sure if it would make me permanently psychotic. Most of us weren't sure about that, but we did LSD anyway. I took the risk because of the experience of taking peyote and smoking marijuana and having seen the immensity of what I'd learned to exclude from my noticing.

If the whole hippie movement had to do with any single, most important thing, that was it: the immensity of the sudden growth in the capacity for noticing. Before we learned from drugs how much we didn't know, we knew that what our elders claimed they knew was the same as what we thought we had known. Drugs taught me a great deal about awareness from the very beginning. Taking those acid trips helped me choose to grow big enough for this larger reality even though I thought I could lose everything I had in my smaller existence when I ventured forth into the fields of the Lord. The drugs and conversations we shared both simply overcame the limitations of cultural belief. We were almost forced to discover that our personalities and cultural surround were mere guesswork constructions of the mind, and that not only were they not sacred, what was, in fact, sacred was much much greater than that. We learned that what usually passes for a human being is a bunch of beliefs organized around an asshole. What makes a culture is a bunch of those. What makes a civilization is a bunch of those cultures. All of them are fundamentally organizations to protect assholes. We knew then that we knew something beyond what our elders knew. That is why "Don't Trust Anyone Over 30" was such a popular bumper sticker for the times.

We were a group of anthropology students who'd read and heard stories about Native Americans who use hallucinogenic substances in their religious rituals. We also discovered that you could buy peyote cactus buds by the bushel at our local neighborhood plant store right there in Austin. As a result, I took peyote before I ever smoked pot. We were terrified, excited, and blown away by the immensity of what had so far not been commonly known about the doors of perception. But once we took a big risk when we thought we might all go crazy and stay that way, we admired ourselves and each other for our courage. We had an experience of fear and trembling and the sickness unto death, but we faced it anyway. We had the courage to step across the threshold into a new world, not knowing if we'd be able to come back. We held hands and leapt. I took acid soon after that first time of tripping on peyote when my friend E.L. Hazelwood brought some from California. But first, it was peyote, in 1961.

I eat the sliced up raw peyote cactus bites that taste like bitter, green snot and chase them with lemon juice to get them down. Over the next forty-five minutes, I keep drinking Pepto-Bismol when I am about to puke, and swallow the contents of my stomach back when it comes up. It goes down again and stays for a while.

Now I am walking outside to get some fresh air. It is a little after sunset. The cars parked on the street are starting to look kind of funny and the grass on the lawns is, too. The cars are starting to vomit. The grass is vomiting now. Suddenly I begin to vomit. I bend down on my knees and vomit. I stand up on my toes and vomit. I am a piece of vomit in a flood of vomit, vomiting. I am totally committed. Vomit are us. Pink and green like I've never seen from stomach and spleen joins the stream of green, and I'm a vomiting machine in a vomiting scene . . .

Now, a little later on, I am just spitting. I keep spitting. Now I am going inside, kind of wobbly. I get through the screen door, though it is strange, very strange. I go in the bathroom and start spitting in the toilet. I see the blood in the water and I taste the salt of my blood. I broke something. I am bleeding. I am spitting my blood out. Maybe this is it. Maybe I am about to die. I went too far this time. I puked until I hemorrhaged, and now I am going to die. I keep spitting. Then, it dawns on me slowly that the blood is coming from inside my nose, down into my throat. I just have a nose bleed! I am not dying!

I drink a little water. I go out into the tiny living room and sit in the butterfly chair. I turn into a chamois cloth, like the ones we used to use to wash cars. There is a breeze blowing through our little living room, and my corners are flapping in the breeze. I am flapping in the breeze. I am free. I am happy and free and I am not going to die. I am a chamois cloth and I can live! What a joy this wonderful life is!

And here is another flashback.

I swallow the twenty-seven triple-ought "horse capsules" filled with dried and ground-up peyote. I'd cut off the buds with stickers in them, washed and sliced the cacti, and then sundried the strips on the roof of the former World War Two barracks that had been converted into married student housing. Then I ground the dried-up chips in a meat grinder by hand. I knew that about five or six cacti amounted to twenty-seven capsules. After swallowing, I resist vomiting for a long time. In about forty-five minutes, I finally vomit a psychedelic vomit.

After I wrestle with God and give up, I begin to hear things that match what I see. I hear the sound of brown and purple and blue. I hear red and white stripes. I hear a crackling static now and then. The walls have little wavy ripples in them, and the ceiling bends like the surface of water or vibrates like heat waves on pavement.

I smell peppermint that matches the flow of red and white stripes that show up to match the sound of "Billy the Kid" by the So-and-so Philharmonic Orchestra conducted by Andrew Cohen. It is pretty flavorful music. It flows with the world and the world flows with it, so nicely; and it is pretty and it smells nice; and it reminds me of sweet times in my sweet, tremulous life.

The kitchen stove is taller than me now and the refrigerator has shrunk. When I reach inside of the refrigerator I have to bend down. When I get something from up on the stove I have to stretch upward to get it. I can't understand this because it doesn't seem right, but there are so many interesting things in the world right now that I don't have time to worry about it.

The cold milk I drink to settle my stomach curls up in my mouth and crawls down to my belly and the curls up there like a snake, but it feels very good.

I smoke a cigarette. It burns and crackles like a Yule log dynamite fuse: bigger than life—louder than life—more explicit than life. I am really alive—particularly when I take a drag and inhale. I am alive. I am alive. This is life and I'm really alive.

Judy cooks food for us. And after we eat, she washes the dishes. We sleep together all wrapped up in each other's arms. We have sex together. We are safe and in love. We live in this tiny place. I am falling asleep…

We bought a Volkswagen Beetle. Our friends Jim and Louise bought one, too, at the same time. We had them both shipped from Germany so they arrived at the same time. We were proud of them. They were our first new cars ever. Both cars were red. We lived in a little place and drove little cars, but we were living in such a bigger space than we'd ever imagined. We read, took speed, smoked dope, drank alcohol, dropped acid, took courses, made discoveries, and had conversations about things no one had ever talked about. We knew we were riding a wave that was changing the world. We knew that. We didn't know how it would turn out, but we knew it was turning.

I take the pink square in my mouth and soak the LSD out onto my tongue and swallow my own saliva. I am a little afraid. I know medicine has a change in how things show up within it, and will probably change how things show up forever. A big integration of all that preceded this moment in my entire life comes into being for me. I can't exactly articulate it, but I know that my life is coming together. I know there is a lot I don't know, and I also know I know more than I ever could have known.

When we were in graduate school and working as project assistants we eventually moved out of the married student housing into a series of apartments for a few years. After that we moved into a house. With each move it was nice to have a bigger space to live. We had offices (or nooks at least) at school. We were both working on doctorates in psychology and educational psychology.

One day we were sitting around in our new house on a Saturday. Jim and Louise were there and our friend John Harrington came over. He walked in and said, "Hello, Hippies!" That was the first time we knew what to call ourselves! We'd found out we were hippies from an article in *Time* magazine. John had read it and come over to tell us. We read the article. *Sonofabitch. We're hippies. We made* Time *magazine.* Time *made us.* We had wondered what the fuck we were!

We are at our house and it is a Saturday morning. We dropped acid a couple of hours ago. Louise is outside sitting in the yard, leaning up against a tree.

All of a sudden, here comes the landlord. Omigod! He is walking in through the front gate. Omigod, we have to try to be cool! Okay, be cool. Be cool. He walks up the walk and sees Louise, who has a short haircut and is sitting there watching God knows what. He says to her, "Oh! . . . I thought you were a boy!"

She looks at him and pauses a little while. Then she replies, "Maybe I was . . ."

We all lose it and start laughing our asses off. The landlord has no idea what is going on, but at least he turns back and goes away.

The computer on campus at the University of Texas was housed in a gigantic room that took up about an acre, near the Tower. Computers before the invention of microprocessors were essentially something you lived in, in a big room. John Harrington worked in one of the big computer rooms in Austin on the night shift, changing gigantic tapes from one tape-spinning stand to the other. The computer on campus at U.T. took up acres of space. There quickly became a new program of study called "computer science," which I got into. The possibilities were endless.

I learned Fortran, the new language of computing, and then, to meet the requirement for my doctorate degree of having familiarity with two languages, I was tested on my ability to read and understand German and Fortran. It was almost like the explosion of knowledge from both educational and personal experiences allowed us to fundamentally identify ourselves as discoverers, whose task it was to learn new things on all fronts and figure them out and integrate them, and we all kind of liked the work.

The University of Texas Tower is where a guy named Charles Whitmore, who was the former youngest Boy Scout ever to make Explorer Scout, as well as a former military man, stood on the rampart in 1966 and shot a bunch of students and then killed himself. I remember that Judy and I were on campus separately that day, and we didn't know if the other got shot or not. The whole scene was just like Texas. When people heard what was going on they brought out their rifles and started trying to be the one that shot Whitmore by using the rifles they had in their trucks and cars. Texas was a hell of a place to attempt to become enlightened.

I loved drinking alcohol, I loved smoking pot, and I loved being in altered states of consciousness most of the time. The years of using speed (Ritalin, Dexamil, and Dexedrine) to research, write, and stay awake when I was working on my dissertation were fine, high times. I loved working. I loved reading and thinking and talking and writing. I think I didn't go overboard with drug experiences themselves, like some of my friends did, and do too much of any substance and hurt or kill myself, because I was using the drugs toward an end beyond just getting high. I was using them to get a Ph.D.

I learned a lot about how to allow things to happen and how to make things happen that I don't think I would have learned without drugs. In the first draft of my dissertation I put in an acknowledgement of Smith, Kline, and French Pharmaceutical Company for having helped me write the dissertation, but Cody Wilson, my major professor, made me take it out. We'd both been arrested for the civil rights movement and he covered my back a number of times to help me get my doctorate. Editing out some of my wilder assertions in my dissertation was one way he helped. (Probably I could use his help right now!) But that reminds me, he was there when this all happened. . .

It is 1965, in the fall, in Austin. The City Council is meeting downtown. There are lots of cops around and lots of press and TV cameras because they know we demonstrators against the war are going there to raise hell about the city having denied us a parade permit to march against the war in Vietnam. It's me and my friend Booker T. Bonner, as usual. We make our way up the huge steps to City Hall, in through the door and into the council chambers. We are accompanied by a fair number of people in suits who we don't know, so before they can surround us and move us out, we charge the council table, shouting at the City Council for denying our right to demonstrate against an illegal and immoral war. We make it right to the edge of the table before the suits and uniformed cops grab us and haul us out of there.

They take us through the doors to the outside and lay us on our backs on the concrete in front of the door to the courthouse. A couple of cops take one of each of our feet and start down the steps, letting our heads bob and bump as we go down the fifty-plus-long number of steps: plunk, plunk, plunk. We hunch our backs and put our hands in the air to try to take the hit on the upper shoulders. They are kind enough to not speed up when we do that, but it may have been because cameras have shown up when our bobbing bodies with our hands in the air draw a lot of attention. The bumping isn't fast enough or hard enough to knock our brains out, but it is clear that we are to get a message that we should not to test authority in this way anymore.

At the bottom of the steps, they let go of us. We get up and walk off. We go down the street and around to the basement of the city building, find an open basement window, crawl in, take the elevator up to the council meeting floor, and when the elevator door opens charge into the council chamber again, yelling like hell. We make it all the way to the front again. They nab us at the edge of the council table again, take us out, lay us down, and drag us down the steps again, but a little faster this time. They "detain" us a bit longer, until the council meeting was over.

The video cameras were rolling both times me and B.T. were dragged down the steps so we were featured all over the country on The Hunt-ley-Brinkley Report, which was the most popular national evening news show in America. The reporters gave a pretty good explanation of what we were protesting (the denial of a parade permit to demonstrate against the war in Vietnam), showed us being bobbed down the steps the first time, and then showed us the second time around—with a kind of amused, grudging acknowledgement of the cops having their hands full, and of our persistence.

Corporate media were unsophisticated in those days. Besides, they thought we were harmless, which mostly we were. It took about eight more God-damned years to end that useless, fucking, stupid slaughterhouse of a war. We should have killed more of the motherfuckers who kept it going, because they sure as hell killed a lot of the leaders on our side. Back then we were suckers.

The Authority of Direct Experience vs. "Constituted" Authority in Various Uniforms

We didn't really give a shit what people supposedly in authority had to say, except perhaps as a guideline of what not to do. I still consider that a pretty good rule of thumb. And I've relied upon this rule of thumb as a therapist advising other people for my whole life. If you don't know what to do, then find out what the fucking Republicans recommend and do the opposite. If you want good psychological advice, but can't come by it with a good therapist or a friend, you can also ask a lawyer what to do and then do the opposite. It works (most of the time). People with their heads up their asses have pretty good intuition sometimes—if you know how to use it.

Judy and I used to go to Mexico from Austin on long weekends and holidays. It was a short four- to five-hour trip to get past the border town at the point of entry and reach the interior. We liked to go to small towns, where we'd stay for days. They fed us food as long as we were drinking beer. They'd just bring out food now and then for us to have a bite or two while we drank. If we drank all day, we ate all day. We could live cheaper there in Mexico than we could by staying at home, and we could drink beer all day long for a quarter per beer. Plus, we could buy amphetamines over the counter there and bring them back to Austin with us, where we'd sell some and have speed to use in graduate school. I would walk into little pharmacias in Saltillo and smaller towns, and say, "Dexedrina!"

They would ask, "Quantos?" (How much.)

I would answer, "Todos!" (All.) Then they would bring out all they had in stock and I would buy it.

Judy and I, and B.T. and his wife, Florence, are in our Volkswagen, driving back from Saltillo to the border. We've bought a lot of speed, and Judy and Florence have opened all the bottles and wrapped up the pills in toilet paper and put them in their bras. B.T. and I bought a bottle of rum. We're taking speed with shots of rum, and then we keep hitting the bottle as we get closer to the Texas border. B.T. is driving and we're high on speed and a little drunk (though not as drunk as we would be without the speed, or so it seems) by the time we hit the border.

As we pull up to the guard, B.T. is in a hell of a good mood. We live for defiance. So, we enter the United States defiantly. We are a black couple and a white couple together in a car. It is just at the height of the civil rights movement in Texas. We are smuggling speed, and we're high and drunk. We're also a little scared, like we've been before with cops and FBI and such, but it is exciting as hell. We get to the little booth and B.T. rolls the window down. The man at the window asks, "Do you have anything to declare?" Well, what kind of a question was that?

B.T. had been on a hunger strike that year, been arrested, been making talks, and been leading demonstrations. Did he have anything to declare? He thought about it for a minute. Then he says, "We have about ten pounds of cocaine in the spare tire, and the two back tires on this vehicle are full of marijuana. That's all I can remember, unless I forgot something."

The official looks at him. He looks at the rest of us in the car. He looks over at the line behind us. He looks at his busy colleagues, and at his watch. He looks at B.T., and me, Judy, and Florence. We just look at him. He decides it's just bullshit that's going to cost him a lot of work. He says, "Just get the hell out of here," and waves us through.

B.T. laughs and pulls on forward across the line. Then we all laugh and holler and have another shot of rum and go on back to Austin.

Aftermath: Or Beforemath ... or Some Kind of Math

We, who were there in the '60s, have all suffered fifty fucking years of some hard, God-damned subsequent disillusionment.

We felt like we'd won the civil rights battles for desegregation, but it turned out that actual integration would take for-fucking-ever, which it has. A lot of our victorious heroes of the civil rights movement either got killed or became photographers, or drug addicts and alcoholics, or depressed people or suicides, or sell-outs and yuppies.

One after the other, disheartening, gut-wrenching, infuriating, hard things continued to happen. Martin Luther King, Jr., got killed. Bobby Kennedy got killed. Nixon, for Christ's sake, got God-damned elected—with our help. Hippiedom flashed up, but then declined due to hard drugs and yuppie compromises. The "almost" overthrow of civilization only strengthened its ability to grow more dominant over the spirit of freedom.

It seemed like even when we won we lost. In fact, it still seems to me that by winning we lost. Some of us began to learn then about what we know now: how the cards are stacked in a corporatist-fascist society where romantic, emotional high ideals work as a cover story to hide thievery, payola, murder, and the work of the CIA and other mafias to protect and enrich the bosses, bankers, and boneheads. Since centuries before the U.S. Constitution was written this has been this way to protect the rights of males who owned property and people; they rule the rest of us, while hiding under the cover story of freedom.

We didn't know then how bad things actually were ... and too God-damned fucking few of us know it now!

Oops! Don't let the rant and minor lack of a fair amount of completion work and forgiveness on my part run you off yet. Consider it a part of the practice I need to go through to get to forgiveness. And also, if you don't mind, consider killing some Nazi motherfucker who is younger than you if you get a chance before you die. Do it on behalf of the next generation.

CHAPTER 14

Texas Nonviolence

My sister, Eleanor, my brother Jimmy, and I had all moved to Texas by 1957, and before long, in late 1958, my mother had followed. Our source family that had fallen apart in Virginia kept trying to fall back together again in Texas, but we weren't very good at it. We made lame attempts to be family, and we were kind to each other most of the time, but the center would not hold. The culture no longer supports families in the old way and vice versa.

Mother moved to Fort Worth to be with her children in the Dallas-Fort Worth area. She kind of followed me after leaving Tommy in Virginia and her own mother in Knoxville, Tennessee. My sister and brother-in-law lived in Arlington, between Dallas and Fort Worth, and Jimmy lived with them for a couple of years before quitting school and going out on his own, in a while joining the Air Force to study electronics and become an airplane mechanic. After splitting up with Marilyn Sue Miller, I moved in with Mother in Fort Worth for a month or two before I went to Houston to sell Bibles.

Soon after I left town, Mother moved in with an alcoholic in Fort Worth who fancied himself to be a writer. Alcoholics fancying themselves to be writers were her main avenue of support.

My sister and her husband, Joe, were busy making their own family, and already had their daughter Tina and son Mark when they were in Arlington.

I am in Fort Worth. I've come home from work late and Mama is not in the apartment. I imagine she's with that bum she met and they're somewhere down on South Main Street. I'm in a bad mood. I go out and start wandering in and out of bars down on South Main. I see her with Edgar, the phony bum who says he's a writer. They're sitting in a booth with two other drunks. She's sloshed.

I go over to the booth and reach right over Edgar, bending down and picking her up in my arms. As I lift her out of the seat, I turn and hit him in the mouth with her high-heeled shoe as I exit with her without saying a word. Her shoe falls off. I just leave it there. I take her out to the car, put her in it, and take her home. She walks upstairs with a little help when we get there, and goes to bed. I go to bed.

My mother wanted to help and support me in my quest to graduate from college, and she wanted to be near her daughter and grandchildren and the boys she'd abandoned when she decided to stay with Tommy until they finished drinking up their relationship. After they lost the house and orchard, she ended that relationship to Tommy, and she then abandoned her youngest son, Mike, as well. Though she didn't plan to be gone forever from his life, she only went back to visit briefly once or twice in the years he was growing up, from age seven to when he graduated from high school.

Mama wanted to help us and contribute to us, and she did at times, at least by sharing the rent. But usually, in the beginning of showing up, she needed money "to get started over." I would come up with the money from my various jobs and loan it to her. And she'd eventually get work as a secretary and pay me back.

In between living in the Christian Faith and Life Community and getting married to Judy, I lived with my mother for a few months again in Austin, Texas. She came to Austin about two years after I arrived.

When Judy and I decided to get married in 1961, when we were both about to get our undergraduate degrees from college, my brother Jimmy and his new wife, Madeline, moved to Austin. They'd been living in Austin for about six months when Judy and I got married. Jimmy came back after getting kicked out of the Air Force. Madeline was pregnant. He also came because I was there and mother was there, and Austin was a truly happening place. They had their daughter there.

After Judy and I got married, mother moved in with another man she met in Austin. She stayed with him until he died, and then stayed in his abandoned place until she herself died in fall 1968. That was a few years after Judy and I left Austin. I went back there after returning from a summer in Europe, and after the riots that occurred in Washington after Martin Luther King, Jr., was shot.

I had asked my friend Neil Schiff to go look in on Mama because I hadn't heard from her. He found her crawling around her apartment, not able to get herself up to go to the bathroom. He called for help and she was committed to Austin State Hospital. By the time I got there she was in a coma she never came out of. She died of cirrhosis of the liver in Austin State Hospital, the hospital part of the mental hospital where I used to work the night shift. She was sixty years old. I always thought I'd be able to help her. But I wasn't.

I felt sorry for my mother for almost as far back as I could remember, at least back to when my father died. I felt sorry for my brother Jimmy, too. I wanted to help them to make up somehow for the raw deal they'd gotten in life. I gave them money a number of times, even though I was "working my way through college" and taking out loans from the Methodist Student Loan fund and the National Defense Education Act. My mother usually paid me back. My brother usually didn't.

During the course of the couple of years of psychotherapy I was going through at the University, I eventually decided to quit giving my brother money and told him he was on his own. Jimmy survived by sometimes doing time, and sometimes by finding another woman to live with and a job. He and Madeline split up a year or so after he left the Air Force and Jimmy moved to California. By the time he became a hippie, he was good at it.

In our family, we tried to help and encourage each other, but we weren't very good at it. Jimmy and I fought when we'd drink. One time when he and a drunken friend came to see me after Judy and I got married I hit him and knocked him down in front of his friend. I still feel bad about that.

I also still feel bad about hitting Judy a bunch of times over the ten years we were married. I never beat her like Tommy did my mother or hit her with my fists. But a number of times I slapped and shoved her, and cussed and yelled at her. I also hurt her feelings and lied to her. Like other physical wife abusers, I'd apologize and try to make it up to her after I hurt her or her feelings.

Over the course of years of therapy, I very gradually became less physically abusive than I once was, but it took me many years. You see, I was comparing my ability to control myself against Tommy's poor example. Compared to him I was doing pretty well. I punched holes in walls and busted up furniture instead of hitting Judy.

I've never put a woman in the hospital or cut or scalded her or bruised her badly or hit her with my fists. By general redneck standards that isn't bad, but compared to any middle-class standard of decency, as well as my own views about the civil rights that we all deserve, I was, not always, but more than I wanted to be, a failure.

As a kid, I used to think restraining my power completely was stupid. I thought, When I am bigger and stronger and madder, I'll use it. God Bless America. Land of the Freaks. In my life, I've been a well-acculturated, moralistic, double-standard, abusive, civilized American male. And I am still in recovery from it. I am responsible for the cultures I have been in, as they live in me; and I am the one responsible for the violence I've perpetrated on the people I love. This has become less as I've become older, but I haven't set any God-damned speed records getting over myself.

Even in the civil rights movement when we were trying to be non-violent, I had trouble with it. I had to be restrained a number of times by my more peaceful friends. Like taking a Catholic out of the Church and then spending years taking the Church out of the ex-Catholic, I took many years to get over my unfair and dictatorial violence, and my threats of violence, which were my form of survival.

In regard to the civil rights movement and anti-War movement, however, I'm not ashamed of hardly any of my threats and actions that were over the line.

B.T. Bonner is on a hunger strike on the Drag just below the University Theatre. He's been there on the sidewalk with his sign for three days now. We bring him water and take shifts to keep an eye on him. I am on duty and several others from the Y like me are standing and talking about a half a block away. Three frat rats with a cheeseburger appear in front of B.T. One takes a big bite out of the burger right in front of B.T. and says, "Ummm. Umm. Want a bite?" and holds it out in front of him. I launch myself in their direction full speed ahead, yelling at the top of my lungs, "Give me that hamburger, you cocksuckers, and I'll stick it so far up your ass you will choke on it!" I am ready to kill.

All three of the frat boys run, though there are three or four people holding me back. Three of my non-violent compatriots have tackled me, and they also hold me up so I don't fall on the ground even as I keep yelling and fighting to get loose and kick some ass. Somewhere in there, with all of them telling me, "We're non-violent. We're non-violent," it occurs to me, Oh yeah, we're supposed to be non-violent.

You can take the asshole out of the jungle, but taking the jungle out of the asshole is another more difficult, painful, and long-lasting project. I am sorry for most of my violence, but not for all of it. I actually had a lot of fun running off those three frat rats. And over the course of my life I still have protected myself and my kids in ways I am not ashamed of, which sometimes involved actual violence and sometimes just the excellent bluff of being completely willing to die in the process of taking on someone who threatened either me or my children.

All of us who are survivors of violence in childhood recognize the signals of shaking and crying and shortness of breath that threaten the outbreak of attempted total annihilation at any second. We'll back down from each other most times when we get those signals, if we can. We know from experience there is hell to give and hell to pay, and hours and hours of pain and suffering in store for one or the other of us (and more likely both) when a real fight happens. We can sometimes hold back when we need to, but sometimes we don't—and you can't really ever know for sure your own self which response is going to be which. It's a dysfunctional way to live, but not entirely . . . because it works in our favor sometimes. Like the food addict, we have to eat; we can't give up eating. Yet we're hard pressed to control how much, how fast, and how unselectively we eat.

There is for me a trigger. In a split second, I then access a fury that lives inside me, and it's like a drug hitting me hard, seconds after an injection. I change suddenly from whatever mood or state of being preceded the trigger to the state of fury. I seldom have to actually act on it, and therefore can maintain a semblance of control. And I'm glad I have my potential for fury because without folks like me in the wings to support Gandhi, King, and Jesus with willingness to die and, in a personal confrontation, perhaps even to kill, love is not enough.

I believe non-violence works best in the context of the threat of violence. Otherwise the socially acceptable perpetrators of violence (the corporations, cops, armies, governments, and so on) just keep killing and stealing and promoting injustice. I don't think I am alone in this belief. Here's an excerpt from Richard Flanagan's novel The Unknown Terrorist (Grove Press, 2007), where he's writing about Friedrich Nietzsche.

"Nietzsche began to fear that what drove the world forward was all that was destructive and evil about it. In his writings he tried to reconcile himself to such a terrible world.

"But one day he saw a cart horse being beaten brutally by its driver. He rushed out and put his arms around the horse's neck, and would not let go.

Promptly diagnosed as mad, he was locked away in an asylum for the rest of his life.

"Nietzsche had even less explanation than Jesus for love and its various manifestations: empathy, kindness, hugging a horse's neck to stop it being beaten. In the end Nietzsche's philosophy could not even explain Nietzsche, a man who sacrificed his life for a horse."

Another flashback.

It's almost eleven at night and B. T. and I are standing outside the Nighthawk Restaurant. I'm tired. I've been up a day and a night, but tonight I don't have to go to work at on the graveyard shift and I'm grateful for it. We're standing outside in the rain talking, and we're a little depressed. We and a lot of our cohorts have been sitting-in at this restaurant periodically for months now. We've put forth a lot of effort, but they just let us occupy the booths and don't do shit about kicking us out, so we just sit there even though they won't serve us. We're both tired.

One of us, I don't remember which one, says, "Let's go talk to this guy." Seems like a good idea. We go around back and knock on the kitchen door. The owner, a big man, comes to the back door, recognizes us, and says, "What do you want?"

I say, "We want to know, when are you gonna integrate this God-damned restaurant!"

He looks at us and says, "I'm a damned mean Swede, and nobody tells me what to do." When he says that I cease being tired and become full of energy.

B.T. says, "Well, I'm a damned mean nigger and I am not leaving you alone until you desegregate."

He barely gets to finish because I can't wait to jump right in there and say, "I'm a mean God-damned redneck, and if you don't integrate this mother-fucker in twenty-four hours I'm coming back here to beat the shit out of you!" I am breathing hard and moving up close to the man. Apparently I look like I mean it, because he closes the door in my face and goes inside.

B.T. and I look at each other, and then we walk away. I go home and sleep. And I'll be a son of a bitch, the next day, and from that day forward, the Nighthawk Restaurant is desegregated! The next day he serves us both when we come into his restaurant.

Honestly, I don't think the Nighthawk Restaurant was desegregated be-cause the owner was afraid of us. I think it was just because no one had ever communicated to him before, clearly, and in terms he understood and that he identified with, as a fellow abused child. Since he was going broke, he seriously considered our seriousness and what he could do.

This is only one of many instances in which my friends and I somehow got across the point that we were serious and didn't mean ever to let up on creating all of the hell we could create until the God-damned justice we wanted was accomplished. When we stopped being polite, the owner of the establishment understood we were serious people, just like him. So the next day he served us food when we came into his restaurant. He didn't really care that other restaurant owners in the area wanted him to keep segregated. He was a damned mean Swede, and nobody told him what to do. And when we, a black man and a white man, went in there and sat down and ate together, nobody said shit, except when we paid the bill. Then we looked at him and said, "Thank you," like we meant it. He looked back at us and said, "You're welcome," like he did, too.

This background threatening attitude and experience of being willing to die in order to destroy is a central part of who I am, just as it is a central part of Dick Cheney and George Bush and the Neo Con Men (their band). Even saying that makes me nauseous. Being like them is the last God-damned thing I ever wanted to be!

If there's anyone I'd just love to beat the shit out of it's those two bastards and Karl Rove. I'd be happy to take them all on at once and give Cheney a shotgun to boot. I'd kick all three of their asses up between their fucking shoulder blades before they could do jack shit about it.

There that little, internal, lame-brained, loudmouthed fucker goes again! I'm seventy years old and still can't keep them fantasies under control for shit.

CHAPTER 15

Another God-damned Serious Rant about Civilization and Its Criminal Intents

Seriously, all I've come up with to use my anger and not just be used by it is to be honest about it, get help to control it, and be willing to experience the experience I've been trying to avoid by doing violence, instead of doing the violence. I use my courage to be present to this experience instead of using my courage to risk my life in order to destroy an enemy. Above all else, I make my anger personal and contactful: I directly and honestly express it, because love has to include dealing with anger.

"Love" as an ideal, as a pose or a phony act, is definitely not enough. Love of children and animals and creatures and plants and environments justifies killing perpetrators of the destruction of those beings one loves. I don't want my anger to use me, but I don't mind using my anger to bring a halt to violence even if it includes killing the enforcers of domination and control who so far are winning and wiping out the planet.

I need to say this here because I am not a believer in non-violence at all costs, and I want you to know this. I am in favor of avoiding violence and controlling violence, and trying everything first other than violence, except in situations in which it appears that nothing but violence will work. I've been struggling with this issue of non-violence vs. violence all of my life. I still think that some people do need killing.

Civilization itself makes us all as sick as we can be. Lots of mothers love their children and don't really want to hurt them. But they hurt the hell out of them anyway by the way they love them and the way they deprive them of love when they get angry at them, or and by the way they moralize to them and control them and punish them on top of loving them.

Particularly when we teach children to be obedient and behave we do them perhaps the greatest disservice of education and acculturation. Love is not enough. (There is a book by Bruno Bettelheim with that title, *Love Is Not Enough,* and the topic is touched on in my book *Radical Parenting*).

For real growing up to happen, rather than extending adolescence forever, some wisdom has to be there in us about not automatically trusting authority and being well behaved no matter what, because that philosophy is a poison that kills the spirit. Being civilized is being poisoned. And all the "civil" wars we constantly interfere with wouldn't have enough troops were it not for the constant poisoning that comes from public education.

The way people love their children damages the children mainly because they're being phony while trying to "be loving" or "set a good example." Parents often withdraw contact and relate to an ideal of being loving rather than continue to relate honestly with their children. By alternating nurturing with depriving their children in order to control them, definite damage gets done.

The problem is not that parents don't love their children; they often do. The problem is that love from a culturally conditioned, hysterical, angry mother or father who really loves her/his child but wants to teach the child something for the child's "own good," is the perpetrator of an always hurtful and long-lasting mixed bag of love and poison. Love is not enough because love mixed with moralism is poison to the wonderful sprits of little children.

All the studies show that constancy is what works best in parenting. If you're even handed and consistently loving, children can handle it. Even constant abuse without much variation works; children can handle that, too. Inconstant love and deprivation of love, or alternation of love and abuse, this is what they can't handle. Kids treated that way turn out the most fucked up as adults: They are more neurotic, do more damage to others, and fuck up their own kids more if this is how they've been raised.

I don't like Marshall Rosenberg's non-violent communication (NVC) movement because NVC involves suppression of one's feelings and the denial of honest self-expression; also because it equates cussing with hitting. I know the God-damned difference between the bullshit category of so-called verbal abuse and real physical abuse. I've expressed my anger and forgiven my enemy enough times as an alternative to violence that I can use that preferred way instead of my totally reactive violent way. *I didn't learn that by avoiding being honest about my intense anger.*

I only limit my expressiveness about anger by not hitting. That works more often than suppression, and more completely. As far as I can tell, Marshall Rosenberg and most other practitioners of NVC are full of shit.

Seven or eight of us are at the police station in Austin again. They've "detained" but not arrested us. They've learned that when we just get picked up and held for a while we don't get newspaper and TV coverage for our movement, and they know nothing has to be put on the police roster about it. As we walk into the holding room, the uniformed guys who detained us turn us over to a detective sitting at a desk on the other side of a fairly big room. I'm out of cigarettes. I walk over to the desk and say to him, "I saw a cigarette machine right outside there. I'm going to go get some cigarettes." He pulls out a pistol, lays it on the desk, and says, "You're not going anywhere. If you walk through that door I'm gonna shoot you."

I am getting that energized feeling again. My heart races and now I am ready to die. This motherfucker is not going to dominate me. I look him straight in the eye and say to him, "Fire away, motherfucker," then turn and walk straight toward the exit door. All the way across the room I'm waiting for the bullet to hit me in the back and for the sound of the gun, or for him to kick back his chair and come after me. It is very exciting.

After what seems like a month or two of walking across that room, I walk right through the door. I go get a pack of cigarettes, open it, take one out, and light it up, but my hands are shaking. I walk back through the door.

The detective is still sitting there and the gun is still on the desk. I walk over and say, "Well, what the fuck happened? Did you lose your nerve?"

He says, "Just sit down and shut the fuck up." So I do.

It has always seemed a little strange to me that we say, "I lost my temper," when we describe loss of control when we're angry. It seems to me that we do anything but "lose" our temper, we "get" our temper—and then we might lose control of our temper or we might not. Sometimes it is appropriate to do so. Most times it isn't. Losing control is definitely not always a bad thing. In fact, when I can lose control a little earlier or I can decrease my controllingness earlier in the process of getting mad, I actually gain more control over being violent.

I've coached a lot of people in how to do this, and written about it extensively. That is one of the ways I've tried to turn the reactive lessons of my life with my source family into something of value for myself and the rest of you. It is also an attempt to compensate for some of the suffering I have caused, by relieving suffering.

Almost by accident, this issue of what to do about anger and vengeance has become the core issue of our time. We are at a crossroads between Empire and Earth Community, and central to our success is the willingness to confront and stop the forces of Empire in order to create the opportunity for community power instead of corporate economic domination.

What I mean to say is: Fuck the God-damned bankers. Screw the wealthy. Shit on the corporations. They can all eat shit and die. Let's make that personal and say it to their faces. Let's be willing to act on it and have a serious conversation with them and see if we're going to have to kick their asses or not. Then we may have to love them enough to actually do what we threaten, and, if possible, not kill them. If not possible, then we need to kill them. We need to act on this, one way or another, quickly.

At this point in writing my first draft of this book, I peeled off and took a year and a half to write a different book on this very subject matter, *The Korporate Kannibal Kookbook* (2011). Once that was published I took this up again. Luckily, that book was a long enough rant for me to be able to spare you from some of what you might have had to put up with had I not done it.

Finally, love is not enough because it's usually not inclusive enough. Here's a short excerpt from an interview I did with Susan Campbell, my friend and colleague in the Radical Honesty movement, on this point.

A Conversation with Susan Campbell

Susan Campbell: What gets in the way of people behaving "for the good of the whole?"

Brad Blanton: That's a great question! I think what gets in the way of people behaving "for the good of the whole" is people behaving for the good of the part! When we mammals distinguished ourselves from our reptilian ancestors by birthing our young out of our own bodies rather than hatching them from eggs we laid, we developed at the same time the limbic brain, over on top of our reptilian brain, and it had to do with caring for our own.

I've said before, as have many others, that the only thing that can save us is love—for *all* of each other and with *all of being*. But now I think love will probably not save us. Most of the time, the love human beings experience is not wide enough. Love for a narrower, smaller family group brings about defense against, and violence toward other groups. In our evolutionary social experiment to get all the goodies or nothing, the limbic brain is failing to integrate with the prefrontal lobes soon enough. We cannot develop the capacity to care for all human beings, much less all beings, as our own. Humankind is coming to an end because of our failure to include all life as our own.

Even when people get in touch with themselves as *beings who notice* as their primary identity (which is the therapeutic goal of Radical Honesty) and they see the similarity between themselves and all other beings, they move away from this awareness because everything in our culture reinforces the more limited view of who they are as their performance. This is the main thing learned in school: You are your performance (meaning, the grades you make, the acceptance you get, recognition from teachers and peers, your status in the eyes of others, how you rank, the college you go to, and so on).

In order to perform well, you must be obedient. Thus obedience training overrules caring for anyone or anything bigger than the trap of your own performance. That's why when I got older and was married to Amy and we did all the work of The Forum, we kept our kids out of school. My daughter Carsie is an independent, powerfully creative person, a musician (hear her music at CarsieBlanton.com) and a gift to humanity. She missed most of her obedience training. So did my son Elijah. Most Americans have taken obedience training and are proud of it.

Our schools are the very heart of fascism. As cultural historian Morris Berman says, "America takes away love and gives its citizens gadgets in return, which most of them regard as a terrific bargain."

Consequently, as environmentalist Dale Allen Pfeiffer says, "People need to understand that we are faced with a madness that will make life miserable for us and for generations to come, if it does not severely damage the viability of this entire planet. Yet they also need to know that each of us has the power to stop this madness, simply by ceasing to take part in the system that perpetuates this madness. We are all armed with monkey wrenches; it is time to use them. It is time to take back our power and to realize that we, ourselves, are our own masters. And let us never delegate that power or that responsibility again."

A Monkey Wrenching Summary

We are driving along, Jimmy and I. I think we're taking someone home from my bachelor party. It's the day before my wedding to Judy. My brother is driving. I am drunk. I ask him to stop. I get out of the car and puke. I'm sitting there, after vomiting, thinking, "I am twenty years old. I'm going to marry Judy Schleyer tomorrow. This is a mistake. I don't know how to love anybody. I'm alone. I'm a fool. I don't know what I'm doing. I am sad. Everyone does the best they can, but nothing really works."

I start crying. I cry and cry and cry. My brother keeps repeating, "What's wrong? Bradley, what's wrong?"

After I cry a while, I get up and tell him, "I'm okay." and we get in the car and drive on.

Had I been more articulate at that age, I would have said...
There is a lot of sadness in this world.
There is a lot of meanness in this world.
There is a lot of love in this world.
Love, and the loss of it, and the poison often mixed with it, is the very source of the sadness and the meanness in the world. People learn to live by what they've learned whether they learned the wrong things or not. Because of what I've learned and learned to live by, I know that the loss of love is inevitable. The consequences are always sad, painful, and infuriating.

While the opportunity of the crises of anger and hurt is the chance to forgive and be whole again, this cannot be seen during the beginning of a crisis. But when we stick with it, an opportunity to feel our way through to forgiveness may show up, if we don't try to fix things with violence or non-violence or other forms of idealism.

In each individual case, maybe it will turn out that "I" transcend what I "know." I've heard it's possible. I have also tasted the possibility. I have even done it a few times. I know that acceptance and a new beginning are possible. I've done it before. I know we can do it together. I've lived all this and I know it is possible.

So did D.H. Lawrence. He wrote a poem about it. It's about the discovery in the depths of despair of "A New Heaven and a New Earth."

I

And so I cross into another world
shyly and in homage linger for an invitation
from this unknown that I would trespass on.

I am very glad, and all alone in the world,
all alone, and very glad, in a new world
where I am disembarked at last.

I could cry with joy, because I am in the new world, just ventured in.
I could cry with joy, and quite freely, there is nobody to know.
And whosoever the unknown people of this unknown world may be
they will never understand my weeping for joy to be adventuring among them
because it will still be a gesture of the old world I am making
which they will not understand, because it is quite, quite foreign to them.

II
I was so weary of the world,
I was so sick of it,
everything was tainted with myself,
skies, trees, flowers, birds, water,
people, houses, streets, vehicles, machines,
nations, armies, war, peace-talking,
work, recreation, governing, anarchy,
it was all tainted with myself, I knew it all to start with
because it was all myself.

When I gathered flowers, I knew it was myself plucking my own flowering.
When I went in a train, I knew it was myself travelling by own invention.
When I heard the cannon of the war, I listened with my own ears to my own
     destruction.
When I saw the torn dead, I knew it was my own torn dead body.
It was all me, I had done it all in my own flesh.

III

I shall never forget the maniacal horror of it all in the end
when everything was me, I knew it all already, I anticipated it all in my soul
because I was the author and the result
I was the God and the creation at once;
creator, I looked at my creation;
created, I looked at myself, the creator;
it was a maniacal horror in the end.

I was a lover, I kissed the woman I loved,
and God of horror, I was kissing also myself.
I was a father and a begetter of children,
and oh, oh horror, I was begetting and conceiving in my own body.

IV

At last came death, sufficiency of death,
and that at last relieved me, I died.
I buried my beloved; it was good, I buried myself and was gone.
War came, and every hand raised to murder;
very good, very good, every hand raised to murder !
Very good, very good, I am a murderer!
It is good, I can murder and murder, and see them fall,
the mutilated, horror-struck youths, a multitude
one on another, and then in clusters together
smashed, all oozing with blood, and burned in heaps
going up in a fetid smoke to get rid of them,
the murdered bodies of youths and men in heaps
and heaps and heaps and horrible reeking heaps
till it is almost enough, till I am reduced perhaps;
thousands and thousands of gaping, hideous foul dead
that are youths and men and me
being burned with oil, and consumed in corrupt thick smoke, that rolls
and taints and blackens the sky, till at last it is dark, dark as night, or death, or hell
and I am dead, and trodden to nought in the smoke sodden tomb;
dead and trodden to nought in the sour black earth
of the tomb; dead and trodden to nought, trodden to nought.

V

God, but it is good to have died and been trodden out,
trodden to nought in sour, dead earth,
quite to nought,
absolutely to nothing
nothing
nothing
nothing.

For when it is quite, quite nothing, then it is everything.
When I am trodden quite out, quite, quite out,
every vestige gone, then I am here
risen and setting my foot on another world
risen, accomplishing a resurrection
risen, not born again, but risen, body the same as before,
new beyond knowledge of newness, alive beyond life,
proud beyond inkling or furthest conception of pride,
living where life was never yet dreamed of, not hinted at,
here, in the other world, still terrestrial
myself, the same as before, yet unaccountably new.

VI

I, in the sour black tomb, trodden to absolute death
I put out my hand in the night, one night, and my hand
touched that which was verily not me,
verily it was not me.
Where I had been was a sudden blaze,
a sudden flaring blaze !
So I put out my hand out further, a little further
and I felt that which was not I,
it verily was not I,
it was the unknown.

Ha, I was a blaze leaping up!
I was a tiger bursting into sunlight.

I was greedy, I was mad for the unknown.
I new-risen, resurrected, starved from the tomb,
starved from a life of devouring always myself,
now here was I, new-awakened, with my hand stretching out
and touching the unknown, the real unknown, the unknown unknown.

My God, but I can only say
I touch, I feel the unknown !
I am the first comer !
Cortes, Pisarro, Columbus, Cabot, they are nothing, nothing!
I am the first comer!
I am the discoverer!
I have found the other world!
The unknown, the unknown!
I am thrown upon the shore.
I am covering myself with the sand.
I am filling my mouth with the earth.
I am burrowing my body into the soil.
The unknown, the new world!

VII

It was the flank of my wife
I touched with my hand, I clutched with my hand,
rising, new-awakened from the tomb!
It was the flank of my wife
whom I married many years ago
at whose side I have lain for over a thousand nights
and all that previous while, she was I, she was I;
I touched here, it was I who touched and I who was touched.

Yet rising from the tomb, from the black oblivion
stretching out my hand, my hand flung like a drowned man's hand on a rock,
I touched her flank and knew I was carried by the current in death
over to the new world, and was climbing out on the shore,
risen, not to the old world, the old, changeless I, the old life,
wakened not to the old knowledge
but to a new earth, a new I, a new knowledge, a new world of time.

Ah no, I cannot tell you what it is, the new world.
I cannot tell you the mad, astounded rapture of its discovery.
I shall be mad with delight before I have done,
and whosoever comes after will find me in the new world
a madman in rapture.

VIII

Green streams that flow from the innermost continent of the new world,
what are they?
Green and illumined and travelling for ever
dissolved with mystery of the innermost heart of the continent,
mystery beyond knowledge or endurance, so sumptuous
out of the well-heads of the new world.

The other, she too had strange green eyes!
White sands and fruits unknown and perfumes that never
can blow across the dark seas to our usual world!
And land that beats with a pulse!
And valleys that draw close in love!
And strange ways where I fall into oblivion of uttermost living!
Also she who is the other has strange-mounded breasts and strange sheer slopes,
    and white levels.

Sightless and strong oblivion in utter life takes possession of me!
The unknown, strong current of life supreme
drowns me and sweeps me away and holds me down
to the sources of mystery, in the depth,
extinguishes there my risen resurrected life
and kindles it further at the core of utter mystery.

CHAPTER 16

Therapy

Growing Up

During those years of being in the Christian Faith and Life Community and the civil rights movement, and of finishing my undergraduate degree and beginning graduate school, I was in psychotherapy. Therapy was offered free or at a deeply reduced rate for students back then, and I wanted it for many reasons. I was often angry and sometimes depressed. I wanted to become a therapist and to learn personally how to heal my own wounds, and to do so before I presumed to help others do the same thing.

I had this feeling like there was a hole in the middle of my chest, a sadness about having lost people I loved in my life: my father when he died, my sister when she left home, my mother when I left home, my little brother Mike when I left home (who I still missed and felt bad about leaving even almost ten years later).

I felt guilty about having gotten married and having it be annulled, and for my baby being born and given away for adoption. I felt guilty about lying to Judy and fucking other women. I felt guilty (well, most of the time) about keeping secrets. I needed help and I wanted to know how to give help to people like me. I didn't know then, like I know now, about how much my secrets and lies were costing me.

One secret I kept and didn't feel guilty about, but which still cost me something in terms of honestly sharing with my friends, was that I was the only one who knew that B.T. Bonner was on the payroll of the FBI. He got $150 a month to keep them informed of what was going on in the civil rights movement. He made sure to tell them of things we knew would be in the paper the next day anyway, or things everyone already knew. I understood why he agreed to do it: The $150 a month was real money in those days. It fed his kids. We were glad that J. Edgar Hoover was helping make it possible for him to be in the civil rights movement with that money, and we felt like we were taking advantage of the lying, racist, segregationist pervert and hypocrite J. Edgar Hoover, which we were. And that is not the first time the dumb assed right wing has sustained the left when they thought they were being so fucking slick.

I didn't mind lying to authority and still don't. But lying to friends, people we know personally, costs us all more than we reckon in terms of contact and intimacy, and limits our ability to be co-hearted, co-intelligent, and sustained by each other rather than depressed. I didn't know that then.

I felt tired a lot, mainly because I was always working, going to school, or demonstrating, and hardly ever sleeping. I was in individual therapy and group therapy at the Student Health Center at the University of Texas for a couple of years. Later on in graduate school, I was in individual therapy at the counseling center run by the psychology and educational psychology department. There I was in temporary groups and in supervised sessions in coursework in group therapy and individual therapy as well.

One of my therapists was a man named Stromberg. A few friends of mine had been seeing him. I remember the first session. He was listening most of the time, and asking a question now and then to show he was listening. Toward the end of the session I was about to cry and I was saying that I felt "a little bit angry a lot of the time," and he said something like, "Oh hell, angry. You're not angry! I've seen angry people before!"

I jumped up, got right in his face, and said, "Yeah! And maybe you're about to see another one, motherfucker!"

He laughed. Then he said, "Okay, I guess maybe you are a little angry."

I felt like he had tricked me, but I also, and more importantly, felt that he actually got me *because* he could trick me. So I stayed in therapy with him. I also joined one of his ongoing therapy groups.

Most of the time throughout my group therapy sessions I felt more like a co-therapist than a client. That's because I was. I am good at "getting" what's really going on with people and it's a great way to avoid having to do work on myself. I needed a lot of therapy for any of it to soak in for me. I was slow to get it because I was so quick to get it.

I had this thing about not feeling sorry for myself. I couldn't stand people who indulged in self-pity. I hated people who whined. It was clearly an issue for me. At another time, around the beginning of graduate school, I was in therapy with a woman at the counseling center and she helped me learn something valuable. She was always kind to me and listened carefully to me; she seemed to care about me. I was, I think, telling her about having gotten an F in Texas History a few semesters back, when I'd had a confrontation with the professor. I'd done poorly on a test and had missed a number of sessions of the class, which took place at eight o'clock in the morning on Tuesdays, Thursdays, and Saturdays. The professor had asked me why I'd missed class on the last two Saturdays. I told him I worked the graveyard shift. One Saturday my replacement came late. The next Saturday I tried to get in a half hour nap before class and didn't get up.

He said he was a Korean War veteran, and that he'd worked his way through school, too, but that he didn't miss classes because of his work. When I said I didn't really give a fuck if he was a veteran or if he worked his way through school or that he didn't miss any fucking classes in the process, he looked at me and said, "You might as well drop out now because an F is all you are going to get."

I said, "Fine!" and walked out.

After telling my therapist this, along with describing a few other instances of arrogant failure because of my temper when anyone moralized or judged me, I realized it wasn't really fine. I had to admit that the behavior was more than a little dysfunctional. I felt like it was unfair that he wasn't sympathetic, but I also could see that I'd set up the conflict in the first place. I saw that I kept kind of pitching myself as a brave, but constant victim of other people's minds. On this day, I said, "Oh well, I think I am just feeling sorry for myself." I was quiet then for a minute.

My therapist looked at me, and then she reached over and touched me, and said, "It's okay if you do. Go ahead and feel sorry for yourself. You've had some pretty hard times in your life. It's okay if you feel sorry for yourself. Go ahead."

All of a sudden I just started crying. Then I cried and cried and cried. No one had ever told me that before. I'd never told myself that before. I never even considered the option. I couldn't believe it was okay to feel sorry for myself, and when I did it a whole floodgate was opened. Grief flowed through me like a river. I cried until my bones ached. That little boy I was trying to take care of all the time wasn't just my younger brother and my baby brother, he was me. The people I helped in the community and in the group therapy groups and wanted to help as a therapist, and the people I was fighting for in the civil rights movement, were who they were, but they were not just who they were—they were me, too.

Up until that moment I could feel sorry for anyone else in the world but myself. And still it was me I was feeling sorry for when I did. *Why not feel sorry for all of us, including me? Why not? It's okay. Go ahead.* So I did. And I do. I am crying right now as I'm writing this. But I am not resisting it. I've never resisted it again like I did before that therapy session. When my sadness deepens and I let myself experience it, I feel better again: less angry, less depressed, and more willing to forgive even myself.

I still hate whiners, particularly when they compare themselves to other people and make themselves the greater victim and try to torture those around them with their indirect bitching and whining. But now I can work with them because I see they're disowning anger in themselves, just as I disowned, and still occasionally disown, my grief. We recognize each other after a while and quit lying about what it is we're really feeling, and it helps us move on to other stuck places instead of staying stuck in just one place, which is practically the whole point of therapy.

Therapy is feeling your way through, and not avoiding anything, and then moving on to the next place of resistance—until there's less resistance altogether and more willingness to be where and how you are.

I am grateful for those years of psychotherapy when I was in college and for the years of therapy, psychoanalysis, and training therapy I did for years during and after receiving my doctorate. The insights I got into what makes me tick were helpful, but not nearly as much as the opportunity to feel what I hadn't let myself feel. My listening improved and my capacity for empathy eventually sometimes included myself.

My disdain for authority wasn't all bad. I think the civil rights movement was therapeutic for me and for a lot of my fellow protesters as well. We were a bunch of neurotic kids. We were doing battle the best we could with a bunch of neurotic so-called adults. But we knew that we'd learned a lot of things those people didn't have a glimmer about, and that they had no right to impose their ignorance on us or on anyone else. By God, we were going to see to it that they didn't. We learned not only from books and therapy, but also from drugs and honesty about our own and society's pretenses—things we knew the "authorities" didn't know shit about.

The same was true of the anti-Vietnam War movement: It was therapeutic. That whole total waste-of-life phony fucking war came and went, and all it did was keep the phony bureaucracy in place along with the phony capitalist-corporate-fascist dictatorship. The problem is, after all these years, that nothing of great substance has really changed. Period. The therapy hasn't worked for society. Most of us never grow up beyond the feelings of being jilted and abused as children, or being invested in denying it, partly because we are swimming in a culture of denial and ignorance in the first God-damned place.

CHAPTER 17

Groan Up

Well, it's about time we got back on the linear theme of my life story. A few more things have come to me that I left out, so briefly now, it's 1964 again. I am in graduate school, in therapy, married to Judy, screwing around in secret on the side, active in the anti-Vietnam War movement, into becoming a hippie, smuggling drugs from Mexico, taking all kinds of drugs, smoking cigarettes and pot, drinking a lot of beer, reading a lot of books, taking speed, writing a lot of papers, playing golf now and again, being a preacher in the Methodist Church with a circuit of three churches every Sunday (two in the morning, one in the evening), working on Don Yarborough's campaign for Governor of Texas against John Connolly (an asshole friend of President LBJ), and starting work on my dissertation. How did I get here?

I got into a special program that was sponsored jointly by the Department of Psychology and the Department of Educational Psychology at the University of Texas. The deal was that if I completed all of the coursework for a master's degree, I could take the qualifying exam for admission to the doctoral program prior to writing the master's thesis. Then, if I passed four written sections and the oral section of the qualifying exam, I could proceed with my doctoral studies and write a doctoral dissertation instead of writing a master's thesis. Passing those exams meant I could get a "Get Out of Jail Free" card a couple of years earlier than usual.

As a junior with only one year left in undergraduate school, I was majoring in psychology with minors in philosophy and anthropology. I went to a lecture given by one of the more famous professors in the counseling department. I can't remember his name now, but I do remember the tremendous length, breadth, and spread of his grand lecture about the developmental themes of human life, regardless of culture, from the womb to the tomb, which was mostly based on Erik Erikson's work. The night I heard that lecture I decided I was going to get into the special program this man and his colleagues had invented. I wanted the grand perspective of the view from the womb to the tomb to be my own focus, along with the brand of big-picture existentialism I'd learned through participating in the Christian Faith and Life Community. His vision was breathtaking to me, and I realized that wide, all-inclusive perspectives on evolution and growth were going to be my cup of tea—probably until I died.

I had not been a very good undergraduate student up to then, and my grade point average showed it. So I had to get to work. I needed to bring my grade point average up. If I could do that, at least for the final two semesters, I could get into graduate school. So I did that. I made all A's one semester, and one B and all the rest A's for the next. When I applied for the graduate program they let me in. Not only that, they gave me a job as a research assistant, which was not quite enough to live on, but it was easy money compared to making money with the work I had been doing.

I felt really lucky and successful. Not only was I getting quite a privileged education from my life in the CFLC, the civil rights movement, the anti-War movement, drugs, sex, and rock and roll, but I was eventually going to be able to get a Ph.D. for it! God damn! If the official world out there knew what I was getting away with they'd lock me up and throw away the key!

Maybe they should have. Certainly a few people in positions of power tried.

Not too long after B.T. and I were featured on The Huntley-Brinkley Report for getting dragged by our feet down the steps of City Hall with our heads bouncing on the steps, the chairman of the Educational Psychology Department sent a message for me to come to his office. I went up and his door was open. I walked past his secretaries and went into his office. He asked me to take a seat. He began by telling me that he'd just been to a national conference. On his return flight he engaged in a conversation with a number of his peers. One of them had asked him if that fellow who was on the national news was in his program. He'd said yes, that I was in a joint program on cognition and motivation. And he told me he felt embarrassed by that admission and my affiliation with the program he ran. He didn't like to have students in his program be an embarrassment to him.

Then he asked, "Do you understand me?"

As you can imagine by now, that question really fucking pissed me off. Before I said anything in reply to him, I stood up, went over, and closed the door so the secretaries in the front office couldn't hear, and then came back in front of his desk, bent over directly in front of him, and got real close to his face. I said, "If you think I give a fuck about whether you got embarrassed or not you have another fucking thought coming. And if you do anything whatsoever to have any effect on anything I do in this program for any reason other than academic reasons, I'll personally have a God-damned piece of your ass! And if I can't get you legally, I will get you physically. Do you understand *me?*"

He went pale, and then said, "Yes."

Pointing my finger at him in a very un-non-violent fashion, I said, "Okay. Don't you ever fucking forget it." Then I walked out and closed the door behind me.

I didn't tell anyone about that whole episode at the time except for my wife Judy and Cody Wilson, my major professor, who'd graduated from Harvard University only a few years earlier. He'd been arrested in a civil rights demonstration in Texas. He told me he had my back, which perhaps he did, because nothing ever came of it. I got my borderline Ph.D. about two years later. Whenever the Chairman and I saw each other in public we were polite and businesslike, and he never tried to threaten me or teach me a lesson about how I should behave again. Nor did I he.

It was typical for conventional people to be upset with my activism. Once I was turned down for a job as an assistant dean at the University of Texas that I applied for in my next to last year of graduate school with no reason given except that they "weren't sure whether my behavior would be appropriate for the job given how much I was in the news."

All the angry confrontations I brag about are protests about the world being the way the world is and about people being the way they are. That's essentially the definition of neurosis: not liking things to be as they are (demanding that the world be other than it is). At the same time, if you aren't neurotic in a sick culture you're even crazier than the other people. I do get angry about any hint of manipulation, and I am glad that I do and that I don't quit being angry and expressing it. I don't know what I would do if I didn't do that.

I do know that the joyfulness I have, like the Sufis, Gestaltists, and even some Christians say, comes from expressiveness and forgiveness. And I know that forgiveness is not an intellectual exercise. For me it only shows up after a process of expressing, experiencing, and getting over anger and hurt by telling the truth about it, being with it, and feeling my way through it until it has come and gone.

The Sufi poet Hafiz wrote a poem about forgiveness that I like. Here it is.

When
The violin
can forgive the past
it starts singing
When the violin can stop worrying
about the future
You will become
such a drunk laughing nuisance
That God
Will then lean down
And start combing you into
His
Hair
When the violin can forgive
Every wound caused by
Others
The heart starts
Singing.

CHAPTER 18
A Man Fit for My Times

From fall 1966 through summer 1967, my last year at the University of Texas, I became more radicalized and active in protests against the war in Vietnam. I ended my student deferment for graduate school by sending a letter in red ink to my Fort Worth, Texas, draft board, saying that I was a homosexual Communist and that I'd move to Canada before I would serve in the God-damned U.S. military. I told them they could go to hell. I got a 1A classification by return mail. That classification meant I was at the head of the line of those who were next to be called up. I destroyed the draft card.

The army never came and got me. I don't know what in the hell happened when I didn't show up, though I imagine all that happened was that some poor black kid from Fort Worth got sent over to Vietnam and killed or maimed for life in my place, simply because it was too much fucking trouble for them to have to deal with a resistant SOB like me. I'd been in a lot of newspapers for leading marches, making speeches against the war, being detained by police, and for suing the City of Austin in federal court for denying a parade permit to our anti-Vietnam War group and other things.

I completed my final oral exam on my dissertation and went to celebrate getting my doctorate at Scholz Garten, the most famous neighborhood bar in Austin, where my friends told stories and toasted me. The day after that was the first time I was officially addressed as Dr. Blanton in public or referred to that way in the press. It happened when I was called to the witness stand by our American Civil Liberties Union (ACLU) lawyer to testify against the government for having denied us our right to peacefully assemble to march against the war. We lost the case, but got a lot of press and the opportunity to speak to lots of people about what a deadly hoax the war was.

We were already over two years into our protest then, and the anti-War movement grew year by year, but it still took eight years of protest by us, and eight years of fighting by the Viet Cong and incompetency by the U.S. corporatocracy, to bring that war to an end. Though the U.S. was clearly defeated, it not only cost the profiteers nothing, but they made a killing from all the killing and remained in power after ruining millions of lives for nothing. Those same bastards are still in power and still supplying both sides in perennial wars that make no sense at all. Any American who doesn't know this by now is an ignorant, brainwashed sonofabitch with his or her head up his or her God-damned ass.

We didn't know it yet, but our movement disowning the ignorance of the past, though slow as hell, was becoming the most significant cultural change movement of the twentieth century. Protesting evolved slowly into changing the way we lived and breathed and had our being. Protesters became hippies. I remember when Bob Dylan's first album came out and a friend brought the record over to our little apartment. We were blown away. From then on, we listened to all of his songs religiously, and to the songs that came after him by The Beatles and The Animals and all other direction-givers of that era. I started learning how to play the guitar and sing during those years. We knew those songs were ours, and those people who wrote them were us, and we also knew they were songs from our direction givers.

God, what a time! Since 1966, Judy and I had been managing an apartment complex in Austin. We'd been doing this at two different complexes for a couple of years while attending grad school full time and also working as research assistants half time. I intensively worked on my dissertation through the first eight months of 1966 while Judy finished up her course work. She was about a year behind me in her graduate program. I finished my dissertation, passed my final oral exam, and got my Ph.D. in August 1966, a month before my twenty-sixth birthday. The times they were achangin' and my personal life was, too.

After fucking around in secret with various women on campus for several years, I confessed to Judy and tearfully promised not to do that anymore. We were letting go of structures that had been traditional for a long time while still pursuing a quite conventional trail of success in the academic and social world. We were actually changing some critical cultural standards about sex, but the main way we experienced it was by jumping back and forth from conventional morality and shame to pride in our new-found freedom to love and let love. We hadn't a clue about how to handle it, but like everything else at the time we took off in that direction without much of a clue about what we were headed for. It was one of the best characteristics of hippiedom.

In fall 1966, I took a job as an associate professor of psychology at Miami University of Ohio in Oxford, Ohio. Judy still had a year to go to finish her dissertation, but when we moved to Oxford, which is near Cincinnati, she also took a job as an instructor in one of the branch campuses of Miami University. She kept writing her dissertation and made trips back to Austin a number of times to finish her work for her Ph.D. that next year.

We drove to Ohio from Texas in our fairly new used Plymouth Barracuda. That car was the prettiest and newest car we'd ever had. I was going to be paid $1,000 a month, way more money than I'd ever made in my life. Because I was called "Dr. Blanton" everyone assumed I was smart and expected me to be so, so being smart was easy.

Judy and I were both pretty happy with what we were accomplishing and happy to be venturing out into a new world. We knew a lot about adventure from the psychedelic drugs we'd taken and the friends and fellow adventurers we'd known. As I said before, we knew that wherever we went we were participants in a really important, really big social change: something new in history was happening to us, and being caused to happen by us.

It was not long before I became the faculty sponsor of an anti-Vietnam War group on campus called Students to Educate and Act for Peace (SEAP).

I taught a large introductory psych section of about 200 freshmen that year. In my lectures I played music from The Animals and The Beatles, and talked about phenomenology, existentialism, and taking risks, and about drugs and turning-on, tuning-in, and dropping out. I was famously infamous within weeks and the students loved me. They smuggled friends into my classes to hear me and I loved it. I was closer in age to my students than I was to most of the faculty and administration. I was a part of the revolution, and someone who could still be "trusted" without breaking the bumper sticker rule "Don't Trust Anyone Over 30."

Judy and I lived in a farmhouse we rented off campus where we threw parties for performers and speakers who came to the University, some invited by our SEAP group. I smoked grass with prominent Beat poet and activist Lawrence Ferlinghetti, who later founded *City Lights* magazine and City Lights Bookstore in San Francisco, and I smoked opiated hash with singer-songwriter Phil Ochs. We loved to hang out with these singers, poets, and speakers on their way from San Francisco to New York via Antioch College in Ohio. We were still on the route! Antioch was close by (about fifty miles away) and a hotbed of social protest and hippiedom.

Our friends Jim and Louise Jordan had moved from Austin to Yellow Springs when Jim took his first job as an art teacher in the Art Department at Antioch. Eventually he would become the chairman of the department. Since we were within an hour's drive of each other and involved in our mutual new beginnings we were happy to get together, get stoned, and report back and forth about our surroundings and our progress in demythologizing the horseshit of America. We had no idea of what it was going to take, and luckily our naiveté allowed us to continue, for soon we started finding out how ingrained cultural ignorance really is.

Miami University of Ohio was an ROTC school, and the Students to Educate and Act for Peace were a big threat to the solid citizens of the State of Ohio. We sponsored a series of events called "Gentle Wednesdays" where we gave out candy, soft drinks, and colored chalk for people to draw pictures on the sidewalks. We sat around, played guitars, and put out blankets for people to sit on right in the middle of the campus. And we hung out and talked to people about being peaceful, about peace, about the war in Vietnam, and about the two worlds we all lived in. Soon TV stations from around the state began coming out to the campus and reporting on our activities. Ordinary people from Ohio were appalled. A congressman from Dayton began an investigation of us forthwith, knowing in his heart that we must be anti-American Communists.

This was a couple of years before the horrific killing of unarmed Kent State University students who were demonstrating against the war by the Ohio National Guard. That event, which took place on May 4, 1970, provoked a significant national response. Hundreds of universities, colleges, and even high schools closed throughout the country due to a strike by four million students. It also rallied anti-War sentiments.

The San Francisco-Austin-New York Educational Corridor

Prior to coming to Ohio and during the time I was participating in the protests in Austin against the war, I was making occasional trips to San Francisco and a lot of people from San Francisco were coming through Austin. Something was afoot. We all knew something was up. We were dropping acid and smoking pot and singing and dancing, and not trusting anyone over thirty, unless they said to us, "Don't trust anyone over thirty." All social norms and morals and standards were questionable, and we were being damned sure they got questioned. This was the two and a half years after John Kennedy was assassinated in Dallas and a year and a half before the "Summer of Love" in Haight-Ashbury, California.

Located somewhere between rage and love and the tremendous psychological and perceptual liberation of psychedelics was this community of friends who no longer wanted to have anything to do with the socially retarded, outdated standards of Middle America. We were free—or at least learning how to be free—and experimenting with our freedom! And we had tons of fellow investigators. We were re-inventing culture and we knew it.

For a while we thought that our ideas and way of being could win out over money and the military-industrial complex. Yes, we were very naïve, but we had a hell of a fine time in the process.

Everyone who was not doing what we were doing had no idea what to do with us, or about us, or how to relate to us. The rest of the people in the country, the "establishment," and the "old guard" knew something was up during those years as well. They did what they knew how to do: control the uncontrollable masses with force and kill their leaders. Our enemies started killing people who were learning from us. All those famous assassinations during those years were related to threatening social experiments going on. It was the formula the masters of war used for handling their social anxiety and reestablishing control. It worked. We lost John Kennedy, Robert Kennedy, Martin Luther King, leaders in the Student Nonviolent Coordinating Committee (SNCC) and Congress of Racial Equality (CORE), Malcolm X, and many much less famous leaders—the list goes on and on. The FBI and other secret agencies that considered themselves the protectors of the *status quo* at any cost were either helping the murderers or simply not helping the followers of the assassinated leaders when they were threatened.

As people were killing the leaders they could identify, a problem emerged: How do you kill a hippie leader? Because . . . where are their leaders? Who the fuck is leading these people?

Can you get by with killing some pitiful dumb-assed kid who puts a flower in your fucking gun barrel? No, you can't get by with that. And it wouldn't do any good anyway.

Besides, how dangerous are these hippies? No one is going to pay any attention to them except as circus freaks, are they?

Still, it is clear to me that the assassinations worked to hold back the progress of real structural social reform fairly effectively for about fifty years. Many of the leaders who were leading at the time, and many who would have followed to lead us in conscious social change were killed, and it worked: In spite of all we learned and all we did, the Republicans and the Dempublicrats kept their power to dominate and control society throughout those years. Our cultural influence continued and brought about some slow change, but political dominance by fascist corporate interests continued, as it has continued to this day.

A New Kind of Teaching and Learning Model

That school year, 1966–67, wasn't the first time I'd taught university courses. I'd been an instructor in psychology at Bergstrom Air Force Base near Austin as a side job while I was in graduate school. I did this even though I had quit ROTC after the first year and was a known anti-Vietnam war activist, which I told my students on the base. (I also offered to assist them if they wanted out of the military. None of them took me up on it.) But despite that earlier job, this new assignment was the first time I had the stature and responsibility of being an associate professor. At the same time I was establishing myself as an anti-establishmentarian, I was teaching a couple of big sessions of introductory psych, a course in developmental psychology, and a graduate course in communications theory. When I became the faculty sponsor for SEAP, one of its student leaders was enrolled in my graduate seminar in communications. I may have learned more from him than he did from me.

There were only eight people in the graduate seminar and I told them in the first session that they'd all passed the course already, just by attending and participating in the conversation, but how good their grade would be was to be based on a paper they'd write over the course of the trimester on a topic in communications theory that interested them.

Pipp, the president of SEAP, was interested, as was I, in the work of Canadian philosopher and communication theorist Marshall McLuhan, author of *The Gutenberg Galaxy*. He is best known as the "medium is the message" guy. (After McLuhan died, he was named the patron saint of *Wired* magazine). McLuhan said that the way we get our information may be as important as the information itself, and that TV is a kind of information that impacts our consciousness in a different way than reading to find things out did. Even though the change that took place when the printing press was invented (from verbal storytelling to reading) was immense, this multimedia electronic expansion, this new medium of television, would have even a greater effect on human consciousness.

After reading the book, Pipp came to me and said that he thought writing a paper was too old-fashioned a way of trying to present the ideas of Marshall McLuhan. He suggested that instead of a paper he'd like to come to my farmhouse and spend a Friday setting up a presentation that he'd give when I came home from work that evening. I thought that was a great idea and agreed.

Judy was in Austin for a week of work on her dissertation and I was on my own, so it was easy for Pipp to come and go at our farmhouse and take as long as he liked to set up. When Friday came around, I came home from being at the campus all day at about six o'clock. Pipp greeted me, led me into a darkened room, and seated me in a comfortable easy chair. He lit up a joint, gave me a few tokes, and asked me to be silent and just experience what was about to happen. Then a whole bunch of TVs came on at once!

Pipp had news shows from several different networks going at the same time, and a variety of other TV programs and radio stations blaring at once. My job was to sit there, be bombarded, and pay attention to the experience. The bombardment of light and sound was a great way to get McLuhan's message that "the medium is the message," and I got it.

After about fifteen minutes of that, Pipp came in, turned off all the machines, and then blindfolded me and led me into another room, and sat me down on the floor. I was told to remain in silence. After a while, when he removed the mask, seated on the floor across from me was a pretty young girl, a friend of Pipp's, who was a student from another college nearby.

He said her name by way of introducing her to me, but asked us both to remain silent and find other ways to communicate. She handed me a joint. I took a toke, she took a toke, Pipp took a toke, and then he left the farm. The young woman and I took another toke and just looked at each other. In front of her were little pots and spots of greasepaint of various colors. She put her finger in one of the paint spots and then reached up and drew a line on my face. Then she took my finger and put it in one of the little hills of paint and guided me to draw a line on her face. We were both smiling and laughing a little, but not speaking. She unbuttoned my shirt and smeared a couple of big lines of paint on my chest. Then she unbuttoned her blouse and with very graceful gestures invited me to paint her upper chest and throat. Then she removed her blouse and invited me to paint anywhere I wanted on her body. I did.

We painted each other all over. Then she started kissing me. I kissed her back. We painted each other's bodies with our bodies. She took my hand and led me upstairs to my bedroom and we made love, and some more art. A little later she left. We never spoke a word.

I gave Pipp an A-plus. I got it.

Our new society and new world was so creative and so wonderful! I had no idea university teaching would turn out to be so much fun!

CHAPTER 19

Jim Bevel

Jim Bevel, Director of Direct Action and Director of Nonviolent Educa-tion for the Southern Christian Leadership Conference, was perhaps the most creative of all the people around Martin Luther King, Jr., during the civil rights movement. Not only that, he had a lot of courage. He died re-cently, in 2008, and since I'm at the place in my story where he was critically involved I want to say a few words about him. Bevel was the one who pushed King out onto the bridge in Selma. He's short and he stood behind King. When King hesitated, Bevel unceremoniously, and not too gently, pushed him out there on the bridge toward the dogs and water hoses.

I have three examples of Bevel's daring and creativity to share. He came to Austin once to advise us civil rights activists who had become anti-Viet-nam War activists, and also to talk to local members of the American Fed-eration of Labor/Congress of Industrial Organizations (AFL/CIO) about how to support Mexican-Americans in organizing for their rights to form unions, demand equal pay, establish worker compensation, and so on, and eventually also help illegal immigrants become legal in a number of ways.

The first suggestion Jim Bevel came up with for us was something none of us, civil rights workers or union organizers alike, had ever come up with to do. He said hundreds of Mexican-Americans should camp out in tents on the grounds of the capital in Austin and demand that the state pass a bill to give official recognition of their right to organize and receive workers' compensation when out of work so that their families wouldn't be in danger of starving. Then, he said, after a week or two, the whole group should apply for foreign aid from Mexico! They should ask the nation of Mexico to help them sustain their efforts in the U.S. to establish their civil rights!

This was an absolutely stunning, outlandish, right-on approach. And it pointed out how we could put Texas legislators on the horns of a terrible dilemma. What an insult it would be if Mexico had to help poor people out in Texas because Texas couldn't even take care of its own Mexicans!

We never did it. There weren't enough Mexican-Americans willing to face all the risks involved, and the AFL/CIO didn't have the courage, but the idea summed up and confronted every single aspect of the problem, and it gave us inspiration to organize and recruit allies for our cause.

One night, I think during that same visit, Jim and I were drinking beer in a Mexican restaurant late at night, just the two of us after all the others had gone. There were a bunch of beer bottles on the table because we'd asked the waitress to leave them there so we could tell how much we'd drunk. (We were already drunk when we asked her to do that.) We were talking about the previous years in the civil rights movement. (This was before King was killed.) I don't know how many beers we'd drunk already, but the table was pretty much covered with bottles.

Jim said to me, "You're a psychologist. Explain something to me. Before I got in this mess, I was set. I had my own church. I got a new Cadillac every year. I was sleeping with half the women in the choir . . . and then I got into the damned civil rights movement! What in the hell is wrong with me?"

I said, "You're a damned fool."

He said, "'Deed I am." We laughed. We both understood the humor and the inevitability of such a choice.

I talked about what Joe Mathews used to say to us about being "fools for Christ" and about my own forays out of safety and comfort into danger and discomfort. We had a real honest conversation and we loved each other. We would not have traded what we'd done or what we knew we were a part of, or what we were doing right at that moment for anything else in the world.

A couple of years later, in early 1967, I was helping organize the upcoming simultaneous East Coast and West Coast marches against the war in Vietnam in New York and San Francisco. We called a big meeting at Case Western Reserve University in Ohio to make plans for a couple of days and coordinate all our efforts in the Midwest to help our committees on the coasts. I persuaded my cohorts to invite Jim Bevel to come and be the keynote speaker at our upcoming rally.

We had about 300 people at the rally, including about thirty Catholic priests and nuns, and a fair number of participants who one might say were "interested," but not certain about the degree of their commitment to being affiliated with folks who "might go too far." I wondered what Jim would say to them, because you could never tell what he might say.

Bevel walks in and just does everything all wrong. First off, he shows up an hour late. He breezes in from the airport, after we'd all been waiting for an hour, gets no briefing at all, comes directly to the podium, and says: "My name is Jim Bevel. I am a social psychiatrist. I just recently passed two bills in the United States Congress that demonstrated my capabilities as a social psychiatrist." (Everyone applauded and cheered.)

He continued: "Now the powers that be are escalating the cruel and stupid war in Vietnam, and it's up to us to do something to bring that to an end. And I think it is important for you to know why we are in Vietnam— the real reason we are in Vietnam. Here it is. We are in Vietnam because Lyndon Johnson thinks that Mao Tse Tung wants to fuck Ladybird."

A few people laughed. Mostly nobody said a word. It was one of those embarrassing moments when people didn't know what to do or how to feel. Bevel was in no hurry to give anybody relief with more explanation. So he just stood there and looked at everyone for a painful pause. A few people walked out. Some of the nuns left. A few others stood up and kind of drifted toward the back.

Bevel went on. "And you know what? Mao *doesn't* want to fuck Ladybird. *Nobody* wants to fuck Ladybird!" Another pause. "So are all these people in Vietnam dyin' for nothin' or what?"

Some people laughed, and some cheered and applauded. A few more people get up to leave and drifted out the doors. Bevel kept going for a bit along the same lines, then waited patiently until the folks who had stood up and walked had exited and closed the doors. We must have lost about twenty or thirty people.

"Okay," he then said, "Now we can get down to business. Our worst enemies throughout the civil rights movement have been the fainthearted amongst us. It's best to try to get rid of them first." He got some applause, and we got down to business.

I've never known for sure what the Holy Spirit is, but I imagine Bevel was it for me. We had a hell of a big demonstration in New York and San Francisco about three months after that meeting because all of us worked our asses off to make it happen.

Jim Bevel had a lot of bad things said about him before he died, and whether or not the rumors are true I have no way of knowing. But he made me laugh and want to dance. He made me believe the Holy Spirit is flowing in all of us through our caring and daring and declaring, and maintaining our bearing through sharing. And that Holy Spirit talking through him used some pretty unholy sounding language now and again. Those of us who have been possessed by Holy Spirit, and are looking to be repossessed whenever we can, are the richest poor folks in the world.

I really wish Bevel could have talked to Lyndon Johnson. It might have relieved poor Lyndon of some stress, and given him courage when his own courage failed him. It could have happened. It was one of those near misses that make history turn right instead of left.

Everybody gets so romantic and teary eyed about Obama, including myself. But I am waiting. I know millions of people like me are waiting. Is the spirit going to remain and recur? No one can know. But we can for God damned sure know whether it is or isn't there when it is or isn't. So far with Obama it seemed like it was going to be but just hasn't turned out. I knew it was over for Clinton when he came up with don't ask don't tell and I think we will know just as certainly that hope is over when gutless folks, like most of Barack's appointees, keep steering the ship of state to avoid the shoals instead of accomplish the goals. If Barack can't be like Bevel, the honeymoon is over and the marriage is on the rocks. No use to start bad habits of compromise before one has been fully self-expressed.

I wrote that last paragraph the first time through on writing this book in 2009. Now it is 2011 and my doubts about Obama are fully confirmed. He is a coward and not a leader. He lacks the courage it takes to deconstruct what clearly doesn't work and reconstruct what does. We can forget him. Another gutless wonder.

CHAPTER 20

Peace?

On April 15, 1967, a couple of months after the planning meeting at Case Western Reserve where Jim Bevel spoke, I was in Kezar Stadium in San Francisco at the peace rally for the West Coast protest against the war in Vietnam. The parade to the stadium and away from the stadium was the gigantic start in Haight-Ashbury to what came to be known as the Summer of Love.

We made a deal with the cops that they would remain outside the stadium while we had our rally and concert inside. Everyone was there from The Fillmore: Janice, The Dead, Jefferson Airplane . . . and many more. There was a big bandstand in the middle of the stadium with sound that reverberated throughout. There were 70,000 hippies packed in there. As we walked among the bleachers to find a seat, people handed us joints. We'd take a toke and pass the joint on to the next person without one. The whole damned stadium had a cloud of marijuana smoke inside and above it. It was a peace rally as well as an anti-war rally. Everyone was high and everyone was happy. Everyone was dancing, and the stadium was literally rocking and near to collapsing.

When the concert, speeches, and dancing were over, we streamed out and headed for the park and Haight-Ashbury. Walking towards us through the flow of people were the "Provos," as we called them, guys wearing big, black hats like Abraham Lincoln used to wear. They held out the hats and said, "If you need money take some. If you have money put some in."

People were doing that. And it worked! Everyone had food and a place to stay that night. And for a while there, at least throughout that summer (I went back later during the Summer of Love, for about a month), there was an economy of love and sharing that really worked. I can't tell you how wonderful it was. For me it is still the best model of a functional economy I've ever experienced or known.

My brother Jimmy was living there then, too, as were many friends of mine from Texas. Everyone rode free bicycles to wherever they were going and dropped them off there. Then others took them and went where they wanted to go. The Provos redistributed bikes and repaired them and kept things going.

People also hitchhiked all over the city and all over California. If you had a car, you gave people rides. If you wanted to go somewhere, you went out on the road and stuck out your thumb.

Sometimes, traveling during those days, people would give everything they owned to each other. One time a hitchhiker in a car I was driving said to me, "I think I'll leave you this backpack. I've had it for a while."

I said, "Great, take mine," and he did.

Once my friend Jim and I were driving up to Mendocino from San Francisco and we picked up a hitchhiker headed for Las Vegas to see his mom who was sick. When we got to the turnoff toward Nevada, Jim pulled over, reached into the glove box, took out the title to the car, signed it, and handed it to the hitchhiker. He said, "I think your need to see your mom is more pressing than any we have. You take the car. We'll hitch the rest of the way to where we're going."

At another time (I can't remember all the times too clearly because we were all stoned a lot of the time. That's why they say if you remember the '60s, you probably weren't there), I was down somewhere south of Big Sur, off Highway 1, a few miles up a creek called Bear Creek. There were a bunch of people there without any clothes on all day and all night (from a dozen to about twenty as the size of the group ebbed and flowed). We would wander around naked and sleep in sleeping bags under the open air or sometimes in tents late at night and in the early morning.

Every day at about noon we'd gather at the fire site and draw straws. The two people who drew short straws would have to go put on some clothes, go get the sack and the sign (it read, "FOOD"), walk the couple of miles out to Highway 1, and hold up the sign at one of the pulloffs or viewing spots. People would pull over and meet us, and stop and drink a beer or smoke a joint with us. Then they'd give us something to put in our sack: something to eat or get high on.

At around five or six o'clock the two people would bring the sack back, the group would open the cans, cut up the veggies, and throw the carrots, tomatoes, or dope into our big cooking pot over the fire, and when it got hot, or just seemed the right time, we'd put it in bowls and eat it, and wait to see what happened to us. I remember one day when we woke up we had all the sleeping bags unzipped and under us or over us, covering everyone in the group. We thought we might have had an orgy the night before, but nobody could remember.

I remember meeting an ex-Episcopal priest there, a man who'd just quit preaching and walked away from the church to become a hippie. He was making his way down Highway 1 in no particular hurry to get anywhere.

One night at Bear Creek, a bunch of us were sitting around the fire talking and playing the guitar. At one of the lulls in the music I noticed the earring the fellow across from me had in his ear. "I like that earring," I said. "It looks good on you." He stood up, came over to me, and took another earring like the one he was wearing out of his pocket. He also had a needle. He stuck the needle through my ear, and inserted the earring. I thanked him, laughed, and bled a little. I wore that earring for several years.

You might say we were very interested in the possibility of what could become a new way of living together for human beings. We didn't know what it would be, but we figured it was more a matter of discovery than thinking, so we went about investigating and researching alternative ways of living. I loved those times and try to keep the possibility of discovery like that open in my life in these times—with varying degrees of success.

CHAPTER 21
Summer 1967

Judy and I decided to go to Europe with our friends, Jim and Louise Jordan, a couple who had been in the Christian Faith and Life Community in Austin with Judy and me before they got married and before we got married. They also lived in married student housing in old military buildings at the same time as us off campus, and they moved to Ohio when we did when I got my first job teaching at Miami University of Ohio and Jim began teaching in the art department at Antioch College in Yellow Springs. He had gotten a master's degree in Art History at the University of Illinois while I was finishing graduate school.

Jim and Louise and Judy and I decided to go to Europe together in the spring at the end of the school year and stay for a couple of months. Jim wanted to tour the cathedrals of Europe and take photographs for a presentation to his classes, and a course, and perhaps a book, and he was glad to have us go along and get a tour from him as an art historian. Judy and I were happy to have the opportunity.

Miami University was on the trimester system, so our classes let out for the summer about a month earlier than at Antioch. Thus, Judy and I took off first for Europe. We flew to Central Europe, rented a car, and traveled around Greece and Yugoslavia for three or four weeks while we waited for Jim and Louise to come meet us. We were there right after the six-day war between Israel and Egypt ended. We gave rides to hitchhikers from Israel going home from the war to Yugoslavia.

Along the way we found out that the hashish dealers who knew people on both sides of the war were the ones who negotiated the cease fire that ended the war and brought about a truce. It's been one of my beliefs ever since that hashish dealers should handle matters of war and peace for all world governments.

We took a five-day cruise of the Dodecanese Islands in Greece along the coast of Turkey, and discovered Patmos. We went back to Patmos after the cruise was over and stayed an extra week because it was our favorite place on the cruise. There were no motorized vehicles on the island then. We fell in love with Patmos and went back many times over the next twenty years. I went to the hillside on Patmos and stood in front of the cave where John, the disciple who was the brother of Jesus, had his vision of the apocalypse and wrote *The Book of Revelation*. A little later on a return trip, I dropped acid there and, after a considerable while wrestling with God in the little field outside the cave, my own vision of the apocalypse showed up. The sea rose up, and the chaos, folly, suffering, and waste of the great uprising and downfall of humankind played out before my eyes and ears. I got it. I got the vision of the end when God's wrath toward humans (or nature's wrath . . .) will come down. Sadly, I may see that again before I die.

I don't know now where I found the foolhardiness to do such things in order to see what I might learn or lose. In those days, a lot of us took chances to learn, even if the methods were scary. Judy and I and our peers and friends on the leading edge of venturing forth, felt like it was up to us to take the risks to be heroes or failures in an ongoing experiment in the possibility of being human in a less stupid way than most humans. We knew it was our job to be the discoverers in life. It was up to us to find out the relationship between the unknown and that which had formerly been believed, and to debunk the bunk of human history. So we did what seemed to need doing.

After a month, we met Jim and Louise in Belgium and the four of us began our driving tour, which took us through France and to Italy. We had great times: We ate great food, drank fine wine, smoked good dope, and looked at beautiful cathedrals. We were young, nouveau riche, and pretty happy. Toward the end of that trip, in Italy, we took the next threatening step to social reform and psychological chaos . . . and adventure . . . and discovery . . .

It's nine or ten at night. We are walking along the coast of Italy on the in-side bay. It is a beautiful evening with the moon out and a nice warm breeze. We're walking near the lagoons of Chioggia and the waves are sparkling. The bioluminescence that happens there in the summers has been admired for cen-

turies. We are blown away by the beauty of the nighttime sea, which lights up when the waves come in or anyone splashes it or swims in it because of glow-in-the-dark lichens.

We've just smoked some pot and consumed some fine wine and wonderful food, and we're happily walking along the beach. Louise suddenly starts running and pulling off her clothes. She drops her blouse on the beach, pulls off her bra, and drops it, then takes off her shorts. Doing as she's done, the rest of us proceed to throw off our clothes. We run into the water and begin to swim out to sea. Our beautiful, silver bodies, our laughter, and the sound of the waves, and the warm breeze, and everything around us is like heaven. After a while we come together, holding each other in a group hug, just standing with our arms intertwined, being rocked and cradled by the waves.

We hug and hold each other, and start to kiss. We all know at about the same time that this night we aren't just going to sleep in the same room, as we have for most nights of the trip, but we are going to have sex together. We can hardly get back to the room fast enough.

When we get to the room, we all kiss for a while, then Judy and I start making love next to Jim and Louise who are fucking there right next to us. We are all really excited and the idea that we are doing what we're doing is also very exciting. Then Jim reaches over and taps me on the shoulder, and we all know the next part of this dance is to switch partners, so we do. It is so hot. Everyone is so aroused. Louise's beautiful tits are outstanding. Her hard nipples thrust against my chest as I thrust into her, and the sounds of our lust magnify what we feel and see—we all make such sounds! We can hear each other all loving fucking and being fucked. It is a new experience of what multiple orgasms mean.

After we are exhausted, and I do mean exhausted, we eventually switch back to our original pairs, but sleep close together in a kind of a big pile for the rest of the night in that bed.

The four of us kept on sleeping together during most of the nights for the rest of the trip. Some nights we switched partners and had sex with our cross-couple partner separately in separate rooms. When that started happening we—meaning, mainly me—had some jealousy issues and conflict occasionally, but, all in all, we stayed pretty excited about our experiment. We felt like the characters in their group marriages from Robert Heinlein's novel *Strangers in a Strange Land*, which we'd all read. We talked about how that may have contributed to our blessed corruption and the terrific breakdown of morality that paved the way to such bliss and trouble for us.

When Jim and Judy wanted to go off together, if I felt jealous, I would nix it and they would do what I wanted. Louise and I were in it for the lust. I think Judy was, too. But I worried about Jim and Judy falling in love and leaving together, so I stayed paranoid about that possibility for some time.

All of us knew that as a result of this experiment in polyamory our world had changed in ways that we couldn't predict or control, and we were still willing to take the risk. When we returned to the U.S., these changes, and others that happened right after losing our moorings in the old ways, were terrifying, but tolerable, except for our need to control.

I was the worst about that.

CHAPTER 22

Sgt. Pepper's Lonely Hearts Club Band and the Murder of our Leaders

We returned to Yellow Springs, Ohio, to the campus of Antioch College. The Summer of Love was now happening there. The Beatle's Sgt. Pepper's Lonely Hearts Club Band, the greatest album of all time, was released in the United States the day after we got home. We'd already heard it in Europe, and loved it. We were back on the campus then, and for many days you could stroll from one end of Yellow Springs to the other and hear the music from the album playing all along the way.

In early June, while still in Europe, I had found out I had been fired by Miami University. I was sorry to hear I'd lost my job, but it wasn't as bad you might think. I was actually kind of proud of my dismissal. Given my background, it's easy to tell why. To me the incredible flow of change that was going on in California, England, Texas, and all over the world was the most wonderful and important thing that could be happening, so me getting fired was a small thing compared to that in which I was a participant.

We went back to Miami University to pick up our things, and I made a speech there with hundreds of students and faculty attending, so I could say my goodbyes and let the world know that I knew I was being fired because of my political beliefs and activities, and for being an inspiration to students to overthrow the outmoded structures of the world. I told the students and faculty that the changes we were a part of were more important than the local traditionalists and retards who just happened to be in control of everything, and would be for a while longer. There were lots of interruptions with applause, cheers of support and standing ovations and the controversy over my dismissal was very much alive and written and talked about and reported on over the next six months, but of course, the status quo won out with only a few small scars.

Since the technicality for which the University's provost had failed to renew my contract was "smoking cigarettes in the classroom," I smoked a few cigarettes there and then while I gave my talk in the auditorium. And afterwards, just for the sake of consistency, I went and got high and drank beer with a whole bunch of students.

I wished the people well who remained to carry on the cause of freedom and were committed to ending the war in Vietnam and changing the stagnant culture of the time. Then Judy and I left and went to Washington, D.C., to the annual meeting of the American Psychological Association, where I got another job (outside academia) with more money and freedom, as the director of psychological services for the Washington, D.C., Head Start Program. Judy, who had just received her doctorate, also got work in D.C. soon thereafter. We rented an apartment for a while and established ourselves in Upper Northwest Washington, near Rock Creek Park, beginning our new lives as change agents for the new frontier—the one we knew about, but the politicians didn't.

Washington was another of those places where big change was happening, and it didn't take us long to find compatriots. David Goldstein, the director of Head Start for D.C., hired me *because* of my civil rights record and my story about how I got fired at Miami University. The friends I found through Dave and those who came to D.C. for other reasons were conscious, intentional participants in radical change, community organizing, and the cultural transformation of our recently desegregated society into a possibly integrated society.

David was a white Jewish liberal. Most of his staff members were young black men and women who were smart enough to get government money to do political organizing. A lot of the teachers and teacher's aides, some white and some black, were folks who were familiar with the ideas and activities of the civil rights movement and the general movement for social change.

I was in charge of the in-service training program for all the teachers and teacher's aides, as well as of providing psychological services to the children and families in twenty-four classrooms. There were fifteen children in each classroom, all four- and five-year-olds. I also helped coordinate and organize research on the effectiveness of Head Start's new, year-long program that grew out of the summer Head Start classes. By the end of the first year, with the help of a lot of wonderful volunteers (liberal Ph.D.'s from the

National Institutes of Health, the Department of Education, Volunteers in Service to America [VISTA], and various private enterprise educational and research facilities), we'd set up a systematic testing and research program that was one of the best in the country to study the short-term effects (over the course of the first year) and the long-term effects (follow-up testing after entry to schools) of the program on the children. Our testing also allowed us to compare differences in teaching modalities and orientations by comparing classrooms that had different kinds of special focuses, such as video feedback with kids, classrooms with mirrors vs. ones without, a Montessori classroom vs. all the others, a classroom with music and dance as a central focus, and numerous other cross-classroom comparisons.

By spring 1968, Judy and I were established in Washington. And both of us were participants, though I more than she, in the burgeoning anti-war movement and the movement for social and political change that was about to be defeated by the regressive disease of the Republicans. We continued our sexual experiments with Jim and Louise, but from a distance, and also decided to have a child. By March that year, Judy was pregnant.

On April 4, 1968, Martin Luther King, Jr., was shot and killed. On April 6, the riots in downtown Washington, Chicago, New York, Los Angeles, and other cities around the country exploded out of incredible frustration felt by so many people (people who thought that we had made, and could still make, positive change happen) at once again being stopped in our tracks by the murder of one of our leaders. We'd dreaded this outcome. King had sensed for a long time he was going to die, as did many of us in the civil rights movement.

Our headquarters for Head Start was in Downtown Washington on Swan Street near Fourteenth and U. All the smoke and the sirens and the days of cop cars, ambulances, and fire trucks screaming all over the place, and the days glued to the TV to find out more about what had happened and was happening, were like a kind of time suspension in a science fiction movie or historical documentary. There was a re-triggering of sadness and crying, just like when JFK was shot. There were alterations of anger, sadness, and fear.

There was some fun, too, because we wanted to bring the whole fucking thing, whatever it was, down. And every time any element of officialdom was thwarted we drank some more beer and took a toke, cheered a little, and then cried again. During the riots, I didn't break into any stores or burn anything (mainly because I was white and could have gotten killed by friendly fire for being out there). But we got some steaks and a lot of canned goods, and some clothes and other shit from friends who had an oversupply of goods taken from grocery stores all over town.

We'd really had a lot of hope. We'd really been quite naïve. We had bought the whole bullshit story of how America was about freedom and love and democracy. We somehow still wanted that to be true so badly that we never got up the gumption to actually overthrow the murderers. We still had hope. Bobby Kennedy was running for President.

After Lyndon Johnson helped pass the Voting Rights Act and the Civil Rights Acts of 1964, even though he fucked over the Freedom Party from Mississippi (and maybe because he had), we were all sure that we actually were going to have a new society. But then LBJ totally fucked up again by continuing the debacle in Vietnam. He turned us all against him soon after he helped us win our civil rights victory. He just didn't get it. He didn't really get what was going on. "Finally now," we hoped, "maybe another Kennedy with some intelligence will take over who can see the insanity of continuing down the stupid path his brother had started of 'killing Communists for Christ,' and finally challenge the military-industrial complex and the God-damned, ridiculous, shit-for-brains Republicans led by the incredibly emotionally unstable crackpot Richard Nixon.

When Martin Luther King, Jr., was shot, we already knew Malcolm X and John Kennedy had been killed, so why in the hell did we keep putting up with it?

Then Bobby Kennedy was killed in June. When he was killed, shit, it was almost less of a surprise than any of the assassinations that had preceded it. Judy and I thought, "I wonder who will be next? Let's hope the world will get better so our child can have a good life."

Hope for change is often a rationale for inaction, and this life history of mine of which I used to be proud, now, upon further reflection, is beginning to stink.

I don't know what kept us from killing some of the killers when Bobby Kennedy was added to the list of casualties. Back when Malcolm X was killed in February 1965, though many of us knew that he was a great reformer of the former fundamentalism of Islam and a growing leader, there was enough propaganda against him, and enough fear of him, that his murder was never really protested. But I cannot, for the life of me, looking back on things, figure out why no one among us started killing some of the reactionary, God-damned, fascist establishmentarians.

I was about to become a new father, I had just gotten a Ph.D., I was establishing myself in the establishment, and I'd spent a number of years now as a part of the non-violent protest movement against racism and the war in Vietnam. I had been, and still considered myself to be, a hippie. But I now think I was an example of the yuppie (young urban professional) failure to stand outside of my poisonous culture. Even though I knew it was poisonous, I didn't ever get any vengeance or justice. We hippies stood by and took our slaughter like most of the Jews under Hitler did. And to this day, I feel like I, of all persons, should have known better.

I no longer believe we should have been so peaceful in our protests. The ones who killed their way to dominance created the delay in human evolution that will soon destroy most, if not all, of humanity. We should have killed back. When I said, back at the beginning of this book, that I was sorry I haven't killed more people, this is one of the times I was talking about where I'm sorry for being peaceful. Like the citizens under the Third Reich in Germany, I am responsible for the slaughter of my neighbors, the killing of children, and the ongoing corruption of society, the continuation of corporate capitalist fascism, global warming, and the downfall of humanity. I did nothing to stop it when I could have. I wish to hell I'd killed J. Edgar Hoover and half a dozen racist, fascist motherfuckers in the Senate from the South, and also a few hundred or so industrialists and defense industry CEOs. It would have made a difference. It still would. And I still don't do it.

Instead, Judy and I bought a row house for $20,500, moved in, and prepared a place for our new baby.

Believe you me, the demonstration in Chicago at the 1968 Democratic Convention was pretty mild considering the fury most of us felt. I didn't go. I cheered the protesters on and gave a little money, but I knew it was useless. I didn't go to the Woodstock Festival either. Both of these things, spoken of by historians and pundits as breakthroughs for new social change, in fact, came at the end of an era. They represented the dying spark of what had once been a promising movement. I didn't vote for president in 1968. It was not only because I couldn't bring myself to bother to vote for Nixon, it was because I chose, with a vengeance, not to vote for Hubert Humphrey.

Many of us were turning inward and becoming depressed; we were pretty much giving up on politics as a method of social change. We supported Nixon instead of another wimpy-assed, warmonger, Caspar Milquetoast liberal with his head up his ass, or we stayed home. As a result, Nixon won. My non-vote, along with millions of other non-votes, elected Richard Nixon president of the United States.

At least (we rationalized) we could have an underground of social change that could happen right under his nose. He and his cronies were probably more out of touch with what was actually going on in the day as any group of people, supposedly in charge, ever has been. The Watergate break-in was just stupid business-as-usual for the arrogant Republican imbeciles playing pretend games like they were in a movie. They were fucking psychotic. The whole fucking country was psychotic.

I was a psychologist. I was twenty-eight years old. When I think about it long and hard, and in all honesty, I didn't really do a thing to help. I kept the machine in place and gave the murderers free rein in a way, because working away at undermining the power of those insane people in our non-violent fashion sustained the poisonous system. Today, those same essential elements are still poisoning humanity and the world. The rich have gotten richer and the poor the world over have gotten poorer and the middle class has gotten smaller and dumber and more obedient than ever to the fascist motherfuckers with the money.

If the end of humanity on Earth, or the near obliteration of humans, comes about in the next decade or two, and we look back on the historical record honestly, it will not reflect well on me and those like me—liberals who called themselves radicals, but played at resistance and rebellion with the luxury of left-wing non-violent ideology while the Earth burned, while the Earth died. The Earth was killed by the right-wing nuts we left in power, who we let get by with the slaughter of our leaders and innocents, and with the rape of the Earth for profit. Were we not, after all, obedient servants of fascism just like the citizens of the Third Reich? We should have killed more of the motherfuckers instead. I was smart and could have gotten away with murder, as many smart people do, yet I didn't have the guts to do it.

With Nixon, just like with Bush Junior, the people eventually figured out what fucking dolts they were through a slow and painful education, and through protest by intelligent, angry, but impotent resisters—but it took so fucking long it didn't count! All of this time we could have been killing the heads of Monsanto, Weyerhaeuser, and General Motors—or shit, just the corporate chairmen of fortune 500 companies belonging to the defense industry—along with right-wing politicians from the South. I was a coward and a fool. And I still am.

In 2009 I sent the following New Years greeting to all my friends in the Radical Honesty community. It's entitled "A Message from One Goddamned Basic Believer in Bullshit to Another."

"Dear Fellow BBs,

"In writing my autobiography it has become very clear to me that for my whole life I've fought to survive and survived to fight. So it should be no surprise to any of us that my life story is about how I was taught to survive, and how it has been the secret to my success and something that has haunted me throughout my life. It's why I've been married and divorced five times, not to mention a few thousand other relationships created by me falling in love with fellow beings with my heart and destroying the relationship to them with my mind. My mind uses its valued method of survival to justify its existence and maintain a bloated view of itself. You could definitely say my mind has been a critical element in the story of my life (heh heh), though it's not always all that useful, come to think of it, if you don't mind. Mind fullness is not always mindfulness. In fact it never is, but never mind.

"I have been a coward and a cop out. I think most of the people throughout human history have been like me—what I call BBBs (basic believers in bullshit) or BBs for short (basic believers) and I am certainly not an exception to that. The number of real thinkers and true value holders throughout so-called American history, as it's reported in schools, for example, can probably be counted on your fingers with a bunch of digits left over. All the rest of all the glorified folk in the history textbooks were fucking BBs like you and me, ginning up their con games and doing sales pitches, just like current-day politicians. Barack Obama is just another fucking BB. In fact he is a BB very much like me: a successful survivor of life who is unable to quit creating conditions that require him to fight to survive because all he knows is how to fight battles and win, and brag, and keep the war going so he can fight more battles and win and brag again. But for Christ's sake (or fill in the religious figure or leader of your choice) don't let the war end or the battles cease or the competition go away, or any real change occur, or we won't know whether to shit or go blind.

"In the battle between nature and man, I am on the side of nature, though I am a worthless soldier and a gutless wonder. I am a turncoat on humanity and on the side of nature, but who cares?

"I have loved living my life, and I still love living my life, and I love my children, and have lots of human friends that I love, but I think humankind is an aberration and a failed experiment that needs to go. (Besides, I like to be on the winning side after a valiant fight and get kudos for having been brave and right. That way I can win the battle when we lose the war. This is standing operating procedure for cowards like me.)

"A fine, current example of what makes the almost exclusively BBB human culture so wonderful is the war-based economy we're currently struggling and fighting to save so that we can survive in the way we've learned and are accustomed to, and keep the system we know going.

"Here is how it works. There exists an excess supply of arms (and people). We need to get rid of some arms to create a need to produce more things that kill and blow up people, and other things to keep the economy going. Luckily, there are currently enough dumb, fucking true believer Muslims, Christian Fundamentalists, Jews, and (fill in the blank)s for each blindly believing group to displace all of our "civilized" aggression onto, and who will volunteer for the brunt of our hatred by shooting off a few rockets now and then, or blowing themselves up in places that are inconvenient to Israeli or oil-wealthy true believer assholes just like themselves (people like Dick Cheney and George Bush: rich, country dumb fucks with the need for a little oil to grease their economy, who have the capability to con even dumber religious fucks into going along with them by using any number of bullshit idealistic con games). Then we are justified in killing off, mutilating, or injuring for life thousands of the other BB's women and children, often by direct bombing of thousands upon thousands of "non-combatants." They're thereby handily creating more "terrorists" to fight them/us later to justify them/us in bombing the shit out of them so we'll have to restock our weaponry for the sake of our economy.

"BBBs love war-based and oil-based economies—particularly the banker BBs, or BBBBs (banker bullshit blind believers)—since they invented them. And now we have all joined the cause by giving the motherfuckers billions of dollars. (Send Billions to the Blind Banker Bullshit Believers! Join the Cause Now!) So aren't we proud to be a BBB, baby? Except from those few aberrant moments in my life when I went from BB to a "be, be" I have an almost perfect record of blind bullshit believing and I know you do too and that you are proud of yours, too.

"Happy New Year! Love and curses, Brad Blanton (BB!), aka Bubba Buddha, Blind Believer, Bullshit Blower . . .

"P.S. The U.S. is the superior military power in the world not because of our nukes, but because we have the biggest God-damned BB guns!"

When I sent the preceding message to friends and family via email, my brother-in-law and friend, Jack Stork, replied:

"Hey Brad,
"Looks like you had a flash of insight and gained a deeper perspective on

yourself. I love it when that happens, especially when it happens to me, but I am more than happy to celebrate the event in others.

"I think that the key word in the definition of BBB is 'believer.' Eric Hoffer did some work on this in his book The True Believer *(Perennial, 1989). Belief is always bullshit. Belief wastes the mind, because belief requires maintenance; it keeps the mind busy on bullshit. Almost every year some idiot goes looking for Noah's ark, as if proving this one myth to be true would make all the rest of them true also. The mind, instinctively wants to know, but it has to struggle with instilled belief. Those few who have escaped belief and assumption also have discovered that they've only been using about 10 percent of their minds. As Buckminster Fuller remarked, 'What use have I of belief? I either know a thing or I don't.'*

"It is easy to assume that it is the variance in belief that causes all of the trouble in the world but it is belief itself. Insight is always a bit embarrassing and often downright humiliating. That is reason enough for most to avoid it.

"As for Barack Obama, I like this guy. If you're cleaning the barn, you are going to get some shit on you. He's going to be knee deep in the bullshit that is Congress. Generally, a politician is a panderer with a tumorous ego disguised in bullshit and demanding respect. It seems to me that the only way to deal with the worst of these is to feign respect and to hide one's disgust. That is enough to make most people throw up, but how else is one to deal with one of these anomalies when killing them is frowned on. Tom DeLay comes to mind.

"Anyway, thanks for including me in your written ruminations, Brad. I find them a good way to start a day.

"With great affection,

"Jack."

I wrote back:

"Thanks, Jack.

"I like Obama, too, in the relative context of this whole discussion, where you can have compassion and even admiration for a fool with shit all over him, trying to clean a barn that should never have been built in the first place. The problem with the hope offered by Obama and his friends, including me and you, is there's not much difference between Barack and Dick Cheney. Though Barack is a truly great improvement, it is not enough of a difference for real change.

"Belief, which I think has to be used by us humans—and there is no way

around it—needs to be used like Kleenex or toilet paper, so that its time of usefulness is extremely limited and it is dispensed with quickly.

"This, I think, is okay, and even necessary. But if you hold on to that piece of toilet paper too long, you're just wiping shit back on your own dumb ass. I think we are barely even capable of seeing how quickly we can get by with dispensing with belief, because believing in belief is so central to our illusion of control, and our belief that we should be, and are, in control, and if we are not we are bad.

"Every day that any of us says, 'I believed this yesterday and I still do today' is a time to search for creative alternatives for that too long-held belief (or to check for shit being smeared from holding on to the toilet paper too long). I believe belief itself is the problem, just as you do and as Bucky Fuller did, but I have never seen anyone live completely without belief, except animals, and I am not too sure about them.

"I haven't changed my belief about beliefs for a while, but my most recurring perspective on belief is that it's a game. If we play at beliefs like we play poker or golf, or backgammon, or monopoly, or something else, there can be an interesting interaction between chance and prediction where you give a shot at determining an outcome given that you are not in charge of the outcome, but might have an impact if you are cagey enough and play skillfully with your beliefs and the beliefs of others. A belief game should never 'really' be taken seriously. Of course, as I said earlier about this, I have never really, except in rare altered states, insights, or meditations, spent time not taking any beliefs seriously for more than a few seconds.

"Beliefs have been the very source of my cowardice, which I now believe is the more accurate self-judgment than courage. But since all of it is bullshit anyway, my disappointment is just disappointment. What does it matter whether I am good or do good, or be good or be, do, am bad? Courageous or cowardly? Significant or insignificant? Smart or dumb? Pretty or ugly? That any of this matters is a belief that is so engrained in our deep cultural identity that even being aware of it requires transcendence. It is hard to be playful when your identity is at stake, but, of course, that is just what can be done, and probably must be done to get over ourselves. Probably this is the meaning of the phrase, 'You have to die to live.'

"Brad"

Well there I went again. I went on a tirade of bragging and self-loathing. Both are arrogance. Now I am leaving it alone. In a way it is as much a description of who I am as my story, and could be a gift to you. If you can get to a place where you feel sorry for me, as in . . . "Poor ignorant arrogant sonofabitch . . ." this pathetic aspect of my story might serve you. Thanks for your patience.

CHAPTER 23

The Work of Stanley Milgram

Before I finish up with the '60s, I must tell you about a man I've never met, though I've seen and heard him and read things he has written. He had a big influence on my life because I was so impressed with his work and writing. I used to talk about his work in speeches against the Vietnam War, and many times since then, when our stupid fucking country kissed the asses of the industrialist profiteers and made war again and again in the name of some fucking anti-something or other in order to keep killing for profit. And all of us dumb-assed, slovenly, ass-kissing suckups went along with them in the name of patriotism or any number of other bullshit beliefs. Bear with me while I tell you about this man, whose influence came over me in1965, and then I will continue my story to the end in a decent linear fashion. (Fat chance!)

I first heard about social psychologist Stanley Milgram when he presented a review of his research done at Yale University during a meeting of the American Psychological Association in Chicago in 1965. Interestingly, Milgram was given an award by one branch of the APA in Chicago, while being censured by another branch on the same day for the same research. Here is how and why he simultaneously got praised and in trouble.

Milgram, several years earlier, had read the book *Eichmann in Jerusalem* (The Viking Press, 1963) by Hannah Arendt about the trial of Adolf Eichmann, Hitler's infamous second-in-command, who had been responsible for overseeing most of the executions of six million Jews and other people judged unacceptable by the Third Reich. Arendt, who covered Eichmann's war crimes trial for *The New York Times* and several other American newspapers, pointed out that his primary defense against the accusation that he was guilty of a crime against mankind was that he should not be held individually responsible for this crime because he was doing his duty in the social system of which he was a part. His lawyers said that a court might judge that the social system was criminal, but not the individual person doing his duty. This argument was rejected. Eichmann's adjudicators concluded that he was individually responsible for the crimes he committed, regardless of the social system of which he was a part, and he was executed.

Arendt then raised another question, which fascinated Stanley Milgram. Was Adolf Eichmann some unusual social deviant, some sadistic exception to common humanity, or was he just a normally functioning bureaucrat? Arendt pointed out that only twice in his entire career had he actually witnessed any executions, which, he said he found "repugnant." What he actually did was shuffle papers in an office, make phone calls, give orders, and obey the orders he received. Outside of work, he seemed to have a normal life with family and friends and associates. *Was he normal?* Milgram wondered.

Milgram designed an experiment to see if he could somewhat simulate the conditions under which Eichmann operated. He drew a random, stratified sample of males from the community around Yale. (In later versions of the original study, he included females, and found no significant differences between males and females in the results of the experiment.) He paid each subject, in advance, seven dollars for participating in an experiment that he told them was a "study of the effects of negative reinforcement on learning."

When Milgram met his subjects, he used a room in a building on the campus of Yale University. He wore a suit and tie and over his suit a white lab coat, and introduced himself as "Dr. Stanley Milgram of Yale University," to establish his credentials and authority.

There were three people in the room: Milgram and two subjects, both of whom were apparently drawn from the same pool of subjects. Though this was assumed to be true, only one of the two was a true subject. (The second was a stooge, a student actor from the drama department at Yale.) Milgram said to them, "I am conducting a study of the effects of negative reinforcement on learning. In this study, one of you will be the teacher and one will be the learner. I will flip a coin to see which is which." The coin was flipped and the true subject from the sample was always designated as the "teacher," because the coin flip was rigged.

After the coin flip, Milgram led both subjects into another room containing a very large and impressive electric chair, and proceeded to strap the "learner" (the stooge) into the chair and apply electrode paste and electrodes to his wrists and head. In later versions of the experiment (which was run several times with numerous groups of subjects before being written up in journals and reported to the APA), Milgram mentioned in passing that the electrode paste was to "keep the flesh from being burnt," and the learner-stooge mentioned that he "had a slight heart condition."

Then the "teacher" (the true subject of Milgram's experiment) was led into a room adjoining the electric chair room, which had a one-way mirror so that the teacher could see the person in the electric chair, though the person could not see him. He was seated in front of a panel of thirty switches, under which were clearly printed labels displaying how the power of the switches increased in fifteen-volt increments. The switches apparently ranged from 15 to 450 volts. Above the switches were verbal labels in graduations of degree, reading: "shock," "dangerous shock," "severely dangerous shock," and two steps before the last switch at the end, an ambiguous, but ominous "XXXX."

Milgram told the "teacher," "I am going to project a list of words on the wall in front of the person in the chair. He will be given several repetitions of the word list in order to learn it. After those initial learning trials, when he sees a word appear on the wall his task will be to name the next word from the list before it is projected, based on having memorized the list. If he makes a mistake, I want you to administer an electric shock and I would like you to increase the voltage of his shock in fifteen-volt increments. Do you understand the instructions?"

When the "teacher" indicated that he or she had fully understood the instructions, the experiment began.

The stooge in the chair was only getting a little light cue every time the switch was thrown, but the "teacher" didn't know that. As the "learner" made mistakes and was shocked, and the apparent "intensity" of the shocks increased, he reacted more and more dramatically. At first, he just jumped a little. As the shocks progressed up the line of apparent intensity, he began jumping and yelling out. Eventually he started screaming when he was shocked, saying, "Stop this! I want out!" And then, further along, he said, "Whoever is doing this, stop! I want to quit! I don't want to do this anymore!" Then, as the voltage got closer to the end of the row of switches (in fact, two steps before the end), the "learner" screamed, convulsed, and then collapsed completely.

When the next word appeared and there was no response, Milgram said, "We'll have to count that as an error; shock him again." When that shock was followed by silence, Milgram said, "Shock him again." So in order to get to the end of the row of the switches the teacher had to shock the learner two more times at the highest voltage while he was apparently completely unconscious.

Prior to actually conducting the study, Milgram had given a questionnaire to a similarly random, stratified sample of people from the community around Yale University in which he asked the respondents, "Would you ever purposely inflict pain on a fellow human being, regardless of the social circumstances?" Over 92 percent said they would not. But when he actually ran the experiment, 68 percent of the people being studied went all the way to the top of the voltage.

The "teachers" sweated excessively, some cried, some went into hysterical laughter, and many begged to be allowed to stop. Many, even though they were later debriefed and told that it was an act and that the "learner" had not actually received any shocks, still reported, when interviewed two weeks later, that they'd had nightmares about what they had done. The subjects obviously had a very hard time doing what they did, but nevertheless they did it. They resisted, they felt bad about it, they felt guilty, but they did what they were told.

Milgram had written down in advance, four statements he could make in response to objections on the part of the teachers—the strongest one being one repeated sometimes during the Third Reich: "The experiment must go on."

Then, in later adaptations of the study, Milgram pointed out that the earlier versions of the experiment were not really fair to Adolf Eichmann because Eichmann had many colleagues who cooperated in his bureaucracy. So Milgram modified the experiment by adding one more stooge, another person in the room with the teacher, who, each time a mistake was made, pulled down a master switch to "turn on the electricity." When the responsibility or blame could be shared with one other person in this way, *92 percent of the subjects went all the way to the top.*

Milgram's presentation at the American Psychological Association annual meeting in Chicago in 1965 was called "A Study in the Legitimation of Evil." He concluded that the people in his sample and, by generalization, the people in the general population "will go against their own individual moral inclinations in order to cooperate with authority."

No sub-group in the sample differed in a statistically significant way from the norm of the whole population. Women did not differ from men, and groupings by ethnic origins, religious orientations, ages, and so on, were not significantly different. One group, however, did approach statistical significance: Catholics. And that difference was in the direction of *more* cooperation with authority, rather than less, in spite of their degree of upset.

One of the things I like about this study is that none of us knows how we would have fared. We would all like to think that we would have been in the 8 percent who said that they would not go on. But obviously, not all of us could have been in the 8 percent.

There were some few subjects, a part of the 8 percent, who not only quit throwing the switches, but proceeded to go talk to the provost at Yale University and to Milgram, saying that not only were they quitting, but that he must stop the experiment. We would all like to think we would have been one of those individuals. But obviously, the great majority of us would have cooperated and felt bad about it, but cooperated nonetheless.

I've been fascinated with this work for over forty years. As I said, I used to report on Milgram's work in speeches I made against the war in Vietnam. I thought it went a long way toward explaining the irresponsible murder of millions of people by the ignorant masses on both sides.

Much of my work as a group leader and psychotherapist has been an attempt to discover and reinforce the kind of independent individuality that might allow for those statistics to change according to an honest person's compassion—the identification, as one being to another, with the person in the electric chair. Clearly, the subjects' compassion made them feel bad about what they did, but it was not enough to overrule their training in obedience to authority.

The people who "went all the way to the top" had compassion for their victim, but lacked the will to act like they wanted to. Their compassion would have to have been stronger or their training in obedience to authority weaker. Their compassion would have to have been stronger than their need to obey the professor from Yale in a white lab coat. Their sense of individual responsibility and their courage to act upon it would have to be stronger than their years of training from school, church, and family to "respect authority" and acquiesce to authority. The integrity of their own feelings would have had to be more powerful in determining their actions than their moral obligation not to challenge the constituted authority or rock the boat of the existing power structure. In 92 percent of the cases that did not happen.

So Adolph Eichmann really was just an average guy. Average guys are just Eichmanns. So are average gals. Most of us would obey Hitler like most people did in Nazi Germany. Most of us are still obeying some questionably constituted authority instead of acting on our own authority most of the time. As children, most of us lined up to go to recess and lined up to go to lunch, and lined up to come back from lunch, and sat in rows and didn't talk, and waited in lines and behaved, and waited for the bell to ring, and most of us are still doing that. Most of us are still teaching our children to do that as well.

Most of us operate from models of what we should and should not do, rather than from models based upon what we feel. What we prefer, and what we are called forth to do based on our empathetic connections with other human beings, is there, but it usually does not determine how we act toward other human beings. And for the most part, we've organized our world to keep it that way. As the Sufis say, 98 percent of the people spend 98 percent of their time at the level of "belief." It's just a part of being civilized.

Honoring Being

Now I ask you, don't you think it very likely that society would be quite different if it was organized around values that honor *being* more than obedience to authority? What changes might occur in how we operate together if we had a world organized around honoring the being of others rather than mere obedience to authority to maintain social order? What if we valued childrearing more than contracts, for example? We might set a maximum of $10 an hour for lawyers (because legal work is not all that important), and a minimum of $300 per hour for childcare workers (because encouraging children to *remain in touch with being* is so much more important than the work of lawyers). Childcare workers and parents and teachers, who are more in touch with children because of their love of the being of young beings, would be getting lawyers' fees, and lawyers would generally be getting the minimum wage.

The world would be quite a different place if we valued compassion more than obedience and order, and if we put our money where our values are.

Suffering Comes from Attachment to Belief

In my personal life and my learning as an intellectual and an activist I BELIEVE that suffering comes from attachment to beliefs to such a degree that the person is avoiding what he or she feels and is trying to convince himself or herself, and others, that the beliefs are reality. What is true about all the successful, but miserable people I have worked with for years who are straining to be functional in a sick system—and suffering from depression, anxiety, and stress—is true on the macrocosmic level for whole groups of people. Whole societies suffer in the same way, and for the same reasons, that the individuals within them suffer.

Learning the distinction between belief and experiential reality relieves suffering for individuals and societies. This distinction is now becoming a part of the public dialogue between all of the people of the world. This distinction is now becoming a part of the world. This distinction is the wooden floor that lets the peasants know a better life is possible. This is the source of the revolution of consciousness.

This is also what radical honesty is about. When enough of us have shared honesty, we discover/invent the possibility of valuing our own minds as instruments of creation rather than as internally programmed do-loops for self-worship or sacred institutional maintenance. This is a revolutionary idea and it terrifies the established mind, as well as the establishment.

The practical implication of this view is that living as a creative independent individual, as well as living with other people in groups, requires frequent restructuring, individually and socially. Frequent restructuring requires frequent re-noticing, and skills developed in noticing and ongoing personal growth at all levels are more important than belief in or adherence to the culture (particularly corporate culture). All models that are relative and temporary models in the world are less important than skills in noticing and grounding in experience, because each time a model for living breaks down or is revised you don't have to be scared to death because your identify is not threatened. Your identity is not your belief system. Your identity is the being who notices what is so in the moment, what is so in the memory, what is so in the body—and has beliefs, but is not self-identified as those beliefs.

Like I said before, we are all organized around an asshole. If you are a body, and a lot of sensations organized around an asshole, your ass is not threatened when beliefs are challenged. If you think you are your story, on the other hand, then you need to learn that you are still there, still living, still noticing, still feeling, still capable of living even when your beliefs have been violated or destroyed.

It seems clear to me that schools, as we have known them from kindergarten through the Ph.D. level, are simply obsolete. Learning is now more valuable than schooling. Skills for learning and continuing to learn with enthusiasm are based on being grounded in our experience, rather than in forcing ourselves to act on beliefs and ideals, and internalized perfectionism. Support of homeschooling and individualized instruction is where the future lies.

More of the practical implications of this, which I outline in my book *Radical Honesty*, made it a bestseller. It is now published in nine languages. I have also written five other books that fundamentally express and elaborate upon this same idea. So I will try to shut up about it now.

CHAPTER 24
Shanti Is Born

My daughter Shanti was born in Washington, D.C., on October 27, 1968. Judy and I had moved into our new row house in Mount Pleasant, near Rock Creek Park. Jim and Louise had come to stay with us and help us lay used carpet in the house.

When the time came and the baby didn't seem to want to come as we'd planned, Judy and I went to the hospital. The doctor determined that the baby had a prolapsed umbilical cord: It was wrapped around the baby's neck, and her heart rate was being affected. An emergency Caesarean section was necessary to save the baby and possibly the mother. They set up to do it, but were delaying because they couldn't find an anesthesiologist. I walked down the hallway of the ward and found an anesthesiologist just finishing with a patient coming out of surgery.

I asked, "Are you an anesthesiologist?"

He said, "Yes."

I said, "Come with me."

He followed me and I explained the situation as we walked back. I told him he was hired and that he was needed right away. I would guarantee he'd be paid, but we had to move fast. He must agree to handle it or I might have to do some damage to him. He said, "Okay." He shook hands with the surgeon and assistant, and they went into the room with Judy. They told me I couldn't be in there for the operation like I'd planned to be in on the childbirth, and I understood. I was relieved because I'd been scared.

I took a seat outside. I prayed. I didn't believe in any God you could pray to then anymore than I do now. Nonetheless prayerful thoughts and requests showed up in the kind of desperate helplessness I was feeling. I wasn't exactly picturing God, I was more or less praying to fate, hoping hard that the great happening of everything flowing with being would give us some luck if I could be clear about alternative kinds of luck that we needed. "Please let Judy be safe. Please let the baby be safe. If they both are in danger, let Judy live, as we can have another baby. If I can die and let them live, let me die." I was desperately looking to make some deal with fate where I had a chance to determine how things could turn out by wishing or begging, or doing something, anything.

We had done preparation and planning, received some instruction, and we were excited and looking forward to a natural childbirth where we both would have some sense of participation and control. Judy was entirely focused and involved with attending to her experience and doing what she had to do during the emergency. I had nothing to do other than desperately pray and hope and be nervous and afraid. So I did that. "O God. O Life. O Fate. O Devil. O Shit. Here come the doctors."

When the surgeon came out and said that everyone was okay and I could go in and see Judy and the baby, it was one of the best moments of my entire life. When I went in I couldn't stop crying and laughing. Judy was okay, and this little baby was there and she was also okay, and she was beautiful. I couldn't believe our luck. I went to make phone calls and tell everyone what happened (finally something I could do). When I told people that we had a little girl I would start laughing and then crying again, and then I would laugh again. Sometimes the person I was speaking with would laugh and cry with me.

Since I couldn't believe everything had turned out okay, I immediately proceeded to start worrying about how to avoid any possible upcoming tragedies in the future. I had to build and maintain my illusion of control again and my role as guardian angel and Lone Ranger papa and protector and defender of the innocent. I loved it though. I was lovin' life. Whether he existed or not, I thanked God with all my heart.

I went home and saw Jim and Louise, and we celebrated and worked to finish putting the used wall-to-wall carpeting in our row house to prepare for Judy to come home with the baby the next day or the day after that. We were happy. Judy was happy. Judy was a great mom from the very beginning, and I loved her for loving Shanti. She loved me for loving Shanti, too.

It was hard though. That first year with the first child is full of bliss and tiredness, and it's like suddenly having your foot nailed to the floor. You're unable to leave and have to go around in circles. We did all right though, that first year. We had some help with cleaning the house and childcare at home when we were both at work, but life out there was still happening so fast. The times they were a changin' with us, between us, and among all of us at the same time. But we had this wonderful little girl who we played with, encouraged, and admired, and called forth into participation in life. She was a shining little light in our lives who taught us how to love all over again in case we had forgotten.

It's late 1969, or early 1970, and it's about 5:30 in the morning. I am downstairs in the house doing my yoga and meditation. I am about at the end and I begin to do the chant that I learned from an Indian guru and have practiced for some time now. I am sitting with my legs crossed, back straight, upturned hands on my knees, and the tips of my thumbs and first fingers touching. I chant: "Aaauuummm Shanti, Shanti, Shanteee . . ." Then sit in silence.

Suddenly I hear a little voice and open my eyes. There before me is my beautiful little girl (a little over a year old), seated just like I am, facing me. She looks right at me and begins chanting, "Oooh Dadeee, Dadeee, Dadeee . . ."

Shanti had awakened and crawled down the stairs. When she saw me seated there, chanting her name, she walked right over and sat down like I did and joined me. She called back to me as clearly as I had called out to her. I took her in my arms and laughed and hugged her, and we rocked back and forth together hugging each other. I loved her with all my heart.

CHAPTER 25

Experiments in Community

I think I found out in 1969 that Judy had been having an affair with Charlie Erikson back in Austin before we left there to move to Ohio. She then met him again each time she went back for visits to finish her dissertation over the course of the year we lived in Miami, Ohio. She had kept it hidden from me. I found out about it after Shanti was born, and though I didn't have a leg to stand on because I'd been doing the same thing (sleeping around outside our marriage) it broke my heart and pissed me off. I just couldn't seem to get over it.

Charlie had been one of my best friends. He was a fellow experimenter with acid and a former rebellious member of The Christian Faith and Life Community. An artist, he'd been traveling in India, stoned, for several years already when I found out about the affair. I hatched a plan to cut off his ear and feed it to him, and I kept that fantasy alive for several years while he remained in India. When I eventually got there, years later, in 1973, after Judy and I were divorced, I'd forgiven them both. Charlie and I became friends again. What I had learned from personal psychological work, psychoanalysis, and training with Gestalt therapists in the interval helped me in the process of forgiveness. I will get into details about it later.

In 1969, I quit Project Head Start when the black women activists I'd helped empower voted that we had to turn back a $50,000 research grant I'd secured for the program with the help of my volunteer professionals, "because it was money so white people can study how to better manipulate and control black children." Though I supported black power, and particularly black women having power to act independently in their own interests regardless of the judgment of white people (males particularly), I was definitely on the horns of a dilemma about the whole thing. I had worked hard to get that grant, and the money meant we could put mirrors and video cameras in a bunch of different classrooms to study the effects of children being able to see themselves in action, and, I thought, gain from knowing who they were and being happy about themselves by seeing themselves in action. It was research that I thought would bring about a breakthrough in the way the yearlong Head Start programs would be run all over the country. At the same time, I thought the right to make their own decisions, mistaken or not, was critical for mothers of Head Start children.

When the mothers group I'd helped organize voted for majority rule in their group, and a majority of them (by a very narrow margin) voted to give the grant back, I did give it back. But not long after that I left the program. That grant had been the main advance I was invested in contributing to the organization. I also thought that a black psychologist, whether or not he or she was as good as me, might be a necessary and viable choice to head up the Washington, D.C., program as the director of psychological services.

I was sad about leaving Head Start, but I was on my way to becoming a full-blown hippie and I'd formed sufficient connections with people in the government that I could now make my living as a consultant. So I left.

Before I leave off talking about this incident, I want to tell about one of the preliminary experiments we engaged in that year, which was critical to the formation of the mothers' group that permitted mothers to determine what went on in the program. In consultation with some of our excellent research volunteers, we set up a plan to test the children in the twenty-four classrooms we oversaw once at the beginning of the year, once about the middle of the year, and once at the end of the year. We used a variety of general IQ tests for three- to five-year-olds in hopes of being able to assess progress in learning as a result of caring and instruction from Head Start.

This gave me the opportunity to investigate something I thought was more critical than the instructional Head Start program for the children: having an impact on their parents big enough to change how the kids were treated at home. Since we had this test series set up, it made it possible for me to select one classroom, do an experiment in parent intervention, and compare the test results of all the kids in that classroom with all the rest of the kids in the other classrooms at the end of the year. I was arrogant and full of piss and vinegar; I wanted to show off how smart I was, be able to brag about my experiences of liberating and being liberated, and test the limits and oppose established authority and, most of all, help those kids. I really loved and identified with the children, along with being the arrogant, redneck, narcissistic asshole that I was.

So I talked to the teacher, the parent assistants, the VISTA volunteers, and some of the central staff at headquarters about setting up a series of parent meetings to create a chance for me to talk to them about parenting. We really worked to get a good turnout for the first of those three meetings. The teacher talked to all the parents about coming when they picked up the kids, a VISTA volunteer visited the home of each kid and told their caretakers, and the parents also told each other. One of the parents agreed to have the meeting at her place. I didn't want it to be held in the classroom. I wanted it to be in one of the homes. The night of the first meeting, nine parents came. Even one father was there. That was a record in itself.

I came to the meeting late, after everyone else was there. I brought a six-pack of cold beer, opened one for myself, and offered the rest to anyone who wanted one. There were only two takers. I started out by introducing myself and saying what I did, and mentioning that I had some hard things to say to everyone, but that these things needed saying.

I talked about the statistics of comparison between Head Start kids and middle-class kids, black and white, living in more privileged neighborhoods. Item by item, I went over the kinds of things privileged four-year-olds knew and could do that Head Start kids couldn't yet. I talked about racism and poverty, and how it was no excuse. I told them about poor kids having the TV on all day long, not having any magazines or books around, not being played with by their parents, not having any mealtime where everyone sits down together, not being talked to, and listened to, and read to. Then I said, "The reason Head Start kids are behind other kids in what they know and can do in the world is not racism. It is not poverty. It is not the conditions of life in the poor areas and the slums. The reason they are behind is they have lousy God-damned parents!" Then I shut up and just looked at them. I opened another beer. You could have heard a pin drop.

Here was a white male, redneck, asshole authority with a Ph.D. bad-mouthing everyone in the room for how they were raising their kids. They didn't like it, but they didn't know what to do. And they recognized that some of the shit I was talking about was real.

Finally, one of the mothers turned to me, and said, "I think you are right." They all turned on her and started giving her hell. "You think we're that bad?" one woman asked. "What does he know?" another said.

I kept quiet for a couple of minutes as the attack on the woman who spoke up escalated. Then I came on again. "You all fight with her, but you won't fight directly with me. You give her hell for saying she thought what I said was right, but you don't give me hell or even question me directly, much less raise hell with me. It's because you know I am a white man and an authority and expert, and you feel have no right to question me because you are being good niggers. There are some differences between a nigger and a black person, and one of them is that, right or wrong, a black person who is not playing 'nigger' can raise hell with anyone in the room, regardless of color. But not you. You kiss ass and kowtow and don't stand up for yourself against me because I am a cracker with some authority."

"Ooohhh shit," said one mother. "We into it now!" exclaimed another. Then I said, "I've gotta go now. But I'll be back next week. Tell everybody to come to that meeting, and we will get into it." Then I left.

The next week's meeting was, and I think still is, a record for parent attendance at a Head Start parents' meeting. There were twelve parents and an uncle in the room. There were even four men there. One of them was carrying a knife on his hip and he didn't look too happy.

I started right in. I told them how happy I was to see them. I told them I wanted to talk about how parents of Head Start children are better at some things than middle-class parents. I wanted to talk about the advantages of being raised by mothers who touch their kids, sing to them, and put their arms around them a lot. I talked about grounding in bodily experience being more important for children than knowing and labeling things. I talked about the characteristics of the country poor and the city poor, and about the advantages of being poor. About fifteen or twenty minutes into my talk one of the men interrupted me and said, "Okay, I hear what you saying now. But what was this shit you was talkin' about last week?"

I said, "Last week I talked about some bad things, and I said things you might have thought were bad. This week I am talking about good things. If you want to learn something and do something other than just take me on, come on back next week. I'll be here. I'll say everything I said last week over again. And I'll say what I said this week, too, and I'll put it all together. And I'll stick around until we are all through. I'll see you then." I left.

I heard a lot of gossip about a lot of conversations that took place over that next week. When we met the third time there were eleven folks, including three men in the room besides me. I repeated everything. We had a hell of a conversation. I told them about my years spent in the civil rights movement. We talked about the 1968 riots. We spoke honestly about all our Southern habits and what bullshit we'd all been raised to believe and put up with. We got down to brass tacks about item-by-item changes they could make in the home environment for their kids. I let them know that if they would invite them, the teacher's aide and the VISTA volunteers would come to their houses and help them re-do what was there for their kids, including bring them free magazines, and help them clean up, make plans for the family to have a meal together each day, put up charts next to the bed so that before they said prayers with their kids they could point to a square, a circle, and a triangle, and other shapes and talk about what they were, and deal with anything else that came to mind when everyone was focusing on the same idea together. After that, a lot of home visits were made and more parent meetings were held.

At the end of the year, the average IQ change for that class was the highest of all the twenty-four classes. The average IQ change measured with two different tests for that class was twenty points. The average for the other classes was about four points. The highest IQ change in that class was forty points, the highest individual change for the whole D.C. program that year. The parent intervention program had worked amazingly well!

I wrote up the results and presented a report on them at the American Psychological Association annual convention the following year. At that meeting I was boycotted and protested by the Black Psychologists Association that was part of the APA because of my "racist" language and impositional style of intervention.

The next year, when I was forced by Head Start Parents' Association to give back the $50,000 grant to study the effects of video feedback and mirrors in Head Start classrooms, the group was chaired by the mother of the child with the forty-IQ point change from the class I'd worked with. If it wasn't for irony we would never be able to iron things out in this world. I think she decided to give this arrogant prick of a white trash psychologist his comeuppance. Good for her. Fuck him if he can't take a joke.

It seems to me that my activist life, and my studies and training in Gestalt therapy and psychoanalysis, my drug experimentation, my love life, learning from my hippie community, my childhood and adolescent conflicts, my adult rebellion against and resentment of authority, and my general unwillingness to compromise were coming together in those years. What was getting born through me was the approach I eventually called "Radical Honesty."

What I now see is that I represent thousands upon thousands of people like me: white trash middle class, kickin' ass, smokin' grass, full of sass, and you can kiss our ass people. That's what led to my superior attitude and mode of operation as a psychotherapist, activist, and writer; and it's also the secret of my great success at marriage, as you might imagine. Obviously it is not all that much fun to live with an arrogant prick.

My son Amos says I am narcissistic. I think he's right, but I worry about what it means for *me*.

CHAPTER 26
Fritz Perls and Training in Gestalt Therapy

In the summer of 1969 I went back to Austin to visit friends and to attend my first workshop with Jim Simkin, a Gestalt therapist from California. Meeting Jim and doing that weekend workshop with him when I went back two years after I'd left Austin was real turnaround in my life. I'd already spent years in therapy, and I was in psychoanalysis in Washington, D.C. with a shrink whose name was Kafka (really!). However, I'd never been so struck by the ability of any therapist as I was by the simplicity and skill Jim showed in doing "hot seat" work with individuals in front of the group. The seat is considered "hot" because everyone's attention is being placed on you while you openly discuss and scrutinize your intimate feelings with the group leader. It made a powerful impact on me and everyone else in the group when we all got the chance to acknowledge, over and over again, with our work in front of others and theirs in front of us, that we were beings lost in our minds, torturing ourselves needlessly based on beliefs formed defensively when we were much younger—some conscious, some unconscious, and some semi-conscious.

At the end of the workshop, Jim found out I had a Ph.D. in psychology. I hadn't mentioned it during the workshop because I was so involved in the process of doing some real work of integration. He said he was happily surprised to find this out and recommended that I do training as a Gestalt therapist. I loved the idea, and in January 1970 I went to Esalen Institute in California to do a ten-day course of training with Fritz Perls, the founder of Gestalt therapy.

Not long before the workshop I'd found out about the secret affair Judy had been having with Charlie Erikson, a secret she'd kept from me even though we'd decided together to have sex with other partners, starting with Jim and Louise. I'd been surprised and hurt both by what had happened and by the secret that was kept about it. At Esalen, I worked on that issue with Fritz. The following is an excerpt from a hot seat session I did with him.

Fritz invited anyone among us to do hot seat work. Our group of twenty was made up of psychiatrists, psychologists, social workers, and a few ministers. I went up and sat on the hot seat, while Fritz lit a cigarette and looked at me. I started explaining about my best friend having had an affair with my wife. As I got into the details in the description, I started to cry. Fritz hardly said a word. Once my crying started it took on a life of its own. I sobbed and sobbed. I was bent over with my elbows on my knees and my head in my hands. Tears were dripping on the floor and snot was running out of my nose, and my grief was mixed with relief. I'd become angry about the situation a lot, but I'd never grieved like this.

After a while, I finally stopped crying. I looked up at Fritz. He had a kind of blank expression on his face. I asked, "Well, what do you think?"

He said, "I think you're a God-damned crybaby."

I leapt up instantly and yelled, "FUCK YOU!" at the top of my voice.

He said, "Oh. Could it be that you're angry?"

I said, "I am angry at *you*, you senile old fart!"

He laughed and said, "Yes. And you are angry, period." Fritz explained to me and the other trainees that anger and grief are sometimes stacked on top of each other. He didn't doubt that I'd been angry before with Judy. Nor did he doubt that my grief was authentic. But he said that underneath the grief and my anger with Judy was more anger.

He was right. I knew he was right, but I was mad about that, too, and still felt mad at him. I didn't want to get off it altogether, but I couldn't help being touched by him and impressed by how well he listened and observed.

That session was the beginning of a quixotic few days between Fritz and me. He picked on me like hell, even during the breaks. He had a remarkable ability to be present. He was trying to teach me how to do that by modeling it, and it still pissed me off. You could see this ability in whatever he'd do. He'd come to the dining room at Esalen, for example, where a lot of women knew and loved him, and they all liked to come up to him and kiss him on the mouth. Not a little peck either. They would stand there and French kiss Fritz for two or three minutes. Fritz would put his tray down to give it his total attention, which was what they, and other women I met later who'd had sex with him, told me was so amazing. They could practically come by kissing him.

So I would be sitting somewhere in the dining room, usually on the periphery of the group, and he'd search me out and come sit next to me. This happened several times. Once he sat next to me and we ate and didn't speak for a long time. Finally he said, "Do you see those waves coming in out there?" pointing to the sea.

"Yes." I said.

"Each one of them comes and goes, and not one of them is thinking about itself."

"Is that supposed to be some kind of pithy God-damned profound fucking statement for my benefit? Kiss my ass," I said.

"Fuck you," he said.

"Fuck you," I said, and then cleared my place, took my dishes to the dishwashing window, and left the dining room.

Despite cussing at each other, I knew Fritz liked me and he knew I liked him. One day he took me to his private house at Esalen. He wanted to show me a sculpture that had been given to him by an artist he'd seen and worked with in workshops over the course of a number of months. The sculpture was a clear glass or plastic globe with some water in it, and sitting in the water was a very thick pair of eyeglasses. Fritz told me that he had worked with this man on his anger a number of times on the hot seat when he came to Gestalt groups at Esalen. He'd used a concentration exercise with him, and had him do the same exercise on his own at home between those weekend workshops. As a result of that artist's work with Fritz on anger and his practice with that exercise, his very severe case of nearsightedness was completely cured, so he'd built his glasses into this clear plastic sculpture and given it to Fritz.

I'd actually seen Fritz do this exercise with someone in our group. He had the man close his eyes, focus his attention on the sensations he noticed in his eyeballs, and describe them in the present tense, while he was noticing the sensations, to Fritz. The person said something like, "I feel pressure at the back of my eyeballs . . . and some movement."

Then Fritz said, "What do you notice now in your hands?" and the guy shifted attention to his hands and reported the sensations he felt there.

Then Fritz said, "Now, your other balls. What do you feel in your other balls?" The guy shifted his attention to his testicles and described a few sensations he noticed there.

Fritz then said, "Now your eyeballs again. What do you notice in your eyeballs?" and the exercise in noticing went on. Eyes. Hands. Balls. Eyes.

Hands. Balls. Over a short period of time, what was being sensed in these locations changed, and the person doing the exercise relaxed into the practice.

Fritz told me, "Particularly if you get a combination of symptoms, like nearsightedness, lower back pain, indirectly expressed anger, or instances of sexual impotency, you can have a noticeable positive impact on all the symptoms at once. It is almost like there are strings that go from somewhere in the middle of the back to the eyes to the hands and the balls, and someone has grabbed hold of those strings, twisted them, and is pulling back on where they're attached at the other end. This causes pressure on the eyeballs so they flatten and the lenses bow out, and the person becomes nearsighted. There is tension and pressure cutting off the blood supply to the hands, as well as pressure pulling back on the balls, and tension in the back sometimes causing impotency or premature ejaculation.

"Psychologically the overruling of the taboos against expressiveness allows for greater self-expression, particularly of anger, which reduces tension. If the place where the strings are twisted, where the pressure and pain in the back are, is relieved, and that area becomes relaxed through paying attention, then the eyesight improves, anger decreases, back pain goes away, and sexual function is restored."

I appreciated that story and Fritz for spending time with me. By the time our training was over, I even appreciated him for picking on me. And in the years of my private practice in D.C., although no one ever threw his or her glasses away completely or built them into a sculpture for me, many times people's eyeglass prescriptions changed to a less corrective set of lenses, and they did have to get new glasses. This outcome came along with their new ways of being in the world, and the new eyes they used to see it with.

Like the lyrics of Kris Kristofferson's song "The Pilgrim," Fritz was a "walking contradiction, partly truth and partly fiction." When he was in Florida, living with his lover there during the years before he came to the Esalen Institute in Big Sur, California, Fritz had taken a lot of LSD and wandered around soaking up the news as well as the new synthesis the acid brought about for him. He told me about that, too, but he didn't like to have conversations about acid trips, as he said, "Because these conversations turn into a pissing contest, about how 'my trip was bigger than your trip' or just stories about experiences on LSD."

Fritz definitely could describe things, but didn't like "talking about things" so much, because it went in the direction of going into our heads and making assessments rather than "being with" our memories to see what would emerge, or having an experience rather than talking about it.

Fritz also put down Buddhism a lot, yet he was close friends with the head of the retreat over at the Zen Center at Tassajara, located across the mountains from Esalen, and they would visit and hang out now and then.

He also pooh-poohed Rolfing and, at the same time, took all twelve sessions from Ida Rolfe when she offered them to him. He said he appreciated her for it and that it did him a lot of good.

I learned a lot from him, as narcissistic and preoccupied with my own shit as I was. I was getting what I wanted and needed from Fritz, and I was grateful to him for it, but not as attuned to him as Jim Simkin, who was a student and close friend of Fritz. I remember Jim crying when he came to sit in at the end of the last session of our ten-day training at Esalen that January. He knew that Fritz was going to leave Esalen soon and also leave the U.S. altogether because, as Fritz said, "I have left two other fascist states in my life, and now it is time to leave a third one." He was referring to Nazi Germany, South Africa, and the United States under Richard Nixon perpetrating a fascist war of empire on the people of Vietnam. Jim was also crying, I think, because he knew that Fritz, then seventy-five, was nearing the end of his life. Fritz said something about "what little time I have left . . ."

Fritz moved to Vancouver Island in Canada and started a "Gestalt commune" there, a community based on the principles of Gestalt therapy. Within a year and a half from the time he left Esalen he was dead.

My friend Bob Klaus, who was also one of Fritz's students, visited the commune in Vancouver not long after Fritz passed away. Bob told me that the rules there were rather stringently enforced for training purposes. He was getting a cup of coffee in the kitchen and asked someone where the sugar was. "Use your God-damned eyes! Not my memory!" the person replied. Later, at the dining table with a bunch of people, someone asked him to pass the salt. Bob reached over and picked up the salt and pepper shakers and passed them both to the person. The fellow stood up and threw the pepper shaker violently on the floor, exclaiming, "I said, 'Pass the salt, God damn it! Don't fucking care-take me, asshole!" Those folks were *serious*. They intended to make new rules of individual responsibility for taking care of oneself in the world rather than continually generating co-dependency and the manipulation we'd all been brainwashed with.

Perhaps that was a noble goal, but Bob nonetheless said he was on pins and needles about violating their taboos the whole time he was there. The contradiction, the dilemma, and the paradox of this is self-evident. One of the leading edges of the counterculture we were trying to create as a substitute for the moralism, self-righteousness, and insanity of the culture we were a part of, had adapted the fascist style of moralistic self-righteousness about the new rules as a teaching method!

The idea is that if we would just confront each other and constantly interrupt our dysfunctional styles of living and ways of being, we might deliver each other into the land of reality, rather than an interpretation of it, or attempt to spin meaning and do a sales pitch for it while claiming to be reporting on reality. If we committed to doing this, we might awaken and support each other in our own attempts to interrupt our minds.

In the end, this particular communal fascistic attempt to correct fascism died fairly soon. But some of us didn't forget the point. Radical Honesty, and a lot of other innovative therapies of the same ilk, was born out of that paradoxical beginning attempt to deliver us from evil. And the evolution of real freedom, the freedom from the jail of one's own mind, continued on its way in our culture: two steps forward, one step back.

CHAPTER 27
1971 May Day Protests

From Wikipedia comes the following report of events.

> *"On Monday, May 3, 1971, one of the most disruptive actions of the Vietnam War era occurred in Washington, D.C., when thousands of anti-war activists tried to shut down the federal government in protest of the Vietnam War. The threat caused by the May Day Protests forced the Nixon Administration to create a virtual state of siege in the nation's capital. Thousands of Federal and National Guard troops, along with local police, suppressed the disorder, and by the time it was over several days later, over 10,000 would be arrested. It would be the largest mass arrest in U.S. history."*

A bunch of people, some from out of town who were staying with Judy and me, and some who were local friends and fellow protestors, stayed up late in the living room of our row house on the night of May 2nd. We were putting roofing nails through flattened sides of cardboard boxes and stacking these flats in preparation for their use the next day on Connecticut Avenue. We intended to spin them under cars, trucks, and buses the next day to blow out their tires. We were smoking dope and drinking beer, as we worked, and everyone was laughing and teasing me about my new look. Until that night I hadn't had a haircut in several years. My beard had been down to my belt and my hair down to my ass. That night I cut it all off. I felt naked, but I had a plan and I liked it.

Like many others fed up to the teeth with the liars in government who now constantly told us they were getting out of Vietnam while they actually escalated the war, my friends and I were preparing to take significant action. We'd warned everyone who worked in Washington, D.C., not to come to work on Monday because they wouldn't be able to get in or out of the city without a very real threat to their personal property and well-being. Nixon had called out the troops and challenged us, and we were readying ourselves to take him on. We were going to shut that city down.

We did. There were 70,000–90,000 of us, and we did as we intended.

My day on May 3rd went like this. I got up at 4:30 A.M. and donned my suit and tie. Then I went out to Rock Creek Park with my axe. By 5:30 A.M. I'd felled two very large trees across Rock Creek Parkway, a major entryway into D.C. from the Maryland suburbs. I brought the trees down in places where I knew it would be a hell of a hard job to clean them up and clear them out. Cars were stacked up and their drivers were trying to turn around and go back the other way before I finished chopping down the second tree. I've never felt better about being good with an axe, one of my survival skills from childhood, not even when I got my Boy Scout badge.

After blocking the parkway, I rode over to Connecticut Avenue with several friends with our big stacks of cardboard squares with roofing nails in them. We began spinning them out, sharp end up and flat head down, into the oncoming traffic on Connecticut Avenue, dispersing them as far north as the Hilton Hotel and as far south as K Street. The effect was immediate. Cars were having blowouts left and right, sliding sideways, stalling, and, in some cases, having their tires come off the rims so that they couldn't be driven out of the way without injury to the wheels.

From that point on, it was every anarchist for himself or herself. We had sacks of potatoes to stuff into the tailpipes of buses. These worked great! You could stuff a potato in a tailpipe and then watch the bus drive along for about 200 yards and then stall out, right where it was. Most of the bus drivers didn't have a clue about what was going on. I told those who did, "Stay on the fucking bus and don't get out." The passengers usually stayed on the bus in the middle of the street for a while, and then got off the bus and left, walking.

I'd brought my motorcycle into the city that morning because I could go anywhere and park anywhere with it. I drove down to K Street and wreaked more havoc alone there than I've ever done before or since. I got so good at judging how long a bus would last before dying that I could gauge when to stuff the potato in the tailpipe to stall the bus where I wanted it to be. I stalled one right in the middle of a left turn onto Sixteenth Street from K, right in the middle of the intersection, and blocking all of the lanes.

Between stuffing potatoes into bus exhaust pipes, I was setting fires in the trash cans up and down K Street by lighting matchbooks and throwing them in the cans. After setting a can ablaze, I'd run into the closest building and set off the fire alarms by breaking the glass on a firebox and pulling the switch inside to call the fire department. Response vehicles sped over, so there was a hell of a traffic jam. The emergency vehicles and their racket contributed to the general merriment of the protestors. The city was full of the sounds of sirens, blocked emergency equipment, and dead buses.

I swear to God, it was easy! Seriously, I alone brought that section of town—K Street from Sixteenth Street up to Vermont Avenue—to its knees. Traffic was fucked up for many hours above and below that point.

None of us had time to listen to the news, but we knew that everyone planning on coming into town was turning around and going back home when they heard about the chaos on the news. When I saw cops collecting, and some of them coming toward me, I hopped onto my motorcycle and took off for Constitution Avenue.

The traffic was brought practically to a standstill everywhere. I couldn't have made my way over to Constitution Avenue without the motorcycle. Once there, I hid the bike and took off walking, and sometimes running. There was tear gas everywhere, and I was using wet handkerchiefs to wipe it away and keep going. People didn't know what in the hell to think about me. Who was I? I looked like a "narc" or an FBI agent. I had on a suit and tie and short hair. At the same time, I seemed to be making some trouble.

When I started pulling out construction barriers and placing them entirely across Constitution Avenue, the few cars that came my way stopped there because I looked official. When I signaled or told drivers to turn their cars around and go back, they started trying to turn around right in front of the barrier and go the other way. At that point I was about four blocks west of the Air and Space Museum, and not far from the Washington Monument.

After observing me for a while, some people inside a federal building nearby came out and walked toward the barriers to remove them. I went over and yelled at them, ordering them back into the building. I told them not to interfere, saying this was "police business." They went back in.

In a while, one of them, a man a little bigger than me, came out again. When he got close to my barriers I warned him not to fuck with the barriers or I'd hurt him. He started to move one and so I kicked him in the balls. He fell down and crawled away. When he'd recovered sufficiently, he stood up and ran back into the building. I put my fucking barrier back.

I maintained my blockade for an hour or so in this way, at which point a whole phalanx of tear-gas cops wearing gas masks came charging my way. I ran away from them, got back on my motorcycle, and rode to the center of the Mall, a little bit west of the Washington Monument.

Here I found a real mess. There were so many protesters and cops, tear-gas brigades, military personnel, National Guardsmen, and buses to haul them to the football stadium . . . and cop cars and ambulances . . . and medical areas and unidentifiable collections of people . . . that it was a hell of a party. There were arrest groups: bunches of protesters encircled by one form or another of the "fuzz," as we called the cops back in the day. For a while I simply charged the circles with my motorcycle, sliding sideways toward the "guardians of the peace" and breaking up the outer circle. Then the protesters (sometimes as many as a hundred or so) would run away and have to be arrested and collected again. The second time I tried it, I lost my bike. Because to retrieve it I would have had to get arrested, I left the fucker there. I never got that bike back, but I never gave a fuck whether I did or not. In fact I was proud to sacrifice it.

Of course, pretty soon I got arrested. I was put in a large, encircled group. I still had my suit on though, so I started walking around the outside edge of the group within the circle and barking commands to the hippies, telling them to straighten the fuck up and back up. After I cleared a few dozen of them back from the edge, I simply went over and touched the arm of one of the cops to signal him to let me out of the circle, and he did. Then I ran like hell.

Half a dozen cops chased me. They were carrying twelve-gauge shotguns with tear gas canisters attached on the end of the barrels so they could shoot their projectiles a long way. They shot at me with tear gas canisters at close range, trying to hit me with them, and just about knocked my Goddamned head off. That pissed me off, so I ran out and grabbed one of the canisters, which was jumping and spewing on the ground where it had landed, and ran back, crying and choking and yelling, and threw the canister right into the midst of the group of six men in uniform who'd been chasing me. Only two of them had on gas masks and when I threw the spewing canister back into them I gassed the whole fucking bunch. Then they were falling all over themselves trying to run away from me.

The big circle broke again and everyone inside it ran away in different directions. I turned and ran again, too, as hard as I could, but blindly, and went into the side streets surrounding the Mall and escaped. I was tear gassed, burned, crying, with blind and swollen eyes, and I was running through, and around, a half a dozen different kinds of cops and troops, but I swear that none of the agents of the law that I ran past knew whether or not to arrest me because I still didn't *look* like a protester. I was laughing through my tears like a God-damned crazy person.

By about four o'clock I was worn out and hurting all over. My eyes were nearly swollen shut and I wondered if I'd be permanently blinded, but I was happy. We had made good on our promises, and I'd done my share that day. The entire city looked like a war zone, and the radio and TV stations had more tape than they could play in days. I found my way home, where I washed my eyes with cold water, collapsed, and went to sleep for a while. Then I got up and went out again to take tons of food downtown to feed any protesters who were still not arrested.

I was an adjunct professor at Antioch College at the time these protests were going on. I taught psychology in the fledgling Columbia, Maryland branch campus. A bunch of my students were in the May Day protest and they got three hours of college credit in social psychology for being there the day. Almost all of them were arrested. One, who is now a professor at American University, got six hours of credit. I gave him an extra three because he helped to quell a riot in the football stadium when it was apparent that a breakout attempt about to happen wouldn't work. He wisely anticipated that the cops in control would be tempted to take vengeance on the protestors inside that enclave, which was protected from the eyes of the public, if the riot took place.

Now, here is the rest of what Wikipedia says about that day.

Course of Events as Described on Wikipedia

"By 1971, many anti-war leaders realized that massive, non-violent political protests were not going to end the Vietnam War. The next step of the protest movement would have to be more aggressive. The planning began in June 1970 when Rennie Davis joined Jerry Coffin of the War Resisters League, and then Michael Lerner later that year. Davis went to Paris for coordination with representatives of the communist North Vietnamese government.

"So the Mayday Tribe was formed. It was made up of Yippies and other more militant members of the anti-war movement. Their tactics

would be non-violent but aggressive. The overall objective of the May-day Tribe was to create such a high level of "social chaos" that the only way the political leaders could end the chaos would be to stop the War. The Mayday Tribe's first and last action would occur on May 3, 1971.

"The Tribe's plan was to 'shut down the Government.' This would be achieved by having small groups of determined protesters block major intersections and bridges in the capital and stop workday traffic from coming into the city on Monday morning. On the weekend prior to the action, about 35,000 activists had camped out in West Potomac Park, not far from the Washington Monument. They had gathered in the park to listen to rock music and plan for the coming mass action. Unfortunately for the protesters, the government had anticipated their actions. Early Sunday morning May 2nd, the Nixon Administration had the park permit canceled. U.S. Park Police and Washington Metropolitan Police, dressed in riot gear, raided the encampment. The police formed up in phalanxes and slowly moved through the park firing tear gas and knocking down tents, forcing out the campers. The campers scattered towards the Reflecting Pool and the Lincoln Memorial.

"After the campsite was closed down, most of the protesters went home, but a hard core of about 10,000 regrouped at various churches and college campuses in the area. Even though their numbers and objectives had been reduced, they still planned to close down the government on Monday morning. Many were forced into the nearest car and ordered to leave the city by police. The mass exodus stopped traffic on the freeways for hours, and there was a big mobile party on the highways leading out of D.C. that day. Police mostly ignored the drugs, concentrating on expelling the mob from the nation's capital.

"The Nixon Administration was determined to keep the capital open at all costs. The federal government already had various plans drawn up to deal with major disruptions in cities throughout the country. These plans had been developed in response to the urban disorders of the 1960s. The government now put one of these plans into action to protect the capital. While protesters listened to music, planned their actions or slept, the authorities quickly moved 10,000 federal troops to various locations in the D.C. area, including 4,000 paratroopers from the U.S. 82nd Airborne Division. At one point, so many soldiers and marines were being moved into the area from bases

along the East Coast that troop transports were landing at the rate of one every three minutes at Andrews Air Force Base in suburban Maryland, about 15 miles from the White House. These troops were to back up the 5,100 D.C. Metropolitan Police and 2,000 D.C. National Guard troops that were already on the streets.

"A state of siege existed in the capital. Thousands of troops and thousands of demonstrators planned to confront each other on Monday, May 3rd. Nixon's internal security forces had moved into place early Monday morning. Every bridge coming into the city was lined with troops. Every monument, park, and traffic circle had troops protecting its perimeters. Paratroopers and marines made helicopter combat assaults onto the grounds of the Washington Monument.

"Hundreds of troops were brought into the city by helicopter to support the police. While the troops were in place and thousands held in reserve, the police clashed with members of the Mayday Tribe. The Yippies engaged in hit-and-run tactics throughout the city, trying to disrupt traffic and cause chaos in the streets. The police responded with tear gas and mass arrests. While Nixon rested in San Clemente, California, thousands of federal workers had to navigate through police lines and Mayday Tribe roadblocks. Nixon had refused to give federal workers the day off because he wanted it to appear as though the government was still operating normally.

"While the troops secured the major intersections and bridges, the police roamed through the city making massive arrest sweeps. They arrested anyone who looked like a demonstrator, rounding up thousands and transporting them to an emergency detention center located at the Washington Redskins' practice field, next to Robert F. Kennedy Stadium, east of the United States Capitol. Skirmishes between protesters and police occurred up until about midday, but by Monday afternoon, the May Day Tribe's actions were mostly over. Against thousands of troops and police, the protesters did not have a chance. On Monday, the police had arrested over 7,000 demonstrators. Over the next few days several thousand more would be arrested during smaller protests, making this the largest mass arrest in U.S. history.

"The May Day action had failed. The government had not shut down. Its leaders were arrested by the FBI on conspiracy charges, and other protesters who had been caught up in the police sweeps were eventually released. Many of those arrested were later financially com-

pensated by the federal government because the massive police arrest sweeps were later declared unconstitutional."

Nope! That version's not correct. *The protestors won.* The crowd-sourced material on Wikipedia is wrong.

We dispersed, but we didn't quit, go away, stop protesting, or let up on the government after May Day, and the whole country, particularly the government in D.C., knew that we were intent on stopping the motherfuckers. We were growing larger and larger, and more and more troublesome to deal with. They brought in 40,000–50,000 troops to arrest about 9,000 of us out of about 30,000 or so who were what we might call "fully committed" demonstrators. By two years later we had won.

Here is one more, brief excerpt from Wikipedia.

> *"In response to the anti-war movement, the U.S. Congress passed the Case-Church Amendment in June 1973, prohibiting further U.S. military intervention. In April 1975, North Vietnam captured Saigon. North Vietnam and South Vietnam were reunified the following year."*

Because we never quit, and never intended to quit, the government and all of the cops and troops, and all of the liberals, and all of the middle-class people, and even all of the newsmen and newswomen, eventually got the message. We were growing stronger by the day and we were not going to go away. Wikipedia is wrong. May Day did not fail to shut down the government. It just took a little longer.

I was glad we could quit when we did, because the next stage of escalation we'd planned was serious. I instigated, and a few friends of mine and I started planning something that would let America get a taste of what it was doing in the world that would definitely have ended up with a bunch of us in prison.

The U.S. war policy in Vietnam for a number of years was to uncover the hiding places of the Viet Cong by destroying the forests and plant life in Vietnam and Cambodia, using the chemical known as "agent orange," which killed and damaged tens of thousands of people in the years following its use, including I don't know how many thousands of U.S. soldiers who came home with permanent disabilities from breathing the shit. Our plan was to defoliate Washington. Had Nixon not called off the bombing of the Haiphong Harbor in North Vietnam when he did, *if he had kept it up even two days longer*, I would have killed all the cherry trees in Washington, D.C., in one night with the help of just a few friends, using something close to agent orange to kill the trees and their roots.

I'm glad we never had to do that. The defoliant we'd have used might have killed some of us with cancer in the ensuing years as well. And if we ever got caught, killing off the cherry trees might have brought us the death penalty. The people of the U.S. do not like to have done to them as they do to others, and that might have been the last straw, so to speak. It was a God-damned good idea though. But I feel lucky we didn't have to do it.

I want to give just two more examples from my own life that tell the people's history of what happened there, and then I'll let this matter rest.

For the rest of 1971 and throughout all of 1972, the year after May Day, my writing in various papers and publications, which was propaganda against the war, focused a lot on tax revolt. I was telling people how they could refuse to pay taxes to support the war and get with not ever having to pay them, or how to cost the government so much to collect taxes that the money would be taken from, rather than given to, the war effort.

I was working pretty much full time against the war then. Well . . . other than my post-doctoral internship at the Group Therapy Center of Washington, conducting occasional weekend workshops at personal growth centers, beginning a private practice, and trying to keep up with all the women who were constantly abusing me sexually. (Believe me, being an anti-war warrior was a fine way to meet some fine women who were as committed to the sexual revolution as a part of the whole social revolution that was going to rid the world of the dilitary-combustible complex.)

One of the things we were working on was the telephone tax. There was a telephone tax, which the God-damned, stupid, fucking Congress had been dumb enough to designate specifically to raise funding for the war in Vietnam. It was only $2 to $4 each month for most people, based on their phone bill, and it was to be collected by the phone company and given to the IRS to give to the Pentagon.

Someone sued the telephone company, saying they could not cut off phone service for refusal to pay taxes because it wasn't their job to collect taxes for the God-damned government. This lawsuit was won. So everyone stopped paying taxes on the phone bill all over the country, and we sent little reminders to the phone company that the growing bill each month was for taxes and they better leave our fucking phones on or something very unclear—but bad and dangerous—would happen to them. We enrolled a lot of fence sitters on this protest, so I guess the gummint decided they had better get some of the leaders to bring this to a halt.

I have always wanted to write an "Alice's Restaurant" kind of song about this story. I noticed I switched into Arlo Guthrie mode in writing about it. Can't you just imagine him sayin', "I guess the gummint must of decided they better try to bring this phone thing to a halt."?

One morning I got up to find square yellow-orange signs posted on the outside of my row house, my school bus, my (smaller) replacement motor-cycle, and my car parked out in front of my house. The signs said that "this residence and these vehicles were U.S. Government Property." (Arlo Guthrie there again . . .)

They didn't know it at the time, but they were closer to pay dirt than anyone imagined. My house had already served as a way station on the Un-derground Railroad to Canada for a few deserters from military service. Just before this thing I am about to tell you came down, I gave a marine who was deserting $300 and the name of a person to contact in Canada, and told him I was a contact for future escapees.

I was actually fairly familiar with my personal tax man at the IRS be-cause I'd met him in person and we'd talked on the phone. I liked telling those folks at the IRS what I was doing and why, and talking with them about what they were doing and ought not to be. I had also met a couple of agents who'd been staking out my house. I went out to them one day and asked them what the fuck they were doing there. I had a friend and a tape recorder with me, so they just left. The next week they came and knocked on the door and we had the tape recorder handy then, too.

When they told us they were there to collect back taxes owed to the IRS I asked them if they really expected me to give them money to burn children to a crisp for no God-damned reason, and asked them how it felt to be baby killers, and asked a few other innovative neutral and objective interview questions, which they dutifully responded to with almost verbatim parallel quotes to those uttered by officials from Nazi Germany.

They left and I transcribed the recording and sent it out to the world of war resisters and almost-war resisters to keep them posted on how the IRS was going to handle our telephone tax rebellion. They told me then, right on my front porch and recorded on my tape recorder, and they also let me know in writing several times soon after, that since they could not figure out how to garnish my wages because I didn't work for anyone who worked for "the man," they could claim my property and sell it to pay the taxes I owed. So, they did that.

Well, "laid claim to it" at least.

I keep hearing the song "Alice's Restaurant" in my mind and I estimate that my sentences are sounding more like Arlo Guthrie than they do me. Can't you imagine him playing in the background and talkin', "They told me right then on my front porch and also recorded on my tape recorder, and it was sent to me in writing several times . . ."? Sorry. I've been repossessed by Arlo Guthrie again.

When I called the telephone number that was conveniently located on the signs the IRS had stuck on my property, the person on the phone told me that I had ten days to pay $283.32 in back taxes, or else. (About $83 or so was for the phone tax. The rest I owed because I'd also refused to pay any tax on anything else. I pretty much didn't work anymore unless I could avoid being taxed before I got the money. But, as all outlaws, probably including you (and if not, why not?) know, living by some form of graft or corruption or avoidance of the gummint is more fun than being an obedient, ass-kissing Nazi bureaucrat.

I said then, to the people on the telephone, "Okay, thanks for the information."

They also told me exactly how to come and see my tax person on the fifth floor of the gigantic IRS building in downtown Washington, D.C. I had ten days. So I waited nine days, and then went down there.

The day before the tenth day, I went to the bank, where I got $283 and 32¢ in change (Arlo again) in nickels, dimes, quarters, pennies, and a few silver dollars, as well as in thirty or forty $1 bills. I came home and friends came over, and we smoked dope, drank beer, and watched the news while we tore open all the packets of coins and made preparations for the next morning. We dumped all the change on a big blanket, and when we had finished I did a test to see if I could carry it if I took all four corners in my hand and slung it across my back like Santa Claus. I could.

The next day everyone (seven of us) packed into my friend Bob Gaines's Volkswagen "Bug" and drove down to the IRS building to pay my taxes. We got there and parked the car, and I hoisted my load just like Santa, and we all went up on the elevator to the fifth floor. When the elevator doors opened, we faced a gigantic, half a football field-sized room with fifty or more desks spread out all over kingdom-come. I walked off the elevator followed by my friends and marched directly to my personal IRS agent's desk over at about the middle of the right-hand side of the room. I said in a loud voice, "I owe you $283 dollars and 32 cents. Here it is!" and I whirled and let loose one, then two, and then three of the four corners of the blanket, spraying money high into the air and across the whole room.

Coins flew everywhere. There was instant chaos. Fifty or sixty people ran to the back walls of the room, some screaming, some yelling, and some just running. I began busying myself by picking up handfuls of change and throwing it into IBM Selectric typewriters at the desks, and some of my friends followed suit. We got by with that for a few minutes (at least two minutes) and then five uniformed cops came and hustled my friends next to the elevator to await further proceedings.

For some reason, they left me until last, so I kept on diligently working away at loading typewriters with change.

The second in command of the whole IRS suddenly appeared before me in an apoplectic fit and a cop got on each side of me waiting for orders. I stopped my work and looked at him. He commanded me, "Pick that money up! Pick it up! We refuse to accept it! You have to pick it up!"

I said, "I'd like to see that. I would like to see you make these hands . . ." (I held them out so he could see them) "pick up that money. I don't think you can do that. I would like to see you try, though."

"We refuse to accept it!" he said, "We will not pick it up!"

"Well," I said, "it may be a little tricky getting these typewriters to work . . ."

He started shaking and shouting. "We refuse to accept this payment! If you have a tax attorney you had better contact him! He can confirm that the IRS does not have to accept more than $10 dollars in coin in payment of any tax! You had better speak to your attorney!" He looked and sounded like he was about to have a stroke.

"Good idea!" I said, "I'll call him. Can I use your phone?" I reached for a phone on the desk.

"NO!" he said.

I said, "Well have you got a dime? I could use that pay phone over there."

"NO!" he said.

I said, "Oh. Here's a dime!" and picked up a dime from the change laying on one of the desks.

I walked over to the pay phone on the wall to the right of the elevator where my friends were encircled by cops. I went to the phone and called information, and in a good, strong voice asked for the phone number for Silverstein and Mullens, the biggest tax firm in D.C. It just happened that

Rich Mullens was a friend of mine (and later on, my father-in-law). Rich wasn't there, but I told his secretary to say hello for me and then I got another attorney on the line.

The Assistant Director of the IRS stood right in front of me, listening to every word I said, nearly foaming at the mouth and telling me, frequently, what to ask my lawyer. Looking right at the IRS guy, I said to the lawyer, "I am at the IRS trying to pay my taxes like a good citizen and they won't let me do it."

The lawyer laughed and said, "Well that's a little unusual."

The Assistant Director was jumping up and down. "Tell him it is COIN!" he said. I still thought he was going to have a stroke.

I said, into the phone, "The Assistant Director of the IRS is here telling me that they don't have to accept more than $10 in coin in payment of a tax debt. Is that true?"

"I don't know," the lawyer said, "but I can check." He went to check, so we waited. While we waited I surveyed the scene. I looked at the Assistant Director and at all of the bunched up IRS agents across the room, and at my friends over at the elevator. I waved at them and they waved back. Finally, the voice came back on the line. "That's correct," the lawyer said. "They do not have to accept more than $10 in coin in payment of a tax debt."

"Okay, thanks," I said and hung up.

"What did he say?! What did he say!?" the Assistant Director demanded.

"He said to tell you to kiss my God-damned ass," I replied calmly. "So I am telling you. You can kiss my God-damned ass! I don't give a fuck about the money, and you're going to have to pick it up . . . Not only that. I am starting to get bored. I am about to leave. I am going to walk over there to that elevator and collect my friends, and we are going to leave by getting on the elevator and pressing the down button. If you attempt to stop me . . . or them . . . you had better know God-damned well what you are doing! You had better know, and maybe you better check with *your* lawyers, because I will give you more shit than you can ever imagine if you screw this up. So here I go . . . I am walking. . . . If you are going to bust me, do it now. . . . I am walking . . ."

The Assistant Director yelled, "We will not accept your money as a tax payment!"

"I don't really give a fuck," I said, "it's only $283. Who gives a shit about $283?" I walked over to the elevator and the doors opened. Me and my friends got on the elevator, we pushed the down button, and the doors closed. Arriving on the ground floor, we left the building.

That all happened by about noon. At about 3 P.M. I got a call at my house. "This is Agent So-and-so from the IRS. Another agent, Mr. So-and-so is on the line. We are recording this conversation for possible future use, if needed, in court. We wish to inform you that we have counted your tax payment and we have found it to be $6 and 37 cents short."

"It is ten dollars short," I said. "Count it again," and hung up.

The phone rang again. I said, "Hello," in a very cheerful voice.

"This is Agent So-and-so of the Internal Revenue Service. Another agent, Mr. So-and-so is . . . (and so on)." At the end of repeating his rap, he said, "If you do not pay the remaining amount owed on your tax debt by the end of this day, we will take possession of your property and auction it off to pay that tax. If you will pay the remainder owed on this bill we will count the debt paid in full."

"Okay," I said. "I'll be down there in a little while."

So I went back to that same room at about 4:30 P.M. When I walked in everybody looked up and stopped working. There were uniformed guards at hand. Some people moved to the back of the room. I walked up to my personal tax collector's desk. He said, "Are you going to pay it?"

"Yes," I said.

"Pay the cashier right there," he said, "and I will sign your receipt here . . ." and he began writing.

I reached for my billfold and walked toward the cashier's window the agent had indicated. Then I paused and walked back over to his desk mumbling something about, "I do, though, have one more little question . . ." and looked down at the receipt he had just written and saw that he had signed it. I reached down and tore it out of the booklet. "Thanks!" I said, and walked away.

I passed by the teller's window and walked to the elevator. As I got to the elevator, I turned to see if I was going to be detained or followed or shot or something. But what I saw, as I looked back when I got on the elevator, was my personal IRS agent walking to the cashier's window, reaching for his wallet.

I called the next day and told them I had paid my God-damned taxes so they had to come take those fucking stickers off my property. They did.

A little later I filed a formal complaint, outlining the highlights of what went on there and for months preceding that. I said I had a complaint with the IRS as a tax-paying citizen, concerning their inefficiency in collecting taxes from me. I made an estimate of what everything must have cost from the very beginning several years earlier, through the disruption of that day, including the expense of mailings, phone calls, agent hours. As a tax-paying citizen, I protested that the manner of collection, according to my calculations, was roughly at least twenty times as expensive as the total amount of my taxes. After I wrote this up I sent it around to people and publications in the anti-war movement to encourage and entertain other tax resisters and people in opposition to the war in Vietnam.

What stands out for me throughout that whole time is how much more creative and playful we were than the troglodytes of straightdom. They were always shocked and appalled, upset, and about to have a cow. We were always having a hell of a time fucking with them and stimulating their systems into systematic crashes.

The depressing part of it all is that the dunderhead murderers continued to stay in power and keep the slaughter-for-nothing-but-profit going year after year, right up to current times. Right up to this very day when the news has reported that Barack Obama just ordered 30,000 more American troops into Afghanistan.

Brief Summary of the Vietnam Protest and Other Protests in My Life

This entire ridiculous tragedy of the as yet untold and unaccounted for slaughter and stupidity in Vietnam started when "advisors" were sent there in 1950. (There are still secrets to be released about this. Obama could get the information released, but of course he won't because the chickenshit bastard doesn't believe in having the truth come out. He's turned out to be just as big a fucking liar and poseur as Lyndon Johnson.)

The Vietnam War finally ended in total defeat and disgrace in April 1975. Twenty-five years of totally paranoid "Cold War" stupidity and the "policy of containment" by narrow-minded, fearful, insane, aggressive, stupid, fucking people continued forward uninterrupted, and the dumb-assed citizens of our country once again were manipulated by, and sustained the American military-industrial complex. That conflict started when I was ten years old and lasted until I was thirty-five.

Twenty-five years of starving and stealing from people at home and all over the world to collect enough money to kill millions more of them for nothing. Makes you proud to be an American, doesn't it?

In addition to our long and stupid history with Israel since the end of World War Two, another, equally poisonous ongoing slaughter-for-nothing has been going on in the Middle East by the bloody hands of corporate capitalism. In 1953, when I was thirteen, the age when I left home and moved to Texas, the CIA backed the reinstatement of the Shah of Iran to start the next in a long series of eternal conflicts cooking. Then, from 1953 until current times, Middle East conflicts continued, stimulated constantly by American secret agreements and interventions. They've continued to line the pockets of gigantic defense industry corporations and all their bribed Senators and Congressmen and affiliated businesses.

So let's just pick 1953 kind of arbitrarily as a starting point for this exemplary, current adventure of the American Empire. Fifty-six years. For fifty-six years we've been fucking over people in the Middle East so that we can steal their oil and maintain our so-called "standard of living."

When I was in Teheran for a week or two in 1973, during my travels around the world for a year just to see the world, I met a man who had just come from Vietnam and was now a special agent of some sort in Teheran. We got moderately drunk together. He said he was there in Teheran to make money from the black market, mainly by buying and selling money as the economy got impacted by American involvement. He told me that while he was in Vietnam he personally made a lot of money in the black market money market there.

I asked him what he was *really* doing in Iran. He said, "This is the next Vietnam," and he explained to me that if you could predict and follow the wars around the world you could make money whether or not you were "working for the government." But since he worked for the government and had inside information, it was like taking candy from a baby.

This was in 1973.

So the wars we kept going and profited by in the U.S., including those we were directly and indirectly involved in—wars between Iraq and Iran, the U.S. and Iran, and the U.S. and Iraq, and so on—and all the presences we maintained all over Europe and the world, were being kept in place and purposefully blown on when they simmered down, and blown up when they simmered up. These things were done by America to keep our military-based economy dominant and our goals intact.

This particular second front is another thing that certainly ought to make us proud to be Americans, is it not?

Our engagements throughout the Middle East have made fortunes for people in the defense industry for decades and decades, and built corporatism to its current state of control even under Barack Obama. And nothing about that has changed in any important way, regardless of anyone's effort, including my own.

I was a psychotherapist in Washington, D.C., for twenty-five years full time and five years part time between 1970 and 2000. One of the ways I became an expert on lying was by having clients who were, or had been, engaged in various clandestine efforts around the world. There were a number of people I treated, for example, who were working for the State Department as their cover, and for the CIA in secret. This is a kind of little pretend game that's well known by all of the nation-states that deal with the United States. Everyone knows that our State Department is full of spies; they're just not always sure who is one and who isn't one, so our so-called "diplomacy" is based on people assuming they're negotiating with the CIA.

There have been some instances where people met, got married, and worked together at the State Department, and one spouse didn't know the other was a double agent. You can imagine how well that worked out for their marriages and family life. Personally I hate the CIA and think it should be abolished. The only thing worse than a bureaucracy is a secret bureaucracy, and particularly one everyone knows about.

This God-damned corporate capitalist-run country sucks and it has sucked all my life. And fuck you if you don't like me saying that.

People with high security clearances (meaning they were approved to lie to hide their secret government activity) who saw me in therapy at The Center for Well Being in Washington, had to sign a form that would be shown to me, that allowed me, and, in fact, required me, to inform the FBI agents who'd be sent when the therapy was over of anything that had gone on with the person or had been revealed by them to me in psychotherapy. The agents who came to visit and question me always asked the same questions. The main one they seemed to be interested in was, "Has this person ever used any illegal drugs?" I always answered the question no, even when I'd been getting stoned with the person myself.

I wasn't fucking born yesterday. I don't advocate telling the truth at all times, blindly—and particularly not to lying representatives of a lying government. As I have often said on talk shows and in interviews, "If you have Anne Frank in the attic and a Nazi knocks on the door and asks, 'Do you have any Jews in this house?' the best answer is no. And kill the dumb fuck if you can get by with it."

One time I asked the FBI agent, right after that question about taking drugs, which was asked toward the end of the interview, "Have you ever smoked any marijuana?"

He said, "No."

I said, "Okay, we're even now. Come on with your next bullshit question." He laughed and I laughed. We both knew the whole fucking boondoggle about security clearance was bullshit. We were just doing our jobs like any other ass-kissing bureaucrat.

CHAPTER 28
What Kind of Hero?

I have been a creative person all of my life with everything, including, but not limited to how I've protested insane government policies. I like how I've lived and how my children have turned out. I like what I've written, and I think I've been just a prince of a guy. I am particularly proud of myself when I compare my life to more conventional lives. I wouldn't trade any conventionally successful person's life for mine, and I don't intend to in the future. Nonetheless, my overall lifetime, when it's judged by history in the future, will be seen as a miserable failure.

I think a lot these days about how clear it will be that I've pissed away forty or so years of my life on being non-violent if two billion or so members of humanity die off, poor people first, in the next decade or so. When I look back on my life in the light of some capitalist armageddon, global warming, warmongering shitstorm that takes most, or all of us, away, it will be clear that I could've killed a lot more of the rich motherfuckers who brought all of it on. I probably would have been able to prevent it, or significantly moderate it, had I not had too much Gandhi in me and too little courage.

The actual process of attempting to tell the descriptive truth about my life, regardless of my practice in honesty, is a grueling experience. I am getting to the hard part now. I am trying to say how I've lived and what I've done, good and bad, right and wrong, honestly and deceitfully, and so forth. Though my biography has characteristics of both the hero's journey and the confessions of a cereal killer, the hero I want to be is a hero of honesty, even if honesty makes me a shitty hero. I want to share what my life actually has been like: what I've done, how I did it, and who I did it with, and what they did, how it was for us, and what I thought then, and how I think of it now, and what I imagine, or know, they thought and now think.

So here is my posterior for posterity.

I think someone is going to want to make a movie of my life, or at least use my life as an excuse to make a movie. I doubt seriously if the movie will reflect more than the sensationalistic possibilities this story has in it, but I really would like to see myself, and people like me, taken apart and looked at carefully. We should be appraised, judged, and plumbed for directions for redirecting civilization—because the way humanity has done it up until now, almost completely unconsciously, doesn't work worth a fuck. Well . . . except possibly in a half-assed way for all the real pricks of the world . . . but they ought to be killed and eaten.

I do want to be a hero of transparency. I'm not proud of all of my exploits or my exploitativeness; I'm ashamed of some of it. And I'm particularly aware right now of having to surrender this story and not have any control over what anyone does with it. So I plod on. I want to get this book out there and have people read it, and give copies away. If I have my druthers, I would rather that poor people read it first and then medium-to-well-off people who are having doubts next. Rich people, as a class, with only a few exceptions, can go fuck themselves.

This reminds me. The City of Berkeley was once overtaken by hippies who were legitimately voted into office in the late '60s or early '70s. Immediately upon taking office, they withdrew Berkeley from the Vietnam War. Then they offered all kinds of courses for all citizens, conducted in City Hall. They had a course offering there for a year or two called "Fucking 101." People could sign up either as couples or individuals to learn about fucking. If they were singles they would be paired up by the instructors with a mate to study and practice fucking. (There was no HIV/AIDS back then.)

A few people I knew took that course and really got a lot out of it—they learned a lot. At the end, couples could fuck on stage if they wanted and get "feedback" from the rest of the students and faculty. A surprising number of participants were regular middle-class people (or as regular as it gets in Berkeley).

Back then, when I heard about this course, I remembering thinking to myself, *Self, isn't this course the cat's meow of compassion? Here, I have been telling rich people to go fuck themselves for years, and Berkeley, lovingly, actually teaches them how!*

Anyway, if there is a movie made about my life somewhat based on this story after I become famous by killing and eating a Republican corporate asshole before I die, I want one thing to be honored or at least argued by a critic, if the movie gets made by a Republican or some fucking corporation. It's this: I want to make of my life story an example of how honesty could work for individuals, families, groups, and the common good. And I want to encourage other people to try it. I think the future of humankind depends on us getting more honest really quickly, and on killing and eating the 1,000 richest people on Earth and redistributing their possessions to the rest of us, and on starting over again with a Main Street economy while letting Wall Street and the banks go fuck themselves.

I was just on a national TV show in Sweden with the prime minister of Sweden (and some actors and a comedian and a talk show host). The show was an hour-long discussion of honesty, including honesty in politics. One of the things I said to the PM was that if he'd lived a relatively uneventful, unadventurous, and fairly uninteresting life (which he probably had since he got elected as a conservative PM in a Socialist, but overly civilized society), it should be easy for him to be honest, because no one would be particularly offended by what he'd done, as they often are by my life. Compared to me, I told him, he should have an easy time of it.

This was said after the TV host asked me if I'd admitted using illegal drugs when I ran for Congress in the U.S. I answered yes and elaborated on that and various other socially taboo topics, and explained that one reason I got only 25 percent of the vote may not have been because I was poor, but honest, but the offensiveness to some people of the topics and behavior about which I'd been honest.

I am an asshole and a thinker and a fool and courageous. My goal is to be all these things out loud, regardless of what emotions and thoughts it triggers in you or me. And I think you might do well to emulate me in doing this for all of our sakes and for the sake of possible, but not certain future generations of human beings.

I think if I report these things honestly, it will give you a chance to get that I am an asshole pretty much like you, and you could be one pretty much like me. Out loud though. Not in secret. I want to be an encouraging asshole. I want to encourage assholes to come out of the closet. I know we can all be magnificent human beings and also that how much we can be magnificent is directly proportionate to not hiding what assholes we are.

CHAPTER 29

When I Was 31

My Personal, Political, and Professional Life

In September 1971, the autumn after the May Day protest, I turned thirty-one. It was a sobering experience. Along with lots of my cohorts, for years I had been saying, "Don't trust anyone over thirty." Now I was.

I was still married to Judy; we'd been married for about nine years then. Shanti was almost two. We lived in Washington, D.C., in the row house we'd purchased the year Shanti was born. I had worked a year and a half for Head Start. Judy was working as an education expert, consultant, and proposal writer for a big corporation. Out of our experience of being polyamorous, drug experimenters, and readers, and alive to our time, we were living a kind of strange life. We worked real jobs, but we didn't keep our private life secret, like we were supposed to.

After I quit that job at Head Start in the middle of my second year of working there, I did some freelance consulting for a while. I worked for the Department of Education checking out people who the department had funded for various educational and testing tasks.

I spent some time in Alaska, using bush pilots to fly me around to check in on remote Bureau of Indian Affairs schools to see if they were doing what they were supposed to do with the gummint money they'd been sent. I got to hang out with Inuit families and their kids, and ride a snow mobile way out onto the frozen ocean flying over frozen waves of ice. My usual bush pilot had a plane with three types of landing apparatus: skis, pontoons, and wheels. When we would be coming in for a landing on a river or on ice, he would turn to me and say, "I wonder if I put the right landing gear down. Whaddaya think?" —just to scare the shit out of me.

I spent a great couple of weeks up there. At one school, in early March, they gave the kids an extra fifteen minutes at recess because it was such a warm day. It was ten degrees below zero. I talked to teachers and counselors about coming out of the long, dark time in winter. I learned that the highest suicide rates occurred was when the light started coming back, not when the dark increased. I saw it proven again that people are adaptive and more capable of handling trouble than they generally know, and then, sometimes, surprisingly less capable.

I had a few other consulting jobs in D.C. and traveled some to a few other states. I played golf some. I spent time with Shanti and Judy some, and with Shanti by herself some when Judy was at work. I spent a lot of time with fellow protesters of the war in Vietnam. Some days I worked against the government. Some days I worked for the government. Some days I was the government. Some days I was a middle-class bureaucrat and business-man. Some days I was an enemy of the state or, as I like to think of it, an enema of the state. Then after a half a year or so, I looked around for another job and found one.

I went to work for J. R. Taft and Associates, a foundation, government, and private philanthropy fundraising institution. I liked working there. Over the course of about a year, I helped design and write a proposal to fund a university called The New University for Peace, which was to be lo-cated in Washington, D.C. I helped raise the first $1 million in pledges from the board of directors of National Training Labs, which was behind the idea. We also got help from the former campaign manager and the staff of the failed campaign of Minnesota Senator Hubert Humphrey (mostly, I thought, because they were now out of a job). But after about ten months of hard work and before the university even got off the ground, I sabotaged it by raising hell when they said they wanted Dean Rusk to head it up. Dean Rusk was the U.S. Secretary of State under President Kennedy and President Johnson. I considered him a war criminal and still do.

We were having a meeting with about twenty people present to plan strategy for the next major fundraising effort for The New University for Peace. We'd been jovial and getting along, and were all enthused with the prospect of designing this university for adult education with re-education for peace being its primary objective. We were all on the same page, and then the Humphrey campaign guys did their little nomination presentation for who would be the president of the university. They nominated Dean Rusk, implying that he would be willing to accept.

I listened for about five minutes. Then I interrupted them. I stood up and said, "I want to say something." You could have heard a pin drop. It was because my voice was trembling and I sounded serious. I am proud of standing up right then and saying in front of the whole group involved at Airlie House Conference Center out in Virginia that I was personally offended that Rusk was even under consideration. Not only had I spent a significant portion of the last six years of my life working in opposition to the idiotic war in Vietnam, but so had all of the people who were likely candidates for participation in any international institution for peace. That they could even consider Rusk was an insult to the intelligence of the entire American public, dumb as they fucking were.

I said that with him at the top, everyone in the world would assume our new creation was no more than a CIA front organization, which I now considered feasible myself. And not only would I call a press conference to *say* that this whole pile of shit was to create a CIA front organization, which it probably was, but that I would undermine everything they attempted to do if they didn't drop Rusk from the list immediately—and maybe even if they did. How in the fuck they thought they could get by with it in the first place was a mystery to me, I said, and I wanted to know where the fuck they had been for the last six years.

My little speech more or less ended the conference. They were not about to proceed to answer me, and it was clear they wouldn't proceed without doing so. The chairperson suggested that we take a break, and when we came back it was quickly decided that it would be best if we just adjourned until a later date. Then the meeting ended. People got the hell out of there, and not many stopped by to shake my hand.

Right after that little speech, I called Dick Taft, my boss and the owner of the company at J.R. Taft and Associates, and told him I'd screwed the deal forever on purpose and that while I was sorry I'd ruined a potential cash cow for him, I wasn't sorry for what I had done. I probably lost him a million dollars on that deal, and a few hundred thousand myself. The project died right after that when the operational director withdrew. Most of the pledges were withdrawn as well.

I killed it. One of my proudest middle-class white trash moments!

CHAPTER 30
On the Road Again

I did a little more fundraising work with Dick Taft on other projects, but pretty soon, in early 1970, I bought a school bus that had already been partly modified to be a camper. I modified it some more, transforming it into a hippie dream bus with wall-to-wall carpet scraps in the interior, a bathroom, a kitchen with a stove, a motorcycle on the front, a generator on the back, two little bedrooms, big twin speakers on the top, and the whole thing painted on the outside to look like a giant bumble bee. We called it the "Let It Bee." I left my job and took off to travel around America.

Judy and Shanti came with me, but they flew back home a lot for Judy to keep working for a week or two at a time at the corporation where she was employed in D.C. Over the next five or six months, we drove across America pulling into hippie encampments and school bus gatherings all over the country while blaring "Let it Be" from our speakers at full volume. Almost every time we stopped someone would come on board and hand us a joint, and we'd hand out some cold beer or warm wine and break out the guitars, then sit down inside or outside and the party that was America then would continue on down the road. We all thought the party might last forever.

I met Steve Gaskin and some of his lovers in their bus in a Safeway parking lot in California, and we hung out together for a few nights way back before they moved to Tennessee and started the commune known as The Farm, which still exists today. I met dozens of busloads of people, picked up every hitchhiker on the road, played guitar, smoked dope, and drank and sang with people I knew I loved though I didn't know their names. We'd all been in and around Haight-Ashbury before, during, and after the Summer of Love. We had read *One Flew over the Cuckoo's Nest, The Electric Kool-*

Aid Acid Test, and *The Whole Earth Catalog,* and shared the music of Bob Dylan, The Beatles, and Janice Joplin, and all the minstrels of the hippie revolution from The Fillmore auditorium and its surrounds.

I didn't get to participate in any of the Great School Bus Races in New Mexico because I never happened to be there at the right times, but I heard about them from those who did. I want to tell you about those races because they so epitomized the times we lived in.

Preceding the big race, school buses and their hippie passengers would gather in a valley in New Mexico and prepare for days. On the day of the race, a whole bunch of buses collected together in the valley, while a few others and a whole lot of people collected on the sides of the hills surrounding the valley. Gallons and gallons of orange juice with LSD in it were passed around and drunk up by spectators and drivers. At 9 or 10 A.M. someone would shoot a gun into the air and the race would begin. The beautiful multicolored, creatively decorated buses would start to move around down in the valley and the people watching them drive around would cheer and clap. After a couple or three hours, people would select the winner. There was no starting gate and no finish line. The winner was unanimously chosen though from some free-acid aesthetic choice everyone made together. Then everyone celebrated for weeks afterwards and it was wonderful. A great time was had by all.

I just love that story. It's the way we were. In the Haight, which I started visiting before I finished grad school, we used to say, "If you walk along the street and happen to find a pill, take it, and see what happens." We figured that whatever happened would be an adventure we could learn from.

CHAPTER 31
The Time of My Fucking Life!

In my time on the road in 1970, I was single as much or more than I was part of a traveling family with Judy and Shanti. Sometimes Shanti traveled with me when Judy went home to work, but most of the time Judy would take Shanti home with her to D.C. I loved traveling with both of them, I loved traveling with just Shanti, and I loved traveling alone. Life really was an adventure inside and out. We began, all of us hippies, to start dreaming about reshaping the world, building community, living a life of freedom and mutual support with sex, drugs, and rock and roll, and a whole lot of lovin'. I started visiting various experimental hippie communes when I heard or read about them along my route. As you can imagine, it was kind of a meandering route going generally east to west to the West Coast, north and south a lot, back across Canada east, back to the Midwest in the U.S. with lots of nonlinear deviations.

Driving up the California coast somewhere in there, I threw a rod in the engine of my old 1953 school bus. Luckily my brother Jimmy, who'd moved to California a while before to become a hippie, too, now lived in Mendocino, right up the road from San Francisco. I went to his camp in the woods, where he, his wife Sharon, and her little girl lived in an old San Francisco city bus, and we overhauled the engine of my bus together. It took us a month, but we had a hell of a fine time doing it.

Jimmy had all the tools, the skill, and the experience of a good shade-tree mechanic, which was very valuable to a lot of hippies besides me. It gave him an elevated status in the community and was a source of trade that kept him in dope, food, and money, in that order. It took us a month to fix the bus engine because we weren't in any hurry. Every day we'd get up about noon, roll five or six cigarettes with fine pipe tobacco and hashish, smoke one, and then have breakfast and some coffee before meandering on out to the worksite. I remember spending two hours washing a piston in kerosene one day. I had to get it clean. And by God that was a good clean job we did on that engine. Long after I left there I attempted to integrate that same work schedule into my daily life.

During all my meandering, Judy and I were in ongoing communication with Jim and Louise (who we went on the trip to Europe with) back in Ohio, and two other couples: Dick and Sharon Johnson who lived in Maine and Texas, and Bob and Ginny Gaines in D.C. We were all in flux in regard to where or how we might settle down, and had begun a discussion of possibly living together communally in Ohio.

By this point, Jim was chairman of the Art Department at Antioch, which was the most stable and best job anyone among our group had. I was working some at The Group Therapy Center in D.C. after having pursued additional training in Gestalt therapy with Fritz Perls after that earlier work I did with Jim Simkin. We set up a post-doctoral internship at the Center so that I could work under supervision and co-lead therapy groups, but I wasn't committed to being there full time. I could come and go as I liked. Judy was working as a consultant and grant writer. And we had a good friend there, Sam Alley, who became Shanti's godfather and who was fascinated by, though scared to death of, our hippie life. He remained a good friend to Judy and co-protector of Shanti for many years after this time.

The three couples decided we needed to have a powwow about the future and agreed to meet on Flat Island in Nova Scotia, a place that Jim, Louise, and a group of their friends had purchased a few years before. Judy would travel to Nova Scotia from Washington. But I was clear across the country, so having set up our meeting a week ahead, I took off from California, and headed across Canada in my fine-running, newly overhauled bus.

As I crossed over into Canada somewhere pretty far out west, the road was full of hippies. I picked up every hitchhiker I saw for a couple of hundred miles until we got to be about fifteen. One was a truck driver who said he liked to drive, so I pulled over immediately and from there forward he drove. Great! I could drink and get stoned and play music! We had plenty of dope, music, and booze on board, so we held a rolling party all the way across Canada. When we wanted to, we stopped and cooked and slept, some outside using their tents and some inside. Various pairings occurred amongst people according to what seemed feasible at the time.

I particularly remember one nice, long, happy stint on the road, where me and a young woman were fucking on the foldout bed right in the living room/kitchen part of the bus, going down the road at sixty miles an hour, surrounded by three guitar-playing and singing musicians, a fiddle player, and a bunch more people keeping time and singing along conducted by us or conducting us, but supporting us and participating in our fine sexual union as they kept a close eye on us. We were laughing, joyful, and fucking our brains out, and we felt like we had our own supporting chorus, and that everyone was in love and being our lovers, too.

There was a little pot, some hash, and maybe a little bit of acid involved. And I did get a case of the clap from her. But, all in all, it was a bliss and a blast. I went out on my motorcycle and got a penicillin shot somewhere up in Canada afterwards, and then wrote a song entitled "I Went and Got Me 900,00 units of Penicsilly—illillillilli—um on My Yama Ha Ha Ha!"

Eventually we got to where we were goin' that way, and it beat the shit out of taking a Greyhound.

When the four couples of friends from Texas and beyond met up on Flat Island and camped out together for a week, we started our time together by taking some acid and spending a day wandering around the island learning from God and nature. That LSD trip was particularly epic, transcendent, and powerful for me. I saw all of life and all of death in the waves and in the plants and glowing, moving vegetation. I saw my own life and my own death in all that was present. With great nostalgia, I saw my whole future going past as well as the lives of those I knew and loved. I felt grateful for my life and for the wisdom that we'd been lucky enough to get from LSD and our community of friends. I was completely open, in love, and free.

We talked about having a community and we decided to start looking around in Ohio for a place. It wasn't long—maybe six months—before we bought a one hundred-acre farm down in Southern Ohio, with a house, a spring house, a barn, and a smokehouse on the property, for $9,000 dollars. Dick, Sharon, and their three kids, me, Judy, and Shanti, and Jim, Louise, and their little boy, Strider (born before Shanti), all came together there.

We had a group marriage. Not entirely every male with every female, but close. I was sleeping with all of the women, although Sharon and I didn't sleep together much. Judy was sleeping with Dick Johnson and some, but not much, with Jim. Dick and Sharon were a little afraid of not having regular work, and worried about how they could live on the farm without jobs and still take care of the kids, and various people were having trouble with various other things. Jim and Louise, for instance, were not getting along too well, and Louise also started spacing out and hallucinating now and then. We made a separate place for her to be alone while Jim took care of Strider for about a week.

I talked with Louise in a number of sessions, and made love to her to get her back in touch with reality, which worked, by the way. I'd always known that locking people up in hospitals and not letting them have sex was a big mistake and the opposite of what people going crazy need. They need to fuck and touch, eat good food, and hear music, and to reconnect to the Earth and life. I knew that and it was confirmed when my efforts brought Louise back and kept her from killing herself over her despair about having a baby she loved with a man she'd learned to hate. It was not, of course, an unusual problem, but it's a serious one for a whole lot of people.

We built a room for the kids to share and made them pretty little bunks and a playroom. We took turns in various couplings taking care of the kids. We started a garden and built an addition onto the house. A guy named John, who was a friend and lover of Louise, and had some carpentry skills, came and helped us and joined in our group. We grew dope and veggies. We also had lots of processing to do, as so many new and old relationships in our group had to be reorganized, re-acknowledged, and re-aligned.

It was the end of the '60s and the beginning of the '70s and everything was in flux and open to question. I was going back to D.C. to run weekend and five-day workshops with another Gestalt therapist, Marcia Hafter, and she and I became lovers. I also had other lovers back there.

The women in our group marriage ganged up on me for screwing around on them with Marcia. They thought I should be monogamous within the community for Christ's sake! I was already getting my brains fucked out by beautiful women who loved me. What the fuck did I want? Of course, I got all indignant and said I wouldn't be taking no henpecking from three anymore than from one . . . typical redneck, hard-ass, braggadocio bullshit, but it worked. Now and then we all mellowed out and let up on our positions, even me. Then the women backed off and commiserated with each other until we'd have some other fight about something. But we'd get through it and keep on going.

Well, that group marriage started out real good, until about five months later, when all at once I was sitting on that farm alone wondering what had gone wrong. The main thing I think we broke up over in the end was that the kids were unhappy because the parents were trying to treat them all equally. Instead of favoring our own kids, like we normally would as parents, we tried to treat all of them as our own, so we treated our own kids like we did the rest of the pack. This bothered them and made them unhappy. When our kids were unhappy, we were unhappy. I really believe it was that more than sexual possessiveness or jealousy or insecurity or previously existing conflicts between couples that caused the breakup, though, of course, that was all still there. We processed a lot and forgave a lot, but the amount of time needed for processing was way beyond what it is for, say, a monogamous couple. The situation was much more exciting than monogamy, and a lot of fun, but there was a hell of a lot of psychological processing needed. Everyone got kind of tired of having to process so much shit so often.

A number of things happened to me in the weekend workshops I went back to D.C. to conduct that greatly impacted our life, my life, and the lives of some others around me. There was a place out in Syria, Virginia, about an hour and a half from D.C., called The Center. I attended Sufi workshops and met Adnan Sarhan, one of my Sufi teachers, there. I conducted Gestalt workshops there, both alone and with other leaders, including Marcia Hafter, who I loved and who was my lover, friend, compatriot, and teacher. She'd spent a lot of time with Fritz Perls and had learned a lot from him both formally and informally. She and a female lover of hers had had an ongoing mutual love affair with Fritz. I watched her be open and loving, and I was open and loving with her, and I think she taught me more than I know how to acknowledge. She loved me and I felt like she acknowledged me as she had Fritz Perls because I was so much like him.

I'll tell you a few things that happened to me in workshops out there at The Center. At the end of one workshop in September, the last day of the workshop was on my birthday. About a half a dozen of the women in the workshop decided to give me a birthday present I wouldn't forget. They plotted in secret and laid out a plan to plan out a lay.

My lover—not Marcia, but another woman who'd come with me to the workshop in my school bus—came and got me at noon on the day the workshop ended. She said she wanted to take me on a blindfold walk, which is something we did sometimes as an exercise in groups. I said, "Okay," and she put a blindfold on me and led me around some before eventually taking me into a room where I could hear other people, even though they weren't talking. She put me on my back on a massage table and took off my clothes. I noticed other hands helping her take off my clothes and putting massage oil on my body. As they began putting oil on my body, they started touching me all over.

Then I felt the strangest thing: The women started massaging me with their breasts. There were women's breasts rubbing up and down all over my body, and the women were making little moaning, delicious sounds. It was wonderful! Their breasts were covered with oil and they were rubbing me all over, including putting their breasts in my face (being careful not to displace my blindfold) and on my arms and legs, on my torso, and on my cock, and they were enjoying themselves as much as me. The women were enjoying turning me on, laughing and muttering little, funny, sweet things, and sticking their tongues in my ears and kissing me.

When I got a hard on, they touched it, and rubbed the tip of it over their nipples. Then my lover mounted me, put my cock inside her, and started fucking me even as the others kept putting their nipples in my mouth and kissing me. Finally they took off my mask so I could see as well as hear and feel what was going on.

The other women kept touching us and rubbing their tits all over both of us and in my face and letting me suck on them as my lover and I fucked. When I came, so did my lover—and so did a few of them. It got louder and louder at the end. Damn it was good! It was, as you can imagine, an unforgettable birthday present, just as they'd intended. And apparently I haven't forgotten.

Damn I miss the '70s! I hardly had time to take a breath for a decade and I loved it!

Another thing that happened during that time of grand liberation out there at The Center was this: I went out for a Sunday afternoon and evening celebration. I was sitting on a blanket by the creek talking to friends and having a sip of wine when a man who was a friend of mine came up and asked if we could talk alone for a minute or two. I said sure we could, and the people I'd been talking to drifted off. Then he said, "I have a request."

I said, "Okay."

He said, "I want to give you to my girlfriend for her birthday, as a present." I knew his girlfriend. She was really beautiful. I had danced with her before, flirted with her, and lusted after her, but kept a little distance from her because this man was my friend and they were a couple. He said, "I asked her what she wanted for her birthday and she said she wanted you. So I said I'd ask you if she could have you. Will you make love to her?"

"Why hell no, of course not," I said, laughing.

He laughed, too. It was just about dusk. He pointed to a tent set up further up along the creek. He said, "Go up there and have a good time. And take your time. It's a present."

I went to that tent and went inside. The woman and I had some wine and a toke of dope. We talked and laughed, and after a while started kissing. Then we got excited and fucked really good. It was energetic and hot, and we came pretty quickly because of the excitement of getting to do what we'd both wanted, but hadn't dared to do until then. We had a little more wine and some munchies, and fucked again. This time was longer and very passionate, and a little louder and even better. Damn I love it when women come! Then we got out of the tent in the dark, went in the cold creek and bathed and shivered, came out, and went back in the tent and fucked again. We saw and heard God that time! If we had fucked one more time it would have killed us both!

We eventually got up and the woman went back to her boyfriend, and (she told me later) fucked him, and really loved him for her present. Lord who could have guessed? A fine time was had by all.

Okay, here's a third and final story about what happened out there in Syria, and then maybe I'll shut up and get on with my life story. This one is probably the most relevant to why our group marriage in Ohio broke up. Marcia and I had just finished conducting a very successful five-day workshop, and afterwards spent the night together. Then she left and went back to D.C. I stayed over an extra day to do a journey on psilocybin mushrooms. I ate the mushrooms in the morning and spent pretty much the whole day wandering around alone on the place.

I've had intense, whole-world experiences in which the environment was part and parcel of my hallucinations. That's what happened on this day. In this one, the farm turned into Vietnam. There I was in Vietnam, hiding in the bushes. Planes and helicopters were flying around and shooting. I was scared and hoped they wouldn't see me and kill me on purpose, or accidentally hit me. It was a very loud, very random, and very out-of-control scene. People were being killed. After that scene receded, I made some resolves to do even more to stop that horrible shit from keeping on.

Next, I entered a period of complete silence. Nothing was going on in the chatter of my mind. Then a voice came. It was clear and specific. It said, "Don't speak for twenty-seven days." I nodded. And that is exactly what I did. I went on a word fast. I made up a little sign I could wear on my shirt or hold up for people to see. It said, "I am on a word fast. "

I fucked up a bunch of times, and accidentally spoke, but every time I caught myself speaking over the next twenty-seven days I quit immediately. It seemed to happen mainly after coming out of a movie. Somehow when I entered into a movie with all my attention and really lived in it, which is what I usually do, I'd slip. Usually after I come out of a movie, back to reality, I never want to talk about the movie right after it is over. But often, when I was on this word fast, I'd walk out of a movie, start to say something, and then realize, "Oh no. I'm not talking, I'm on a word fast," and shut up.

For twenty-seven days I was on a word fast, conscientiously. God spoke to me and what he had to say was, "Shut the fuck up." Now I realize that what I am calling "God" here is some aspect of me that is a little bigger than my mind or my concept of me, but whatever it was, the message, when all the chatter was off, was, "Don't speak for twenty-seven days." I figured it was important and I would find out why, and I think I did.

All my life I'd been the one holding things together. On all the acid trips back in Austin when a bunch of us would drop acid together, if anyone had a hard time or an accident, needed grounding, or got scared, paranoid, or whatever, or if someone called or showed up unexpectedly, or the cops showed up, or anything else unexpected happened, I was always the one to handle the emergency. All my life I'd volunteered or been asked to take over when somebody needed to do something to keep things together, guard the camp, or defend the innocent, and so on.

I imagined that if I didn't keep talking the whole world would fall apart. Well, it did. I was right. I shut up and, sure enough, my whole world fell apart. When that twenty-seven days was up and I could talk again, I was sitting up next to the barn at the farm in Ohio, the last one left, and there was no one to talk to. I had to laugh. The joke was on me. The joke *was* me. I finally got it.

My wife had left me. My community had fallen apart. My friends had moved away. A bunch of them went to California where there was some work for Judy and for Dick Johnson. Just before they left, Judy told me, "You just say the word, and I'll stay."

Ha ha. Funny. The twenty-seven days wasn't up yet. I kept my mouth shut.

My life fell apart and it was one of the best things that ever happened to me! I got it. Life goes on within you and without you. Management at the level I'd been doing it was an effortful waste of time. It hurt to lose and fail at all we'd been dreaming about together. But the lesson was badly needed. Even though I'm still a control freak by nature and a pain in the ass to live with, it has never again been as serious a thing as it used to be, and I did, in fact, learn to shut the fuck up now and then.

I moved back to D.C. into the row house Judy and I owned, and I took up where I had left off running groups and a private practice. But now I was single. I was liberated. I was free. I was less of a control freak. I was rich. I was smart. I was good looking. I was funny. I was thirty-one years old, it was 1972, and the whole world was liberated from the conventional wisdom of the past! And a lot of beautiful, horny, liberated, horny, sophisticated, horny women loved to play with me whenever we could find the time!

Thank ya, Jezis! Thank ya, Jezis!

Right after I got back, I took care of Shanti, who was not quite three, for a couple of weeks while Judy was getting herself settled in California. But soon Judy took Shanti out there to live with her. I turned our old place into a fine bachelor pad and, except for visits to and from seeing Shanti, I never looked back. I truly began a harder working, deeper experience of my life of service to others. Thank ya, Jeziz, again!

Over the course of the next year and a half to two years I slept with literally hundreds of women. I loved it. I slept with a new woman two or three, or four, nights a week. I had lots of repeaters as well, and in fact not many one-night stands, and it all was really, really fun! When I particularly liked someone I would ask her out, or over, again, or ask her to join me on my next date. I had a lot of ongoing relationships with women who knew all about my ongoing exploits with other women but didn't care. I was busy as a bee.

I had so much new sex that after about a year or so, believe it or not, the waxing began to wane. I started thinking I had a job servicing the women of Washington and its surrounds. I thought I might have to hire somebody to help me. I got to where I started looking forward to a night off like I used to look forward to getting laid by a new woman. That made me a little worried and I began to wonder about it. I decided I needed to stabilize my life some, settle down a little bit, take things a little bit under control—maybe find a way of being grounded in a relationship in some way . . . So I came up with this idea: I would get married on Monday nights!

Polly Armstrong and I had an ongoing loving, sexual friendship. She and I had done bioenergetics training together. We'd learned how to come bioenergetically through intense study and mutual instruction and a lot of stressful exercises where you put your body in strange positions until you start vibrating and achieve breakthroughs so the energy in your body would flow past where it used to stop. And we practiced what we learned sexually. She bucked me clear off her once when she came and I flew off the bed through the air to the floor ejaculating while she was coming like a train all by herself in the bed. We thought about taking that act onstage, but didn't because we couldn't be sure enough about the timing each time! Besides that, we laughed a lot and we loved each other. I asked Polly to marry me on Monday nights. She thought it was a good idea, so we did that. We got married on Monday nights.

Our Mondays were reserved for each other. We'd meet kind of early and go out to eat. She'd then come over to my place. We'd go to bed, make love, talk, watch TV, make love again, and go to sleep in each other's arms. We'd get up the next morning and make love then, too, if we wanted, and then hang out a while, have breakfast, and get ready for the day. We arranged things so neither of us had to be anywhere before noon on Tuesday.

That was *mahvelous!* It really worked out great. We both liked it. When we'd meet on Mondays we were both excited to catch up with what we'd been doing during the week and what had been going on with each other. We had fun with each other and we could depend on seeing each other, and we liked the hell out of it. In fact, after a while, I liked it so much I decided to get married on Thursday nights to another woman. So I did that.

My Thursday night wife, June, knew about all my shenanigans with other women and about my Monday night wife. She thought it was funny and fun, and that we were pioneers. So did I. In fact, one time at a party we went to on a Monday night, Polly and I ran into June, and I introduced them. We all had a great conversation and connection, smoked a little pot and drank and danced, and talked with the same group of friends. The two of them really liked each other and cracked a lot of jokes about sharing me around. So we went home together that night and they made love to each other as well as to me. In fact, more with each other than with me! (Women are so superior to men in their ability to come again and again and to make each other come again and again; it gave me an inferiority complex. And women who love other women are the best lovers in all of human history . . . . But I won't even mention it . . . never mind, forget I ever said anything.)

Well, hell, I thought. *That is a fine thing.* So I got married to another woman on Friday nights. Sandy. Sandy had beautiful long, long, blonde hair that would hang down over her perfect breasts. She looked like Lady Godiva. And when her nipples got hard they would peek through the curtain of her beautiful hair, and when I kissed them she'd take my head in her hands and pull me close and put the mantle of her long hair completely over me and take me into her. She loved to fuck and she loved to laugh. I was so happy when Friday rolled around each week.

Well, that was enough. Three marriages at the same time were enough. Too much monogamy is hard on a fellow. After all I was married three nights a week! That ought to be enough! So I left the other nights open so I could fuck around a little bit in case all that monogamy might start getting to me.

Unless you were there, or unless you are gay, you may have a hard time believing me when I talk about how much everyone had sex in the early '70s. Believe me, we took our liberation seriously. I was there. There was no AIDS. There was no herpes. (There was the clap, which I got about six times over four or five years, but it would go away right quick with 900,000 units of penicillin and we could be on the road again in a few days.) We knew there were sexually transmitted diseases around, but STDs didn't worry us or inhibit our behavior.

That sounds a little cavalier. But that's how we were. We all were admitting that we loved to fuck, and we wanted to be sure everyone had the chance to know that they could, too, if they wanted and try it out themselves. And the women! Jesus the women were worse than the men once they got a good taste of freedom and fucking, we almost upset the balance where men were supposed to be the pursuers and the women the guardians of withholding out of virtue.

I also had threesomes with two women and me maybe twenty or thirty times. I didn't mind and still don't mind the inferiority complex I got from it. It was worth it, considering how much excitement and fun it was. But there is no doubt about it: Women are entirely superior to men in terms of their ability to enjoy sex over and over again. They can do it hundreds of times more frequently than we can. And in case you didn't get it yet, I love that.

I've also had a whole lot of threesomes with me and another man and one woman. All of those were very exciting, too. When I was with two women they did a lot of kissing and touching and fucking each other. But when another man and I were with one woman, even though I'd had some homosexual experience before, and didn't mind being touched or kissed by a man, I was much more strongly attracted to women loving being fucked in turn and repeatedly. So when it was me and another guy, the attention was always from us to the woman much more than it was to each other. The women really liked that a lot, too.

I love to watch a woman loving being fucked by a man, and it makes me want to fuck her, too, and then when I do, and the man who has just come inside her watches us, he wants more pretty soon, too. After a couple of times each of us trading out, the woman can get to feeling almost satisfied, like, "Finally! A really good fuck!" And it is also fun to finger her and kiss her and fuck her from behind, so she is kind of fucking and fucking around with both of us at the same time. That tends to be right good, too.

Oh yeah, I forgot. One time when Louise and John and I fucked, when Louise was on top of me fucking me, and I was holding still while she went up and down on my cock, really enjoying it, just as she was starting to speed up John came up behind her and put his cock inside her vagina from behind while my cock was still in her. The base of his prick was right against the base of my prick and we both went all the way inside, stretching her pretty tight, but still fucking her rhythmically together and feeling each other's pricks pressed against each other, and the tightness and movement of her entirely engorged, gorgeous pussy. She really, really liked it and made such wonderful sounds saying, "OOoOOoOOh GodddddddYesss," with the greatest tremulousness in her voice and movement of her body. In just a minute or two we all came at the same time.

It was like fireworks and cannons. I could feel John's ejaculation and mine pumping against each other and squirting into Louise with alternating force as we ejaculated inside her and her whole vagina and whole body convulsed like a kind of seizure, but like nothing so much as a climax . . . an orgasm, a really big one . . . a mutual explosion that damn near knocked us all out. We laughed and cried together after that. We were in a big, cuddly, exhausted, happy heap, and we fell asleep without a peep.

Oh yeah, one more. I was in San Francisco, staying in a cheap hotel. I went outside and found a woman on the street, a hooker. I went up and talked to her and said I wanted to have sex with two women at once who would make love to each other while I made love to them. She said, "Okay," and pointed out a friend of hers on the other corner. We went and talked to her and then a guy, their pimp, came and picked the three of us up and took us to my room, got some money from me, and left. We started messing around some and as we took off our clothes it turned out that one of the women was a hermaphrodite. He/she had a rather small, but fully functioning prick and balls, and underneath that a normal-sized vagina.

When they started to kiss and touch, they both got excited and pretty enthusiastic, really from when they first started kissing. They were rubbing their breasts together and feeling each other up, and sucking and kissing each other enthusiastically. The hermaphrodite man/woman put his/her prick in the woman and started fucking her from on top, and then I started fucking him/her in her vagina from behind, at the same time he/she was penetrating the other woman. He/she really, really, really liked it.

I think the other woman and I both were really excited by her excitement, imagining what fun it must be to be being fucked in the vagina and be fucking someone else at the same time with a hard cock! But it was so good to hear and imagine what it felt like that we didn't get to imagine it for long because, within about three or four minutes, we all came at the same time. We were all really into it and they even stayed with it a little longer past when the two males of us came.

I suggested that was so much fun we ought to take a little break and do it again. They asked, "Will you pay again?" I said, "No, but we could do it for fun." They laughed and said, "Nice try," but they didn't buy it if I didn't buy it, so to speak. We were all pretty happy though, and I thought I was pretty lucky. And I still think so.

Anyway, the point of all this, other than bragging and pornography, is that we were living in a hitch-in-the-get-a-long of Western cultural moralism, and whether it was intimate and loving, like with Louise and John and me, or just exciting, like with the prostitutes and me, it was really sharing in mutual ecstasy—and more fucking fun than a barrel of bonobos.

CHAPTER 32
Psycho Therapy

Meanwhile, back at the ranch, at my place of work, I was becoming a professional. I worked and was paid for doing a post-doctoral internship for a couple of years at The Group Therapy Center of Washington, D.C. After becoming licensed to practice as a clinical psychologist I ended up working there for a few years after that. Paul Weisberg, M.D., was the psychiatrist, founder, and leader of this big center for group psychotherapy, which was affiliated with The Psychiatric Institute of Washington, D.C., and with George Washington University. There were plans to develop centers like it in various other places. Paul was brilliant and he was aberrant. Even compared to me, he was out there. He was smarter than me and much crazier than me. He was also more immoral than me and more manipulative. He was challenging and exciting to work with, but not someone to trust with the family jewels.

He recruited therapists and trainees from Ph.D.s and M.D.s doing psychiatric residencies and post-docs, and practicing therapists who were willing to affiliate and participate in the large client draw of The Group Therapy Center, and put them to work leading group therapy groups with an ever-growing population of people wanting to do serious work in personal growth. We were recruited to assist in running lots of groups under supervision and on our own, and to build a therapeutic empire in Washington, and perhaps in a number of other cities in the United States.

Paul was a megalomaniac with half a dozen chronic physical illnesses, chief among them diabetes. He was sure he was going to die within a few years. He was brave, bright, funny, cynical, and charming, very much like the Devil himself. He was in a position of power and influence, seeing clients and running groups sixty hours a week or so while he maintained a family life of sorts in Georgetown. He took a fair amount of drugs, including acid and pot, in addition to a selection of pharmaceuticals, and fucked around a fair amount, including with patients and female colleagues (and as I later found out—and stopped—even the female partners of couples in couples therapy, while keeping the secret from the husband). He was generally set on living it up while he could, given that he was sick and not long for this world.

The Group Therapy Center became a real gathering place for local practitioners who were participating in a revolution in group therapy, where the work of paying attention and experience was taking over from the world of figuring out and analysis as the solution to psychological problems. A group of us who were training with Fritz Perls and other Gestalt therapists in California, and a number of other partially trained Gestalt therapists began having meetings at The Group Therapy Center.

Together these individuals and I eventually founded The Gestalt Institute of Washington, and I became its first president. We designed a Gestalt therapy training program, and taught and booked other teachers from around the country to teach there, usually in weekend workshops. But that wasn't until a few years later.

It was an exciting time and the shift to paying attention to sensation as a more reliable indication of what was really going on with people, rather than trying to interpret emotion and meaning made out of it, was a breakthrough with dramatic results in short-term therapy. We were dedicated to working ourselves out of a job with clients to make room for new ones recruited by the testimony of the clients with real-life results in a short period of time.

I was also affiliated with Bob Caldwell. I did evening presentations and weekend and weeklong workshops to introduce people to Gestalt Therapy and at Quest, his growth center, in Bethesda, Maryland. I also gave talks at brown bag lunches held by various government departments and agencies, talking to staff members about how there was a revolution going on right under the eyes of Nixon and his fellow blind Republican fools, who had not a clue about what was really going on in the world. Again, I felt I was on the leading edge of change and I expected to take over the world in a few weeks. And again, it took decades before what was leading-edge work then became more or less the standard operating procedure now.

When Paul and I co-led groups, people often experienced more honesty than they were used to. We sometimes took risks by being honest in groups, which put us in jeopardy at times. But when people were given the opportunity to bring us down if they chose to through us voluntarily making ourselves vulnerable, they didn't. They admired us for it.

Here's an example of what I mean. One time we had an assistant district attorney for the City of Washington in a group therapy group with a number of people who smoked pot, and the issue of him participating in prosecuting people for marijuana use came up as an issue both for him and for other members of the group. At the beginning of the next therapy session I brought in an ounce of pot and began the group by rolling a joint. I lit it and passed it to Paul, who took a toke and passed it on to someone else.

Then I took back the joint from the next person it was passed to and handed it to the assistant district attorney. I said, "Either take a toke of this or bust me." He looked at me, then at the group, and then back at me. When he took a toke everyone in the group cheered. We all got stoned and had a hell of a fine therapy session. That man eventually moved on from law enforcement prosecution to another form of lawyering. Obviously we saved one there.

After only a few years of operation, The Group Therapy Center of Washington folded. Paul, along with me and a few other part-timers had to move out of the big space we'd had. This happened after I returned from a year-long trip around the world. Paul and I then shared an office space together and developed our mutual private practices independently, and interdependently; we still ran a group or two together on occasion. Paul did die young, though not quite as young as he thought he would. He moved to the West Coast and I lost touch with him for a few years, then found out about his death when it happened. Only a few years after he departed he departed. He would have liked that little joke. It was nice to have a colleague who was as daring as me and even crazier and I learned a lot from him about mental illness both through instruction and by example.

CHAPTER 33

On the Road Again, Again

(1973–74)

I n 1973, before The Group Therapy Center folded, I took off on a year-long trip around the world. I took a backpack full mostly of books with a change of clothes, my guitar, and a round-the-world ticket from Pan American Airlines with open dates for departures and landings. I bought the ticket for $1,250, and I took $5,000 with me in cash for spending money. On the trip, I supplemented my funds now and then by playing music on street corners and in cafés in exchange for tips, food, and drinks.

June, my Thursday night wife, decided she wanted to go around the world with me or, as we worked it out, traveling at the same time as me: for various periods of time she was with me and sometimes she was alone. We'd go our separate ways for a few weeks, and then meet up again. If one of us had found a particularly good place or friends when were venturing alone, we might travel back to the same together for another stay or go on to some new adventure together.

A few weeks before we left, we had dinner at June's parents' house in D.C. Her father was wealthy and good friends with Lyndon Johnson and involved in politics in Washington. At dinner he wished us well and gave June an American Express Card. He said, "While you all are traveling, have a dinner on us now and then, wherever you like." This was a wonderful gift! We were usually staying in campgrounds or fairly cheap hotels and living free, but parsimoniously. It was great to be able to splurge at the best restaurant in town now and then. It also allowed for us to go up and down on the social scale as we went to new places on the geographical plane, with more variety of friends and classes to venture into contact with. We had a fine time lots of times in lots of different places.

We had a kind of a plan. We started out in Lisbon, where we stayed in a pretty nice hotel and got oriented, and then we rented a car for a month to travel around Portugal and Spain. We went into the interior of Portugal and then along the coast and then on up along the coast of Spain. We stayed at campgrounds in a tent sometimes and met, played music, and sang with lots of groups of traveling hippies on the way to somewhere from somewhere else. We learned about how traveling was for them, about how it could be for us, about places we could go to, and people we could meet, and things we could do in places we were headed. If we particularly liked some people or someplace we'd just stay there until we felt like leaving.

As we began to settle into living on the road over the first month, we were gently welcomed into the travelers' communities. We met lots of folks who were on the road for short times as well as for long open-ended times like us. I got better at playing the guitar and singing songs because I played the guitar every day. I learned many songs I'd been meaning to learn and a lot of new songs on the road. I performed in informal settings around campfires, in front of fireplaces, on street corners, out on docks, and on the beach. I also listened to other people's performances and learned a bit about playing along with others, though mostly I wasn't skilled enough to keep up. Others more skilled would play along to support me now and then, and I felt grateful for it and happy to feel for the first time that I was finally learning how to put a song out there so people could get it. I sang a lot of songs by Bob Dylan and Kris Kristofferson, as well as a few I'd written or that had been written by people on the road. The music was so much a part of how we were getting our inner directions that it seemed right to pass songs back and forth in the magnificent ongoing conversation of the time.

I read all the books I had with me and then traded them for others. That, and working on my novel, *The Eternal Split-second Sound-light Being*, which I wrote by hand, was my ongoing educational plan. It was a great joy to read all four volumes of *The Alexandria Quartet* by Lawrence Durrell straight through with no interruptions. It was also possible to pursue one after another of the new books by authors I loved, like Kurt Vonnegut, Ursula K. Le Guin, and many others. It was lovely to discover books, poems, and music from friends we met on the road and to have our only agenda be to pursue anything we found that caught our interest and curiosity.

Everyone on the road knew we were schooling each other in the ongoing process of discovering who we were and who we were becoming. I was discovering a kind of home schooling, which for me continues to this day, and my love of people who love to learn, which started back in the Christian Faith and Life Community in Texas, grew. June and I gradually settled into being on the road together with a lot of help from our friends.

From Spain, we decided to go to Morocco and take a look at North Africa, because of some things we heard about what we could do there. Here is one of the things we found out about from fellow travelers: Because of the ongoing wars and conflict between Israel and various Arab states, Israel had stopped allowing people to enter Israel who had passports stamped at the borders of Arab states. The Arab states had followed suit. So if you'd been or planned to go to Israel or an Arab state, the border folks with the stamps had decided to let us put a blank piece of paper inside our passports to be stamped for proof of approved entry, which could be thrown away once you left. Your passport itself would not be stamped and you could go on anywhere else you wanted in the Middle East.

An ingenious scheme to smuggle hashish from North Africa to Europe and America had resulted. We met a few couples who had done it, and one couple was doing it for a second time. The typical scenario was that an American hippie couple decided they wanted to travel and develop a nest egg at the same time, and have a little dope for their trouble, would follow a plan. (Then they could have another little dope and be able to support him or her as well. Heh heh.) The couple would get haircuts, wear "straight" clothes, and bring money for the purchase of a car and a special travel plan from the Mercedes-Benz Company in Germany.

The Mercedes plant would put 150 miles on a new Mercedes, making it a "used" car, and then sell it at a discounted rate to Americans, along with a bunch of coupons for stays at various hotels and resorts around Europe when the Americans took "an auto tour of Europe." The couple would fly over, pick up their Mercedes at the plant, travel around Europe, and then go back home on the Queen Mary from Marseilles a few months later. The whole package deal cost less than the list price cost of a brand-new Mercedes.

Well, these enterprising hippies combined that offer with the way of handling passports by the Middle Eastern states and came up with a scam that worked for years. They would pick up their auto, do their tour, go to Spain, take the ferry to Spanish Morocco on the northern tip of Africa, get their little blank page stamped by Moroccan authorities, and eventually drive on up into the mountains of Katama where the hashish farms are.

After hearing about this plan, June and I decided to check out doing it for ourselves. We met a young man who was a guide for this project and he rode with us from Tangier, so he could explain to cops along the way that we had free passage. These cops were in on the deal; he was a member of a family that paid them bribes. He was a trip! He was personal friends with Alice Cooper (a male rock star), and he was entirely imbued in American hippie culture. These virtues were the essence of good salesmanship for what he was selling at the time. I should mention that we hadn't invested in the plan yet; we had no Mercedes-Benz vehicle or special travel plan, only the rental car we'd been driving since we'd left Lisbon.

We got to the hash farm after dark. He took us to a tent where we would sleep that night, and then to a meal at his house, where there was hashish aplenty in everything we ate or drank. Everyone was high and shouting in Arabic. We were stoned, full of wonder, and a little scared, but soon we escaped to our tent. When we woke up in the morning and looked outside, we saw fields of marijuana planted in rows and rows like corn, going up and over the hills for what seemed like forever. We were served a breakfast of hashish tea, fruit, bread, and hummus with a little hashish in it. We then got taken on a tour of the factory and the garage, and we were told how we might invest in the business in the future if we liked the plan.

The factory was turning out flat, quarter-inch thick, black Moroccan hashish wrapped in tinfoil in strips about a foot wide and many feet long. Our guide explained to us was that when a couple came with a Mercedes they stayed overnight much as we had, and in the morning drove away with their car. Overnight, the car would be pulled into the garage and taken apart by six mechanics, and then put back together with about 400 pounds of hash in it. Curled up tinfoil-covered circles of hash would be placed in the main drive train, in the oil pan, behind the brake shoes on the wheels, and in various parts of the body and engine not easily accessible to the uninformed. The auto would also be weight balanced by removing 400 pounds of unnecessary metal; in the end it would weigh the same when it left the garage as when it had come in the night before.

The straight-looking American couple would then drive to the coast and take a ferry to Marseilles, where their passports would be stamped to show that they had gone from Spain to France. Their car would be loaded onto the Queen Mary, and they would cruise back to New York. The car would be unloaded at the dock there, where they would pick it up and drive anywhere in America to unpack and distribute the hash to local dealers with little risk to themselves of getting caught. They would be allowed to keep a few pounds of hash for themselves until taking their next trip to Morocco. The take for them was a new Mercedes-Benz and up to a quarter of a million dollars. As several of our friends had told us, "It was a lot of fun!"

When we left, since we didn't give the hash dealers a down payment for a future trip, and maybe because I looked far from straight then, our guide didn't escort us to the ferry to Marseilles. My hair was down to my ass and my beard down to my tits. I wore a big knife on my hip and a cowboy hat, and carried a guitar strapped over my back and a backpack that looked full of anything but clothes. I had a mean look on my face when approaching authority of any kind, and there were maybe a few hundred other telltale signs of us not being a good front for their business. Or maybe it was because I was just checking out the deal, and possibly not a serious client and partner for the scam yet, but these hash dealers let us continue to the coast alone and without protection from the police or informing the cops in advance to let us pass untouched.

On our way to the coast, we were stopped and searched. And I mean, *searched.* They looked through my stuff, patted me down, and examined everything I had on me, including my knife, which I had to show them how to remove from the secret haft lock strap I kept on it so that only I could draw it out quickly. They took the car completely apart, spreading the seats and the contents of our luggage all over the ground, but they didn't find anything. They didn't check June's bra, which was where we had hidden some hash, so we were okay. They were civilized Arabs after all, and they didn't have any females along with them to feel her up, though she might have enjoyed that. Fortunately, it meant that our stash wasn't discovered.

We took seasick pills, smoked hash, and fucked all night on the overnight ferry to Marseilles. It could be that being in danger and risking your life is an aphrodisiac—or maybe we were just happy and horny. From Marseilles, we drove our rental car back to Lisbon and flew to somewhere else to venture forth on the ground again for a while before separating again. I was thinking, *I love it when a plan comes together!*

So I don't want to do a country-by-country travelogue here, but in the next few chapters I will hit upon the high spots of some of the places I went and the things I did over the rest of the course of that year on the road when I was thirty-three and thirty-four. It wasn't all bliss and there were times of being sick with the shits in various places, a little stress now and then, and a case of the hemorrhoids that I remember well, but compared to my regular life at home there were a lot of perks, wonderful lessons, and incredible experiences on the road that I wouldn't trade for anything.

CHAPTER 34

American Express

After our adventures in Portugal and North Africa, June and I went to Paris. There we had a fine time doing things tourists do, including meeting people at the American Express office. Travelers from all over the world would go to the American Express office to collect mail sent to them from home or receive and leave messages from other travelers they'd told where they were headed. It's hard to imagine in our current cell-phone era how our antiquated communication systems worked back then—and how well—but this service was essential in terms of meeting up with friends on the road and finding out news from home and in places we were headed.

We took a little flat in Paris for a week or ten days and ventured out from there on daily excursions to museums, cathedrals, and restaurants. I'd been to Paris before with Judy, Jim, and Louise in 1968, but on this visit I got to indulge myself longer in certain places I'd loved seeing then.

After about a week, when we were thoroughly settled and happy, we decided to use Daddy's American Express Card to go have a fine meal. We'd met another young woman we both liked and we'd spent the night before with her. The next day we proposed that the three of us go out to the finest restaurant in Paris for a meal. That evening stands out in my memory as a measure of how great life can be. I have told this story many times, bragging about my luck. "I did this," I say. "How is this for a fine time?"

I was in Paris with two beautiful women. They were lovers with each other and with me. We smoked hashish and went to the best restaurant in Paris. We had drinks and two $400 bottles of wine (in 1973) and a seven-course meal spread over a two and a half hour period, delighting in the most wonderful French food in all of heaven. After which, we went home full and full of happiness, and tipsy, and we got stoned again, made love, and fell asleep in each other's arms. We stayed in bed half of the next day, and then sang songs and wandered out and back, and laughed and read, and sang again. Had I died then, with the memory of the best bottle of Pommard I've ever tasted and the best Saint-Émilion in the world still ringing in my palette, along with the best food I've ever eaten and some of the best sex (stoned on some of the world's best hashish) still titillating its last titillations in the hallways of my mind, while listening to the sweet sounds of the voices of sexually sated, grateful, loving, beautiful women, I would have died happy.

Other than that not much happened in Paris.

CHAPTER 35
Song of Affirmation

Here are the lyrics to "Footloose and Free" a song I wrote in 1974, on the road.

I met a longhaired man in Amsterdam, living on a boat out there.
I asked him if he was content or if he had any care.
He said, "I want to be footloose and free and taken by surprise,
Not tied down and runnin' round like all these other guys.
But it gets my goat. I've gotta fix my boat. So I gotta go into town.
After the store, we'll talk some more, if you keep on hangin' round."

I spent a month and a day in old Norway, tryin' to get laid.
A sweet young girl I met out there listened to me sing and play.
She said to me, "Sex is free! Just anytime you holler.
But the pat on the head and breakfast in bed cost a hundred and
*   fifty dollars."*

Chorus: We all want to be footloose and free and taken by surprise,
Not tied down and runnin' round like all these other guys.
And I don't know whether we're alone together or if I'm the only
*   man.*
But I keep on tryin' to keep from cryin', doin' the best I can.

On a hashish farm with more than charm in the mountains of
*   Maroc*
I saw a man leading a mule and he chose my place to stop.

He was poor and tired and uninspired, and rags was all he wore.
He said, "Hello son. Are you havin' fun? If not, I'll give you some
*   more.*
'Cause we all wanna be, footloose and free . . ." (last two lines mod-
    ified)
And I ain't no fool, I'm leadin' this mule, and I'm doin' the best that
*   I can."*

Quiet as a mouse in a little white house on an island down in Greece
I looked at the sea and it talked to me just a pretty as you please.
It said, "Life behaves like the wind and the waves and the stars up in
*   the sky.*
It rolls and blows, then it glows, and then you have to die."

Chorus: *I keep on tryin' to keep from lyin', doin' the best that I can.*

That song was written to my fellow travelers, including those who
thought they lived in the places where I stopped. One of the things I came
to understand on that trip was that we're all doing the best that we can given
the conditions we were born into. And if we are to do better (and because
of the suffering we cause each other, we could do better), we could do so by
getting that we're all doing the best that we can—and maybe we could col-
laborate. Starting there, we could love being as we are, and then we'd be able
to come up with something with less suffering in it for all of us. There could
be a difference between lives lived in reaction to history and circumstance,
and lives lived out of creative collaboration between people who identify
with each other in compassion, good humor, and mutual respect.

Even with all the horrible shit that has happened in the almost forty
years since then, all in all, as Jeremy Rifkin, author of *The Empathic Civilization*, says, we are moving in that direction. Slow as snails, but moving
in that direction.

After Paris, June and I went our separate ways for three weeks. I went
to Amsterdam, then Scandinavia, and then back to Amsterdam. In Norway,
I played music on the street in Oslo and discovered Flam, a beautiful, little
village at the innermost point of the fjords, inland from Bergen, where I fell
in love with a beautiful woman who laughed a lot and loved me a lot, but
nonetheless wouldn't give me a tumble. Flam is one of the most beautiful
places I've ever been, with its tiny seaport and mountains rising straight up

high above it. I have been back there several times. That's where I read all four volumes of *The Alexandria Quartet*, sitting outside, surrounded by all that beauty.

I had a great time in Amsterdam the first time around, so I wrote June at the American Express in Brussels, I think, and suggested we meet up back there and stay for a while. We met and stayed another ten days or so.

The first time there I lived in a caboose car from a train on a barge in the canals. And when I went back, I ended up playing music each day with a small group of guitar players and singers on a different barge set up to serve marijuana tea to middle-class travelers from around the world. The barge was called "The Heads Tour of Amsterdam" and I acted like I lived there and was welcoming them into the world of Amsterdam and the world of pot. It was a listed tour at the train station, airport, and docks. People paid a price and signed up, and then got to go on a tour bus, drink tea, get stoned, and hear music, and go to cafés and head shops, and be introduced to the counterculture over the counter, so to speak. Those of us who worked there had a fine time because we were getting paid a little for getting stoned and playing music. I mean, life was really tough! I had to learn how to play almost all of Bob Dylan's songs and a bunch of Beatles' songs to boot!

They had this place in Amsterdam called The Oasis, or The Cosmos, or something wonderful like that, which seemed welcoming, new, multi-faceted, and multicultural, and grounded, sensate, and sexy, and a few other good things. You'd go there and buy a ticket for the day. Inside it had a gigantic sauna that could hold thirty people. You'd go into a dressing room, take off all your clothes, and then go into the sauna. There were lots of people in there, including a lot of very beautiful women. Everyone was naked and sweating. There was not much talking, instead people were focusing mostly on just sweating and staying in there as long as they could stand it.

When you left the sauna, there was a gigantic barrel the size of a small pool, full of water with ice cubes floating in it. It had a ladder so you could climb up the side of the barrel and take the plunge. That sudden shock and surround of ice water was curiously refreshing. But it's not the kind of thing you might want to indulge in for a long time if you're some dumb-assed hillbilly from Virginia, like me. It took a little more getting used to than I ever could get used to, but it did turn on the lights of the mind and body for a bit.

After the plunge, there was a place with lots of pads to lie down on in a big, flat space up on the top of the sauna. There was room for maybe forty people to go lie down and just reverberate from the sauna and the plunge.

You could relax, do yoga, meditate, or take a nap as you recovered from your shock treatment. At The Oasis you could talk some with people if you and they wanted, and you could also go for a stroll on an outdoor patio, a kind of courtyard surrounded by the building. It would usually be misting with a little rain outside, and this was pleasant and refreshing.

On the way out to the courtyard there was a gigantic hookah with about thirty stems coming from it to a circle of cushions surrounding it. You could go and sit on a cushion and take a few tokes of hash as you proceeded back or forth from the sauna and the resting area to the courtyard.

After about an eon of overindulgence in those experiences, if you'd had enough of that, you could put on some clothes and go to the bar, café, restaurant, or dance hall, where a live band was playing in the afternoon and evening. You could eat, drink, dance, talk, play backgammon or chess, read, or do whatever you liked in there for as long as you liked whenever you liked. If you met someone and wanted to leave for a while, you could do that and come back later without having to get another ticket.

All of Amsterdam back then was such a trip. I kept hearing and, when I got the chance, playing, Kris Kristofferson's song "Me and Bobby McGee," which was made famous by Janice Joplin. We were singin' it and livin' it:

Freedom's just another word for nothin' left to lose,
Nothin' ain't worth nothin', but it's free.
Feeling good was easy Lord, when Bobby sang the blues.
And feelin good was good enough for me,
Good enough for me and Bobby McGee.

In Amsterdam in 1973 we were living free as best as we could. And if I do say so myself, doing a damned fine job of it. That's why I had suggested to June we return to Amsterdam to meet up.

One of the things we did together in Amsterdam was go to a live sex show. Over in the infamous Red Light District there were several places where you could go to watch people fuck on stage. They got paid for it, and people who attended bought tickets to watch. Some of what happened in the audience was sexier than what was on stage at the time.

Some of the couples performing on stage were pretty, but were going through a routine, and, kind of like in porno movies, they weren't too exciting because they were doing a ritual to hit the high spots of what is supposed to be exciting to an audience. So they would kiss, feel each other up, undress, touch, suck, and fuck pretty much by the numbers.

Every now and then a young couple of first-timers would get up there on stage, ignore the script, and follow their passion. They'd be excited by being watched and actually have a lot of fun fucking and doing what they wanted to do next instead of following a plan. And the couples in the audience would then start making out, eating each other, or sometimes fucking in their theater-style seats while they were watching the couple fuck on stage. That was pretty exciting.

I can't remember what June and I did, but I think she gave me a blow job and I touched her some, though she didn't come. Then we went home after the show and fucked. The whole show was exciting both sexually and as another glorious aspect of liberation. We thought we were pretty cool to go there, and we had a hell of a lot of fun doing it. Liberation, libation, inebriation, and co-creation were us.

I mean, it was a hard life, but we bore up under the pressure of it, so to speak. That is why we went to Amsterdam—to toughen up for our trek northward along the coast of Norway to the Land of the Midnight Sun, living forever on a freighter with a few cabins for travelers.

CHAPTER 36

Sound of Fog Horn, Picture of Fog, Feel of Limbo

Onboard our Norwegian freighter, we live in an eternal white fog. It goes on for days. No day. No night. Just grey and cool, drizzly and wet, with a constant dull background hum. We play cards, two-person Bridge, for hours at a time. We finish books. We talk. We read again.

We are lying in our bunks reading. We've slept and awoken and gone to breakfast and come back with the same, constant background noise of engines, regular, pulsing—invariant—accompanying us. We are comfortable, but not too excited. The highlight of our day is drinks and dinner in the bar café in what we used to call "the evening." The boat goes on and on.

After a long time, we stop in a port for an evening, docking "overnight," and go to a movie. It's a John Wayne movie from America. This is a small town with a nice, big theatre with comfy seats, and the movie is like a taste of home. I can't remember the name of the movie, but John Wayne is his mucho-macho self and we're enjoying it. I am sitting on the outside seat next to the aisle and June is sitting on the first seat next to me. Somewhere in the middle of the movie, an usher suddenly comes by and kicks June's foot off of the top of the seat in front of her. June had put her foot up with her heel resting on top of the next row, a seat that had nobody in it. She was just relaxing and there was no chance she would mess up the seat or get it dirty, but this guy, about my size, just came by, and kicked his foot right in front of me and knocked her foot off the top of the seat.

Well shit! I'm in the middle of a John Wayne movie! I stand up instantly, grab him by his usher-suit lapels, jerk him straight up in the air, and throw him about ten feet down the aisle! He bounces and rolls, scrambles and jumps up, and then runs like hell out of the theater through the doors to the concession *stand. I realize then, that I am not John Wayne. I am in a movie theater, not in a movie, so I sit down and watch the movie again.*

When we leave the movie I look around for the usher and see him hiding behind the popcorn stand. I just laugh and wave at him and we leave. It is a small interlude to our constant trip into the eternal fog.

Another interlude stands out in my memory for a different reason. Somewhere during our five days and nights of traveling that were neither day nor night, June was in the cabin while I was drinking beer in the bar. I met a man I liked and we talked for a while. He was from Norway and was taking the freighter up along the coast to a town it came to port in. After a while, he left and went out on the deck. After ordering another beer, I went out there, too. I found him standing at the rail alone, looking at the coastline and crying. I went over to him and asked what was wrong. He looked at me, and then he pointed over to a small light on the shore. He said, "I am sad when I see that light." I waited. Then he told me his story.

"Over twenty years ago now," he said, "I was a young soldier in the Resistance. The Nazis had taken over Norway and small contingents of their troops were guarding ports to keep us from sending volunteers down and across the English Channel to join the war against Germany. We got together a large group of volunteers to go over, and we attacked the small garrison, stationed there where that little light was. There were only three soldiers. We killed two in the attack and captured one young soldier, who was about my age, eighteen years old.

"After the attack, we quickly loaded our boat to the maximum capacity, and there was no room left for a prisoner. I was to be the last to get on, and before I did, my commander told me that we couldn't take the young man we'd captured. But we couldn't leave him behind either because there was too big a chance that he'd notify German vessels that could intercept or overtake and destroy us. He told me I had to go back in and kill the soldier, and then come aboard our boat.

"I went inside and told the boy what my commander had told me, and asked him if there was anything he wanted me to do for him after the war. He asked that if I survived I go to his hometown and tell his parents how he'd died. He gave me their names and told me how to contact them. Then I killed him."

He stopped and cried some more. Then he said, "After the war I did go back and found his parents and told them how their son had died. We all cried together. They asked me to stay for a while and I did. "When I was leaving, the boy's parents asked me to return again. I said yes, that I would. And I have. I have visited them over the years when I can and they have, in a way, adopted me and treat me now as though I am their son."

Then he cried some more. And I cried too. We just stood there for a while. Finally he said, "War is a God-damned, rotten, hell of a thing."

I nodded.

Our freighter pulled into his port of call. We shook hands and he left.

I went and told June the story. We cried. The freighter backed out and we went on our way through the fog. Sometimes it seemed like the fog might just go on forever.

We went up past Finland to the Land of the All-time Clouds with Drizzle and Light and stayed a little while, and then took the long journey back. We got a lot of books read and played a lot of Bridge under the bridge. By the time we got back to Southern Europe, we were ready to travel separately again.

CHAPTER 37
From the Land of the Midnight Sun to a Place of Peace in Greece

I headed for Greece, planning to go to the Island of Patmos again. Before-hand, I stopped in Athens and rented a typewriter. I stayed in Athens a bit to get mail from the American Express office and hear the news from America. The Watergate scandal was going on right then. I bought a short-wave radio so I could hear The Voice of America on Patmos. I took that and my typewriter and went on the eleven-hour-long voyage to Patmos by ferry. The long, sunny day, blue sky, warm breeze, and lovely memories of where I was headed and my plans to finally get fully underway in writing my novel, The Eternal Split-second Sound-light Being, all made me happy. I felt very much alive. I went there in late August and stayed until sometime in November. I rented a house on a bay and settled into writing.

In the mornings after working on my novel, I'd take what I had written and walk across to another bay where a woman friend of mine was staying and I'd give the pages to her to read. In the next day or two, I'd go back and trade those pages, which she had now read and commented on, for what I had newly written. We'd talk some and I'd try to get her to sleep with me; she wouldn't, so I'd go back to my house and write some more.

Spiro Agnew resigned as Vice President of the United States in October. And he wasn't the only Greek with troubles at the time. The Greek govern-ment was having its own problems right then, too. I was in Patmos when Taxiarkhos Dimitrios Ioannides, a disgruntled Junta hardliner, overthrew George Papadopoulos the same year. Military law was reinstated, and Ioan-nides remained the behind-the-scenes strongman.

All the young communists from Athens fled to the islands following the coup d'état. The military pursued them and set up a temporary prison on the island of Lesbos as a place to corral them once they were found.

The military sent a whole company of troops to Patmos to enforce martial law. This was a big event for the island, which had never had police or a jail or anything like it. There had been a Greek Orthodox monastery on top of the hill above the harbor for 300 years or so, and the main tourist attraction on the island was the cave right below the monastery where John, the brother of Jesus, had his vision of the Apocalypse and wrote *The Book of Revelation,* and I'd had my parallel hallucinogenic vision years before.

The island always had a population of less than 5,000 people, and the only semi-law enforcement official ever to have any authority there at all was the harbor master, who was a drunk. But he had a hat: the harbor master's hat. He was the only law anyone had any familiarity with other than the head of the monastery.

Having troops on Patmos to enforce a curfew was the first event in which military force had been seen on the island since the Italians had captured it before World War Two and then lost it back again 30 years later. This was an island that, in 1968, when I first visited it, had no gasoline-powered motor vehicles on it whatsoever, whose sole forms of entertainment from the outside world were a few radios and a single jukebox in front of the harbor building. In 1973, as of yet, it still had only a few automobiles. When tourists came to visit the monastery, they went up the hill on donkeys.

Law enforcement in the few scattered villages on the five-mile-long island consisted of simply adding an addendum to the names of those caught breaking the law so that for the rest of their lives whenever they were introduced or spoken of, they'd be called something like, "Yannis, who got drunk when he was nineteen and stole his grandfather Pericles' clock, and then hauled it away on Stephanos' mule." At times this would be shortened to "Yannis, the clock and mule thief." The likelihood of such a thing being remembered and reported this way seemed to be all the law enforcement needed in a place where everyone knew everyone or at least knew of them. I think one of the reasons I so loved Greece is that it reminded me so much of the hillbillies and small-town folk I knew back in the mountains of Virginia as a child.

So the military, in attempting to establish their authority, put a lot of young communists in jail or in exile on the Island of Lesbos established a curfew for cities and towns, and did a number of other things to demonstrate their intent to establish control. One of the more bizarre things they did was to outlaw the playing of any music by Theodrakis, the most famous kind of Bob Dylan type of figure in Greece, an advocate of freedom and a songwriter and singer literally everyone knew and admired.

I had been on Patmos for about six weeks then and had, because I played a lot of Dylan songs in an outdoor café, befriended a number of young greeks whose sympathies were for greater freedom and against the dictatorship. So when the taboo came down from Athens we happily went to the mountaintop to celebrate violating the dictates of the Colonels. We took bottles of wine and guitars to the top of the mountain, one bay over from the main town, invited a few others, and drank wine and played only Theodrakis songs and Bob Dylan songs late into the night. And on that night, it just happened that one of the very unusual combination of circumstances came about, that occur so infrequently no one could really say when it had ever occurred before or not. Mainly, these two things happened at the same time: It was the night of the full moon, and it was also a time when the Aegean sea had had no wind and no waves for three or four days preceding the night of the full moon.

The water had settled so that there were no waves and the impression in the moonlight was of a big still quiet lake as far as one could see. We had been standing and talking some, looking out at the sea. When the moon got directly overhead, all of a sudden we all stopped talking, struck dumb by the event. As the moon got straight overhead the entire sea reflected the silver white face of the moon, like a mirror. You could see, it seemed, forever. All the other islands, that you could usually only see in the daylight, were clearly out there on the mirror. They looked like little piles of sand—like anthills of different sizes and distances away, placed on the surface of a gigantic beautiful larger-than-life silvery white mirror. In that great stillness in which being reflected upon itself not a word was spoken by any of us and the spell was not broken. Tears began running down my face. I felt such gratitude for being, such fullness and awe and breathlessness and carefulness to not cause a pin to drop. I don't know how long I stood like that because my mind stopped, or time stopped, or time stood still or something happened so profound any words to point to could only sound like some cliché... I breathed breath after breath after breath, and when I thought next it seemed like it had been a lot of breaths. I looked over at the faces of the others, all of whom had grown up on this island, been here all their lives, wondering if they somehow might be familiar with such a thing, maybe used to it. And I was surprised to see tears running down all their faces too. No one spoke a word. Even when the moon passed it's peak overhead and the sea became just the merely beautiful full moon night sea again and the mirror disappeared, there were a few "My God"'s but we spoke very little even after the fact ,in Greek or English. We gathered our instruments and walked home in silence. We were sated. We didn't want to talk. I was grateful again for that, and smiled inside, as I did for days after. No one tried to speak of what we had shared, though I am sure no one doubted it either. We didn't want to cheapen it by trying to praise or talk or brag about it. Some day maybe one of us will write a song about It. (Every time I have tried so far, I hear, "In the light...of the silvery moon...da da da da da"... so I might be blocked forever.)

Sometimes the light just breaks through. Sometimes the wind blows right through. I understand the hesitancy of all purveyors of the ecstatic love of reality to move or think or distort in any way the light that enlightens the light but to just pray to it to allow you to be it's instrument and promise to be the very best of servants.

Leonard Cohen gets it. Affirmation includes all despair and all futility into the great joy of imperfection perfectly.

"Anthem"

The birds they sang
at the break of day
Start again
I heard them say
Don't dwell on what
has passed away
or what is yet to be.
Ah the wars they will
be fought again
The holy dove

She will be caught again
bought and sold
and bought again
the dove is never free.

Ring the bells that still can ring
Forget your perfect offering
There is a crack in everything
That's how the light gets in.

We asked for signs
the signs were sent:
the birth betrayed
the marriage spent
Yeah the widowhood
of every government —
signs for all to see.

I can't run no more
with that lawless crowd
while the killers in high places
say their prayers out loud.
But they've summoned, they've summoned up
a thundercloud
and they're going to hear from me.

Ring the bells that still can ring ...

You can add up the parts
but you won't have the sum
You can strike up the march,
there is no drum
Every heart, every heart
to love will come
but like a refugee.

Ring the bells that still can ring
Forget your perfect offering

There is a crack, a crack in everything
That's how the light gets in.

Ring the bells that still can ring
Forget your perfect offering
There is a crack, a crack in everything
That's how the light gets in.
That's how the light gets in.
That's how the light gets in.

My son Elijah was talking to me recently about chaos theory and he said that they say that creation comes from the edges of chaos, where chaos and order meet. In terms of the light that enlightens the light—our consciousness that allows us to see the light—the eternal split second sound light way of being while being on the way—includes all the dark and all of the struggle and all of the shitty and the less than perfect! Without the dark we can't see the light in more ways than one.

Anyway, during the coup, we all knew that singer-songwriter Mikis Theodrakis' album *Songs of Freedom* was outlawed. But by God, mine weren't, and neither were those of Bob Dylan, Kris Kristofferson, The Beatles, or John Prine or the many other songwriters whose lyrics I knew, as did Theodrakis.

So, a few nights after the light lit me up, when I performed in an outdoor café on the night of the troops arriving in Patmos to enforce the curfew, I played and sang songs of freedom to a particularly diverse and somewhat strange audience. There were a number of Australians still in town, a few Americans, a bunch of Germans, and a larger number than usual of recently arrived, young Greek guys. The group surrounded me and people bought me drinks or came and poured liquid into my glass from their vessels in support of my performance. I had a few ouzos, some beer, and some retsina—in whatever order they arrived from whoever sent them over—and I ate whatever showed up in about the same way.

When nine o'clock rolled around, the waiters came out and said it was last call because of the curfew. I was slightly more than half drunk and I said to everyone, "You'd better order a lot, because I'm not going anywhere! I don't like curfews and l don't like cops! I don't like troops! I don't even like the priests up on the hill because they are cops, too! Fuck 'em! I'm not going anywhere!" Then I had another drink or two, played another song or two, and repeated myself more than once or twice, shouting the same rap.

I didn't quite understand what was going on, but the young Greek guys on the periphery of the circle of foreign tourists were shouting to the crowd in Greek each time I spoke, and the number of people surrounding me grew from the original fifteen or twenty to about seventy people or so. I kept singing and preaching until 11:00 or 11:30, when I was too drunk to do it anymore. The twenty soldiers gathered about a block away under some trees retreated a little further from us the larger my audience grew.

When I left to walk home with an Aussie friend who I'd rented a room in my house to, we walked right by them and happily waved, and they waved back. Or I should say "we staggered by," because about halfway back on the mile or so walk to the bay where my house was, I lay down on the ground and vomited and passed out. I awoke early the next morning with my face covered in mud from having slept with my face in the wet spot where I puked. I still didn't feel too good. I meandered down next to the sea and washed up a little bit, then jumped in and swam around for a while, then went home, fell into bed, and slept until sometime in the early afternoon. I woke up feeling okay, but kind of hungry, so I cleaned up, changed clothes, put my cowboy hat on, and headed back into town toward the taverna to get a meal.

I headed up the pathway from my house to the dirt road leading into town and passed a little white house that belonged to a small family I knew only by sight. Usually we just waved to each other, but on this day they came out shouting my name. Everyone in town called me "Texas" because my hat, beard, long hair, and blue jeans reminded them of the cowboy movies they'd seen from America. "Tex-Sass! Tex-Sass!" my neighbors shouted as I tried to pass. They patted me on the back, led me into their house, and gave me a shot of ouzo and some feta cheese and a bite to eat. They kept slapping me on the back, dancing, and shaking my hand. They were refilling my little glass of ouzo whenever I took a sip.

Pretty soon I escaped. But at the next house I came to on my route the same thing happened! And on and on it went. Each house I tried to pass I couldn't get by without going in, being congratulated, and being given a drink! I couldn't understand enough Greek to grasp what was going on, but it was kind of fun so I went along. By the time I got back to town I was drunk again. Finally, I found a waiter I knew, in the first restaurant at the edge of town, who spoke English. I was finally able to ask him, "What in the hell is going on?" He laughed and slapped me on the back. "You are a hero," he said. "Last night you overthrew the government!" He pulled me into the taverna and everyone there came out and acted just like all the folks along the way to town had acted.

The young Greek guys from Athens who were shouting the night before, were translating what I'd said and yelling it to the crowd and gathering people around me in support and defiance of the government's soldiers. Even though the troops were armed and we weren't, they were hesitant to try to actually enforce the curfew for fear of being overcome by the crowd! We outnumbered them, so we sat and drank, sang and danced, and in the process defied the curfew and we won.

For days, and I mean *days*, I went into restaurants and bars and took friends along and we had meals, drinks, and a regular ongoing party, and when we'd finished, and I said, *"Logariasmo?* (Check?), the owners wouldn't hear of it. "Oh no, Texas!" they would say, "No *Logariasmo*, Tex-Sass! No *Logariasmo!"* I literally couldn't pay for a thing, nor could anyone who came in with me. I'd defeated the Colonels! The troops actually left the day after I sang and didn't ever return. That made me a hero. Personally, I was just drunk and obliviously bitching about the authorities as usual. But apparently my spirit was in the right place at the right time.

Even when I came back to Patmos a couple of years later, as I came into the harbor on a big ship, standing at the rail with my cowboy hat on, some of the kids recognized me and ran into town. A crowd came running out to meet me. They took my bags and guitar for me and then lifted me up on their shoulders and carried me into town. Again, I wasn't allowed to pay for a thing for days.

After that, June came and joined me for a couple of weeks in Patmos, and she fell in love with Greece too. She had also traveled to other islands in Greece and she decided she wanted to spend the winter at an artists' colony on the island of Paros. For myself, I decided I wanted to go through the Middle East alone. So we did that. We left open the possibility of meeting up someplace before going home to the U.S., but in the end we didn't. She met a man with whom she wanted to be monogamous, and a year or two later they got married and settled down.

I left Patmos then, full of the great gift of the light and went to Turkey and then on to Iran, Afghanistan, Pakistan, and India. I was footloose and free, and the whole world was trying to join me.

CHAPTER 38
Istanbul, Teheran, Kabul

Near the end of November, Istanbul was my next stop. I met some travelers going by bus from Amsterdam to India and we hung out for a few nights playing music and getting to know each other. I also met a French woman who couldn't speak English, but knew the lyrics to all the Bob Dylan songs I knew and sang along with me with great delight. Her name was Marie. She was paired up with a man on the bus trek, but she asked me to check for a message from her in New Delhi at the American Express office whenever I got there, so that maybe I could hang out with her and her boyfriend. She was slim, blonde, and pretty, and she spoke French, which in and of itself made me horny. I suspected that her pairing at the time was a matter of convenience.

When Marie and the other travelers from Amsterdam left on their bus, I took off for Teheran. I wasn't feeling very good, but I flew to Iran anyway. Once I landed, it was clear I had dysentery. I checked into an expensive hotel so I'd have a comfortable place to get over my fever and the shits. I stayed a couple of days, drank a lot of water, took some pills, and went through the flu-like symptoms until I got over it. I moved to cheaper digs after I recovered and stayed about a week more there, mostly hanging out with some people I met at an artisans' co-operative.

This is where I met the special agent I mentioned before who'd just come from Vietnam, and told me he was buying and selling money on the black market. At first, he couldn't tell me exactly what he was doing or he'd have to kill me . . . blah blah blah. Then we got moderately drunk together, and he said that if you could predict and follow the wars around the world you could make money whether or not you were "working for the government." But since he did work for the government and had inside information, making money was like taking candy from a baby.

After only a little over a week in Teheran, I flew to Kabul. I'd heard from other hippies coming my way that Afghanistan was a place to be wary of. Various tales of hippies being captured at the border and given haircuts against their will were mixed in with stories of how the jails were, using adjectives that ranged from "terrible" to "magnificent." Some junkies then, the stories went, stayed in jail because their jailers (who only made ten cents a day for pay) would wait on them hand and foot, and bring them food, drugs, and women to have sex with them for only a dollar more per day. But the kind of treatment prisoners got seemed to be the luck of the draw.

I knew I was coming into the airport, which was probably safer than coming into the country on a bus, but I was geared up for possible trouble anyway. I had a bad attitude and a mean fucking look. I wrote a song for me or my friends to play if the officials detained me, in hopes of rallying folks around me if needed. What the hell? It had worked in Greece.

Here's part of the song.

I was in the East travelin' along
They didn't like me at the border cause my hair's too long
So I thought I'd write those folks a song
To let 'em know I think that they're wrong

Chorus: *You can keep your mountains and you can keep your grass*
Keep your dictator and keep kissin' his ass
Keep law and order and marital bliss, and keep your God-damned
nose outta my bizness!

I had that song going through my head when I approached the table in the airport with the customs agents at it. I also had a long beard, a lot of hair, and a cowboy hat that had seen better days. At my side was my great big knife with a handle that made you infer a hell of a blade in the scabbard, which disappeared into my pocket. (It's amazing, but you were allowed to carry shit like that on a plane in those days.) I wore my usual combination of boots and jeans, and was carrying my usual load of a backpack and a guitar over my shoulder. I stood up tall and tromped right up to the gendarmes' table looking like I was looking for a fight. I looked them in the eye and answered their questions in a voice that said basically, "Don't fuck with me unless you want to get fucked with back." Surprisingly they let me right through.

I was a little disappointed. But I didn't press my luck. My delusions could have been reversed quite easily, and I knew it was a bluff in the first place.

In 2011, the time of this writing, Egyptian president Hosni Mubarak has just been overthrown in Egypt. He came to power there ten years after I was in Afghanistan and remained in power for all those thirty plus years during the fuckups of the Soviet Union and U.S in Afghanistan, which are still going on to this day. It occurs to me that the last verse of my song for the East was predictive of those future events. It goes:

Me and your people been walkin' through the rice
And we don't think you been actin' too nice
And one of these days when you're under the weather
We're gonna come down the road singin' this song together
We want the mountains and we want the grass
Don't want no dictator he can kiss our ass
Keep law and order and marital bliss, But keep your God-damned
      nose outta our bizness!

A few Afghani hippies that hung out with traveling hippies like me liked that song back in 1973. Perhaps it was a butterfly wing that helped change the weather in Egypt almost forty years down the road. In any case, it sure made me rejoice on January 25, 2011, when the people of Egypt came out in Tahrir Square in Cairo and refused to go back home until Mubarak was gone.

There wasn't any American Express office in Kabul then. I forget why. But there was a post office and that was a kind of substitute gathering place. There were also teahouses where hippies would gather and drink hash tea, and eat munchies of various kinds. One teahouse had a giant, courtyard-sized chess set with three-foot-by-three foot squares and chess pieces made of carved wood that weighed about sixty pounds each. There were large, throne-like chairs on either side of the board. Players would sit on these thrones so they could look down upon the battlefield and make up their minds about their next move. Then they would stand up, march over to a piece, heft it up, and move it to another square. It was kind of exercise for health—aerobic chess—and an important demonstration of scale.

I met a woman there from Australia. We started living together to save money, but she didn't want to sleep with me. She was on a kind of sex fast.

She asked if I had a guru I was following. I said no, but that there were several I liked. I asked her if she had a guru. She said, "Yes. Joseph Campbell. He's an American." I said, "I know. I've read his work and I like him very much." I had first heard of Campbell when I was in the CFLC in Austin, when one of the former residents came back and gave us a presentation about Campbell's book about the hero's journey, or mono-myth. We became friends and talked long into the nights about what we'd read and what we thought about it. Years later Campbell's work became central to the design of the Radical Honesty workshop I still teach.

One day when we were walking back to our digs from the post office, one of the teen-aged boys in the crowd near the market ran forward and grabbed one of my friend's breasts. She grabbed him instantly and, falling down, pulled him down, too, and threw him on the ground. The boy jumped up and I grabbed him, lifted him up by his coat lapels, and held him up against a wall off the ground. I asked her, "What do you want me to do with him?" She said, "You can let him go now," so I did, and he ran away.

She told me, "I have to do that. In traveling through these Muslim countries, I've found that even though I wear a shawl and keep my body covered up by long sleeves and long dresses, sometimes when young men see my face and know I am a foreigner they consider me free game to cop a feel. But I get so mad when they invade me like that I have to fight them back so I can drop it sooner. Otherwise I carry it around with me all the rest of the day or sometimes for many days."

I understood completely. She told me that, not knowing I was a Gestalt therapist or that I taught folks to express themselves when they are angry and experience their experience to get through it. She'd learned that on her own and taught me about it again. Later on, I told her that my teacher Fritz Perls would have been proud of her.

Another thing happened to me early one afternoon in Kabul when I was breezing through the market and headed for the teahouse stoned on hash. All of a sudden three men grabbed me. One stood on either side of me holding my arms, and the other one got behind me and put his left arm around my front across my stomach and tried to pull my knife from its haft on my right side. I had a hidden clamp on the knife so that when he tugged on it several times in rapid succession it wouldn't come out. His tugging gave me some adrenaline right quick. I whirled to my left, stabilized by the guy on my right holding onto me, and threw the guy on my right through the air into a bunch of baskets at a stall in the market, knocking the canopy down.

I elbowed the guy behind me in the gut and he turned me loose, and so did the guy on my left when I knocked him into the same mess of bouncing baskets. Of course there was an instant crowd of one hundred-plus people around us. Then, in the distance, I saw two cops running our way. I ran like hell the other way, because to be rescued by cops in Kabul is as bad as being robbed and could have meant anything from paying a costly bribe to incarceration.

I was running zigzag all over hell. It was like the movies! I was on hash and adrenalin! And I escaped!

After the incident I went and drank some hash tea at the teahouse, and played a game of giant chess.

CHAPTER 39

India

As soon as I got to New Delhi I went to the American Express office and picked up a note from Marie, the French woman from Istanbul who was a Bob Dylan fan. She told me that she was no longer paired with the male traveling companion she'd had, and how to find her. We met up and moved in together for a while, and then took off together to go see the Taj Mahal. Marie had been a speed freak in Paris, she said, and had gone on the road to escape her addiction. (She said all this using only Bob Dylan lyrics, the only English she knew, and through hand signals and touching.) We laughed a lot and had sex a lot, and it felt quite communicative.

We spent a few days at the Taj Mahal, and used these as a chance to travel to various places nearby the monument. We had the good luck of being there during the full moon. On the night of the full moon, the Taj Mahal is left open all night so visitors can see how it looks in the moonlight. We got stoned and stayed out most of the night. It was incredibly beautiful.

We went back to Delhi and headed south together, and then Marie headed east. We said our goodbyes after that couple of weeks, and departed having loved being together. But we were happily off on the road again. Our language limitations had been perfect.

About six weeks or so later, I was in Katmandu, Nepal, walking down the street and I saw a slim, pretty, blonde woman from a far away distance. She looked right at me and we walked towards each other and then as we got closer we ran and hugged each other. It was Marie! So we took up together again for a few more weeks before we said goodbye forever.

Both before and after traveling with Marie in Nepal, I got to see lots of special places in India and to visit a few ashrams that I'd heard about from roadies and other folks I knew before my trip. For one of the highlights of my whole trip, I got to see Shanti, my little girl, who was four years old then, right there in South India! Judy and Shanti had come to visit Charlie Erikson, my former best friend and her former lover, who'd been in India for many years by then. We all met at an ashram in South India and hung out there for a few days together. I had forgiven Charlie and Judy by then and no longer harbored the fantasy of cutting off his left ear and feeding it to him, as I'd promised to do in a letter I sent to him a few years earlier. (He was an artist, and he liked Van Gogh, so that seemed like a good idea at the time.) Judy and he were lovers there and I was the third wheel, more or less reversing our previous arrangement in Texas. Because they wanted some time alone and I wanted to be with Shanti, I left with Shanti and we traveled around South India alone together for two weeks.

Shanti and I went by bus and on foot. We visited small, interior villages where they'd never seen a blonde child before. We were in places where poor folks fed us and put us up for the night because there was no place to stay except at someone's house. They fed us whatever they themselves were eating for supper. They couldn't speak English and we couldn't speak their language, but they were kind to us and sweet to Shanti. They liked her name and knew it meant "peace" in Sanskrit, and they treated her with reverence as though she were a little goddess, which to me she was. Shanti was tough. When all there was to eat was rice and dal, and the dal was very spicy, she just took rice the first day. By the second day, however, she was eating the spicy dal like it was American home cooking.

One of the places Shanti and I stopped for five days was in a small village in Bangalore, the name of which I can't remember, at the home of a couple from America. We had a fine time there. There were two children about Shanti's age there for her to play with, and adults into Vedanta and spiritual growth for me to play with. There was even a jungle *sadhu,* or holy man, to play with, who the couple had invited to build his ritual fireplace in their backyard. In the evening, he would build his fire and prepare his pipe for the evening. He also prepared a kind of sweet for the children to eat, which caused them to become very energetic and a little bit high, laughing and running around even more than usual. I permitted it for Shanti because the parents of the other kids and of the few Indian kids said it was okay. It was. They and we had a lot of fun.

The kids generally ate and fell asleep before we got started with our activities around the fire pit. After carefully building his ritual fire, our guru prepared a hookah for the evening that held a variety of herbs, spices, hashish, and leaves from various jungle plants. He would fill the bowl of the hookah with about the same amount of contents each evening, and before the main part of the instruction started we had to smoke all of what was in there. If there were twenty people on a particular evening, we smoked it all; if there were nine, we smoked it all, too.

Our teacher taught mostly by playing beautiful music. He had an instrument much like a sitar with front strings that he plucked and back strings that produced sympathetic vibrations, and a drum-like attachment he could play a rhythm on at the same time he plucked the strings. The music was especially entrancing because we were zonked on the hash and herbs, but I am certain that it would have been wonderful regardless of our state of mind. He would usually play for an hour and a half and then we'd take a break and after a short while eat. Then he'd play again for an hour or two and we would disperse.

Some nights the guru would say only a sentence or two while we waited for the food that was being prepared for us by the host family and the local people who came to learn from him. Some nights he wouldn't say a single word.

One night, the guru turned and looked at me, and said, "You went many places when I played that music."

I said, "Yes, I did."

He said, "I took you there."

I said, "Thank you."

He said, "You are welcome."

That was it. That was the verbal lesson for everyone that evening.

Then, several nights later, he seemed to be in a kind of jovial mood. Again, at the pause after the music and before eating, he looked at me and began to speak. He said this. "I was a physician in Delhi. A surgeon. I had a good medical practice. I also had a teacher. One evening my guru said to me, 'Take all of your surgical instruments and put them into your medical bag, walk across the bridge leaving Delhi, throw the bag into the river, go into the jungle for fifteen years, and then return to me for further instructions.' So I did. I took my medical bag and instruments, threw them into the river, and spent fifteen years in the jungle. When I returned my guru was dead. HAHAHAHAHAHAHAHAHAHAHA!"

He really thought it was funny. We all laughed at him laughing at his story, and laughed at the story ourselves. I got it. His music for the second set was particularly beautiful. The next day I left.

I kept smiling inside myself for days and days.

A few days later, I took my little girl back to her mother and my friend Charlie at their ashram and headed for Bombay on my way to Goa.

CHAPTER 40

Goa at Christmas

The next time I ran into Marie, it was in the streets of Bombay. So much for saying goodbye "forever." I was about to start believing in La La Land. I was walking down the street, again in the middle of the day, and she came walking toward me again just like she did in Katmandu! We hugged and laughed and joined arms and walked along together discussing whether to go back to her place or mine to take up together again. I told her I'd been hearing from lots of fellow travelers and American and European residents of India about Goa as the best place to go to for Christmas. She said she'd heard the same stories.

One of the reasons Goa was a Mecca for Euro-Aussie-Ameri-spirit-junkie-hippies was that it was a former Portuguese colony and still partly Christian, so they served wine and Portuguese food! And there were hippies on the beach with all kinds of drugs, and music gatherings at night, and it was cheap as hell. Particularly after having been in India for nearly three months without similar amenities, the prospect of meeting up on beautiful beaches with fellow travelers from the West . . . well, what's not to like? So we headed out for Goa together, with a plan to get there before Christmas and stay there until after Christmas.

We rode a long way on a freight ship and sat on the hard, wooden deck for a day or two. I got hemorrhoids and had to get one lanced by a doctor in his office somewhere in a small village. It was such a relief that I had another burst of days-long gratitude. And then we got to Goa.

You know how you can get your expectations up and look forward to something so much that when you finally get it it's a disappointment? Well, this wasn't like that. In fact, our friends hadn't told us enough about how great Goa was. And we hadn't imagined how great it could be!

When we got there, the white beaches that just went on forever north and south along the coastline afforded us enough joy in and of themselves. There were perfect waves at a perfect temperature and a perfect breeze. But add to them wine, Portuguese food, and the best jungle ganja, and Westerners with musical instruments and paperback books to trade, and just an ever-expanding list of pleasantries like sweet jungle honey and teas of all kinds, and . . . it was sheer heaven.

We found a house that cost about 25 cents a day and moved in. After a day or two, we met other visitors, including another French woman on her way back to France from a stint in Hong Kong as a high-class prostitute. She and Marie liked each other, so she moved in with us. Marie and I were still communicating mostly through Bob Dylan lyrics and since this woman, also named Marie (we called her "Marie 2"), could speak English a bit more, we got to know each other better at the same time. Of course, we all started sleeping together. Both Maries loved having sex with each other and with me.

Here was our typical schedule. We'd awaken in the mornings at about nine o'clock to the sound of a bicycle bell ringing outside our door. One or all of us would go outside, naked as God's own children, and pay a few rupees for a big, hot loaf of freshly baked bread. We'd bring it inside and boil water for tea on our little bottled-gas stove, smoke a little ganja, pour ghee and sweet honey over our bread, feed it to each other, while laughing, drinking our tea, and licking the excess honey off of each other. Then we'd fall into bed again, make love, and sleep for another hour or two. Sometime pretty close to noon we'd go out to the beach, often completely nude, sometimes the girls would wear little g-strings (formal wear). As we walked along the beach, we'd come across little collectives of other tourists, usually smoking something, who would give us a toke or a taste of whatever they were doing in the way of drugs that day. We'd find ourselves a fine little spot on some beautiful dune within sight and sound of the wonderful rolling waves, spread out our towels, get out our books, and read, swim, sunbathe, and body surf to wile away the early afternoon. At about 3 P.M. we'd wander down the beach to a seaside Portuguese restaurant, have a fine meal and some great wine in a leisurely fashion, then wander home and take a nap together again with more sex if anyone wanted any.

At six o'clock in the evening we'd usually get up and dress in a shirt or jacket to keep us warm from the evening breeze and go to a place of music. I would bring my guitar and other tourists would bring musical instruments of different kinds. We then played music and danced together, talked, listened to each other's performances, and got stoned together. It was a fine time. Somewhere in there we might go and eat again. At 1 or 2 A.M. we'd go home together and fall into bed again, make love, fall asleep, and wait for the bicycle bell to do it all again the next day.

It was wonderful! I could barely stand it. After five or six days I had to take a day off and spend the whole day taking a taxi into town, buying a sixty-gallon oil drum, having its top cut off and a hole burnt into it at the bottom with a torch, and having a faucet installed with a showerhead welded to it at the base of the drum. I brought it all back and put it up in a tree near the well, so we could draw water and fill it in the mornings. This way everyone could take showers in fresh water after it had been warmed by the sun all day. I gave it to the little village to use as one more feature to draw hippies and tourists and provide a convenience, both so they could make a little more money and to make life easier for everyone. It was a great improvement and let me give something back.

After that I tolerated about another week or so of bliss, and then I fled. I couldn't take it anymore. It was wonderful and there was nothing to complain about, and that was as hard to take as all heaven!

CHAPTER 41
End of Travelogue, End of Trail

I said goodbye to Marie and Marie 2 and went to Sri Lanka to get a new visa to return to India because I'd used up the time on my current visa for India. I spent a little more time in India, but left pretty soon. I had been on the road then for eleven months and still had airplane tickets left on my around-the-world deal from Pan Am for trips to Tokyo, Bangkok, Australia, Honolulu, and other potential side trips.

I went to Sri Lanka for New Year's Eve and celebrated with a lot of German tourists, including a woman who molested me wonderfully. Then I was off again to Southeast Asia. I must admit though that I was running out of money, my novel was almost finished, and I was starting to yearn for home. My row house, which I'd rented out for a year to a tenant, would be vacant in a month, and I would either have to get someone new to rent it to cover the payment or else go back and live there myself. I decided I was ready to go home. So I remade my plans, leaving Australia out of them and focusing on Bangkok for the longest period of time, because life was cheaper there, and barely touching down in Tokyo and Honolulu.

When I arrived in Bangkok, I happened upon a woman from Europe who lived there and was hooked on heroin. Heroin was cheap and plentiful and a lot of people used it casually. There were no syringes or needles involved, because they weren't necessary. The heroin in Bangkok was pure enough that you could kill yourself from snorting it if you did too much. People who lived there kept little lockets filled with powder hanging around their necks on chains, with tiny spoons attached. They'd open their locket, dip out a little spoonful, and snort heroin in public anywhere they happened to be, often after meals while still sitting in a restaurant.

I took up with my beautiful junkie and told her I'd like to match her habit for three or four days and then quit. She said she thought I could do that. So I did. The only difference between her and me over those days was that she could go out and function when she was high, whereas I'd usually stay in one place, namely our apartment. It was without a doubt one of the most wonderful highs I've ever experienced, one that was all-encompassing. I remember the second day or so, we snorted the same amount in the morning. I stayed home all day until she came back, five hours later. She'd run errands and taken care of her business. When she returned, she laughed and laughed at me because I was sitting exactly the same way in the bed as when she'd left. She asked if I ever got up. I said yes, that I got up to pee and to puke a few times, but when I returned I carefully reassumed my previous mildly slanted, cockeyed, upright position and blissed out again.

Puking, by the way, was a very pleasant experience when high on heroin. I would discharge some yellow fluid and be interested in the experience so much that I forgot to be worried about it. That was a first for me. Another time, on one of those days, she and I were making love. We were in the middle and enjoying it when I became mildly distracted by noticing something interesting about the texture of her skin. We both focused on that, and then on a conversation about it, and we quit fucking and started talking, still enjoying ourselves immensely, but no longer focused on fucking. I had never done that before, either. After about three days I quit the experiment because I was scared of how much I loved being high on heroin. We separated and I went somewhere else, outside of Bangkok, to live for a while.

At my next stop I met and took up with an Australian woman and fell in love with her. I met plenty of beautiful Aussies on that part of the trek, some I slept with, some I did not, but all were experienced road professionals, open to what could happen on short notice. They were headed toward Europe and I toward Australia, but we were familiar with not being in any hurry on the road and we knew how to make the best of what happened to turn up on any given day. I met one of these women in Bangkok. She was so wonderful that she captured and kept me for the whole rest of my time there. And though I'd had fantasies of hooking up with a beautiful Asian woman in Thailand, I didn't mind changing my plans.

About a week after leaving Thailand, I landed in San Francisco in the middle of the night. I was happy to be home. I went to a bar for an after-hours beer to see what it would be like to hear people around me speaking American English. A group of transvestites were just coming in from their evening's work. One of them said to another, "Could you loan me a quarter? I mean, did you do five tricks tonight?" The other said, "Oh I guess so, since maybe one of your five didn't pay you."

Damn! I thought. *I'm home. It sure is good to be back.*

When I took off around the world I'd started my trip from Mount Tamalpais on the coast north of San Francisco, taking pictures facing East. So I returned to Mt. Tamalpais and took pictures facing West when I returned. I still have those pictures, but I got them mixed up and I can't tell which ones are which. So it goes.

After a few days in San Francisco and a week in Berkeley, where I got to see Shanti again, and had someone type up the manuscript of my novel, I finally flew home to Washington, D.C. My journey around the world was over. I was now thirty-four years old. According to my internal time clock, which said I'd die the same way as my daddy, I had three years left to live. I was glad to have done the trip so I could say I'd seen the world and so I'd have an idea about what the world was like. I knew that my perspective from a thin little trip like that was limited. And even though I swam up and down in class structure, and spent a lot of times outside the usual range for tourists, I was happy to have seen so many places and met so many different types people during that year. I was proud that I just up and took off with a backpack and a guitar to go look at what it was like. In that year, I read all the books I'd been waiting to read, I got better on the guitar than I had ever been or have ever been since, I wrote some good songs, and I had adventures I could never have had without being on the road.

I was proud to have written my novel while on the road. Writing that story was the first time I tried to say what my life was about, and its theme turns out to have been the theme of the rest of my life. I didn't publish it until thirty-five years later. In fact, it was the next to last thing I published before writing this autobiography, but at least I got it done.

CHAPTER 42
The Rest of 1974 and 1975
Home Again, Home Again

I came back, moved into my place, got my backlog of mail and other things that had been collected for me by my friend Rita, who took care of things for me while I was gone, and I jumped back into life as I'd known it. The Group Therapy Center of Washington had folded by now, but when I went back to work in private practice I was renting office space from Paul Weisberg again in a building near the corner of Twenty-fourth and M Streets. I started co-leading a group with Paul and started up some ongoing groups of my own. I also reconnected with friends and former lovers and was soon in the social and professional groove again.

A lot had happened politically while I was gone: Watergate, Spiro Agnew's resignation, Gerald Ford becoming Vice President, Nixon being nixed, and then Ford becoming President. The more naïve among us, including me, thought there was an opening for the possibility of actual reform in the system.

A lot of my friends had started studying a spiritual system called Arica from its founder, Oscar Ichazo, who now was offering training in Washington. I enrolled in the forty-day training program, taking classes in the evenings and on weekends over a several-month period. Arica was a mixture of wisdom from a number of meditative, self-defense, and spiritual growth disciplines, with a kind of Sufi bias, which, of course, was my cup of tea. The meditations often were visualizations aided by drawings and assisted by audiotapes of electronic music—and it worked. This was the formalization of the hippie lifestyle into an almost acceptable middle-class mode. It's my belief that hard work on disciplined physical and mental development could help us develop capacities and skills for living and loving. With Arica we were developing yet another alternative community and, for a while there, it was working pretty well.

It turned out that Joanie, daughter of Barbara Mullens, who was one of my former Gestalt Therapy Center colleagues, and the wife of my friend Rich Mullens, was teaching the exercise class in some of our sessions in Arica. Joanie always wore a beautiful, body-molding, stretchy outfit that made it hard not to follow her every move, and made it hard if you followed every move as well. She and I went out on a date and did a little coke and got a little stoned, and then had a lot of sex. It was high and happy. I told her that I'd had sex with her mother and father once at their cottage in the mountains when I had gone to visit them on my motorcycle and spent the night. Rich and I both had sex with her mom, taking turns several times, and we had a great time. Joanie and I went to talk it over with mom and dad, and they admitted it to Joanie, and we all wondered what the world was coming to, so to speak. They were kind of happy that Joanie and I had taken up together, but pretty much told her to be careful about her heart, because I was not a model of monogamy.

When we settled into an ongoing thing, Joanie told me that we didn't have to worry about using contraception because she worked at Planned Parenthood, and if she got pregnant she could have a free abortion. So, of course, she got pregnant during the first month we were together. We weren't too worried about it and said we would get an abortion after the first month of pregnancy. But by then, we decided to go ahead and have the baby, get married, and raise him together.

I made that decision cavalierly. *What the hell?* I thought. *I love Joanie and I love living here and I love being back home and I love children and I love Joanie's parents, so why not?* Joanie was fine with whatever we came up with as a plan, so we decided to join up and she moved in with me. We got married in Rich and Barbara's house next to their big indoor pool in a kind of Arica wedding where we wrote our own vows and designed our own service. We pledged and toasted and vowed. We were going to be a family in which our little boy could be raised. We all agreed to that.

On April 8, 1975, on Buddha's birthday, Amos Benjamin Richard Gautama Warren Hunuman Lightnin' Bokonen Blanton was born. And even though Joanie and I stopped living together about a year and a half later, we did, in fact, stay together in intention and raised that boy together pretty well. Now he is thirty-six years old and a father himself, and a great one.

It was my third time around for marriage and procreation. I had failed with my first marriage completely and that child was given up for adoption. I still have never found him or found out what happened to him in the world. I felt I'd not done too poorly with my second marriage, which had lasted ten years, or with raising Shanti, who was seven and a half by then and very much willing to help with the raising of her brother (she loved him with such kindness and sweetness that I was often moved to tears by overhearing or watching the two of them together.) *This time,* I thought, *maybe I can get it more right than ever.*

CHAPTER 43

1976 and 1977

When Amos was born Joanie and I took on the job of raising him as consciously as we could, but that first year together with a new baby without much practice was hard on Joanie and me both. I was working already, but trying to build up my private practice and do workshops to generate money for the enterprise was a task at the time. Joanie, who had been very independent and productive, with three jobs she maintained and enjoyed, suddenly became exclusively a mom. She loved being a mom and she took to it as a full-time job so well that I started complaining about her not helping with adjunct things, like taking the car in for maintenance or now and then helping me out with the things I had to do to make a living. We were both tired a lot, but we got through the first several months okay. In the summer of 1976, we went to Greece for a few weeks to try to get a break from the routine at home, but taking a four-month-old on a trip was pretty hard, too.

On Patmos, we stayed in the same house I'd rented before over on a bay a little removed from the main town of Scala where my friend Stephanos had a restaurant. We had some fun there, but got into some big conflicts as well, with me being angry about Joanie's level of attention to Amos when he cried. I've always had trouble with being judgmental about mothers in the first year of their children's lives for being in their minds about what needs to be done to care for the little one rather than just doing what is needed right now. It is a theme. I get frustrated with their frustration at the baby's insatiable demands, which I see as something they often create by delaying in preparing to meet the demands. That's what happened with Joanie.

I remember once, in that little Greek house, that Joanie kind of threw Amos on the bed when she was frustrated with him. It was not hard, but it was scary to him, I thought. So I pushed her hard enough for her to fall down. Then she was crying and he was crying. I walked him around some and then left, and when I came back I was crying. I apologized to Joanie and she said she was sorry, she just got so mad and knew I did, too. We made up. But the anger never got completely settled. I kept getting mad at her for wanting more and more from me to make up for her having less time to herself when I felt like I only had enough time to work and take care of her and the baby already.

I don't think I ever have really understood why Joanie and I split up. I mean, she and I have various theories, but when Amos was less than a year old she moved out and lived nearby. We were monogamous during her pregnancy and the first year of his life. It didn't seem fair to me that I not be, considering that she was tied up with the baby. Besides we were both focused on the baby and getting a lot of joy, as well as fatigue, from raising him. We didn't have much sex. She was nursing and we slept with the baby in our bed. Our trip to Greece was harder than we thought, but it was still fun to go back there and be in the sun, and not be consumed by the usual habits of life, though sometimes such habits are comforting.

Back home in D.C., one day Joanie said she wouldn't drop me off at work or take the car for maintenance even though I had appointments. She said she didn't have time because she wanted to see her mother and sister. She suggested I could just cancel the appointments and take the car to the shop myself. In return I suggested that she could just leave, and I could just take care of everything myself. And we did those suggested things.

We did think of Joanie's departure as a temporary relief. We weren't sure it was a real separation, but knew it could be. It turned out that we liked our new arrangement better than the previous one. She moved into an Arica group house with a number of other students and trainers, including a few others who'd recently separated like her.

When Amos was almost two, we were working out a real separation agreement and helping each other take him to daycare and pick him up, trading out days or evenings of care on occasion so she could work a little bit and I could work. Of course, she needed to be with the baby more than I did in order to nurse him, put him to sleep, and do a lot more of the work of child care that mothers have to do during the first couple of years.

I thought we were working things out fine. There were little problems that emerged now and then, but all in all we were doing okay, and the fellow Aricans living in the group house with Joanie were helping take care of

Amos and us some, too. When I'd go visit Joanie and Amos, or go to take care of Amos over at the group house when Joanie wanted some time to go do something, it just happened that I was introduced to the daughter of Gloria Silverman. Gloria had just split up with her husband. She was a client of mine and a former fellow student in the forty-day Arica training. Her daughter Amy came to visit her now and then.

Amy, who was eighteen, was learning to be a pretty good guitar player, and loved the real music of liberation of the era. She was very pretty and independent, and very attractive to me. She liked my songs and she liked me. One night after Amos was asleep we were playing guitar and singing songs back and forth to each other. One song I sang, which was one of my favorites, was a song by Kris Kristofferson called "To Beat the Devil." It turned out to be her favorite song by her favorite singer, too. It is as relevant to our times as it was then.

> Voice: *It was winter time in Nashville, down on music city row*
> *And I was looking for a place to get myself out of the cold, to warm*
> *The frozen feeling that was eating at my soul, and keep the chilly*
> *Wind off my guitar; my thirsty wanted whiskey, my hungry needed*
> *Beans; but it'd been a month of pay days since I'd heard that eagle*
> *Scream; so with a stomach full of empty and pocket full of dreams*
> *I left my pride and stepped inside a bar (actually I guess you'd*
> *Call it a tavern). Cigarette smoke to the ceiling and sawdust on the*
>   *floor.*
>
> *Friendly shadows. I saw that there was just one old man sitting*
> *At the bar; and in the mirror I could see him checking me with my*
> *Guitar; he turned and said, "Come up here boy and show us what you*
> *Are." I said, "I'm dry," and he bought me a beer. He nodded at my*
> *Guitar and said, "It's a tough life ain't it?" I just looked at him*
> *And he said, "You ain't making any money, are you?" I said, "You've*
> *Been reading my mail." he just smiled and said, "Let me see that*
> *Guitar: I got something you ought to hear." Then he laid*
> *It on me . . .]*
>
> *If you waste your time a-talking to the people who don't listen*
> *To the things that you are saying who do you think's going to hear?*

And if you should die explaining how the things that they complain about
Are things they could be changing, who d'you think's goin' to care?

There were other lonely singers in a world turned deaf and blind who
Were crucified for what they tried to show,
And their voices have been scattered by the swirling winds of time,
'cause the truth remains that no-one wants to know!

Voice: well, the old man was a stranger, but I'd heard his song before;
Back when failure had me locked out on the wrong side of the door; when
No-one stood behind me but my shadow on the floor and lonesome was more
Than a state of mind. you see, the devil haunts a hungry man; if you
Don't want to join him you've got to beat him. I ain't sayin' I beat the
Devil, but I drank his beer for nothing, and then I stole his song!]

And you still can hear me singing to the people who don't listen
To the things that I am saying, praying someone's going to hear;
And I guess I'll die explaining how the things that they complain about
Are things they could be changing, hoping someone's goin' to care.

I was born a lonely singer and I'm bound to die the same
But I've got to feed the hunger in my soul;
And if I never have a nickel I won't ever die of shame
'cause I don't believe that no-one wants to know!

I'd played that song a lot on my trip around the world, and I loved Kris Kristofferson like a brother because of his lyrics and his way of being. Amy loved him, too. And she loved me. And I loved her. We didn't actually say it then, but we both were infatuated.

There was quite a bit of time between that evening and us finally getting together. Her mother suggested Amy have a couple of appointments with me to do polarity therapy for her lower back pain, and for me to teach her self-hypnosis. We did. And what I did helped. She could work again, after she had not been able to work for a while. Then we had some more sessions about Amy's issues with her family, and then we started snuggling, and then kissing, and then humping during therapy.

It wasn't long before I left to go to Patmos to run a workshop there for people from the U.S. I had some sexual adventures with someone I met while I was away and I told Amy about it when I came back. During my absence, she'd gone on a date or two with a friend.

I finally asked Amy, "Why don't we stop messing around and go ahead and move in together?" She said, "Fine." So we did.

Meanwhile, back at the ongoing relationship between me and Joanie. We had decided our separation was going to be for real and for good, and that we were both committed to loving Amos and providing the best for him. We'd also committed to helping each other raise him. When Joanie had moved into the Arica house, we'd already agreed that she would keep the best of our cars, a station wagon, and we had moved the furniture she needed from our house to the shared Arica house. When she subsequently moved into an apartment she rented in a neighborhood closer to where her parents lived and about fifteen minutes away from where I lived, I had helped her move the furniture there. I was paying for child care for Amos at our friend Gail's nursery school near my row house.

Totally out of the blue, one morning in my mailbox at home I received a notice from a lawyer that Joanie was suing me for divorce, full custody of Amos, and an incredible amount of child support. I went immediately up to the daycare, parked my car, and met her when she was coming out after she had dropped off Amos. I said I'd received her God-damned lawyer's notice in the mail and I was taking my car back. All arrangements were canceled! And I asked her, *"What the fuck do you think you're doing?"*

I grabbed the keys from her. She grabbed them back. I jerked them out of her hand, and she fell down in the street. Then I got in the station wagon, drove it off, and hid it a few blocks away, came back, and got my car where I had parked it. I went home and made an appointment with the most well-known bitch lawyer in the District.

Rich Mullens, Joanie's father and my friend, came by to see me a couple of hours later. Joanie had called him and he came straight over from work. I let him in and we talked. He was kind about it, but he said he'd heard I knocked Joanie down in the street. I told him exactly what happened and admitted my responsibility for knocking her down while jerking away the keys. He said he thought we'd probably have to get the police involved for both of our protection or that there would need to be a restraining order. And he said he imagined we'd be able to work things out because all of us loved Amos and each other, really.

I said okay, but that I did not give a shit whether the police, a judge, him, or anyone else got involved. I wasn't going to get screwed by the God-damned court system or anybody using the court system to screw me, and that I would not do any shit demanded that I did not agree with, period, win, lose, or draw, fuck, fight, or run. I also told him that I would beat the shit out of any enforcer whatsoever who tried to screw me, including him, a man I considered to be a friend, whether or not the law was involved.

There I went again. The world was full of Tommy Heveners, people who would try to dominate and control me and who would have to be taught a lesson. I was protecting my son and myself from him again. I was pissed off at the system that ignores real trouble and creates trouble on its own, and so forth.

We agreed that it would be a good idea for whoever the hell got involved or pursued anything further to understand just who in the fuck they were dealing with. Maybe it would save us all some trouble. I told him I thought Joanie knew she could trust me, and that he could trust me, and that I trusted him to work out what was best for Amos, Joanie, and me without either of us pissing away our money on lawyers and both of us ending up getting screwed. I gave him Joanie's car keys to give them back to her and told him where her car was parked. I asked him to tell Joanie that I would be willing to go to mediation with a therapist we both trusted, or with a judge and two lawyers, and see if we could work something out to avoid going to trial over the divorce. She agreed and we ended up doing both counseling and working with lawyers, and we worked out an arrangement that honored what we both wanted. We saw the therapist we both trusted first and worked out the arrangements after discussing our resentments, our appreciations, and doing a lot of crying. After letting go and letting the grieving process happen, we shared a fair amount of laughter. Then at the end, we worked out the details.

While he was growing up, I had shared custody of Amos. I paid Joanie child support that covered all of his care and took care of him for three days and nights a week, as arranged each week by us together, and trading off or making special arrangements if either of us had to work or travel. We cared for each other and were involved in each other's lives to some extent from then on. We both loved Amos and shared what was going on with him and what was going on with us.

Joanie worked doing bookkeeping for her mother's therapy practice, and for a few other therapists, and she eventually went to school again to become a counselor, too. We came to love each other again, mostly from the joy of each other loving Amos, but also due to what we knew of each other and what we'd been through together.

A few years later, after Amy had already moved in with me and we'd been together several years, after Joanie had been through a long spell of celibacy not exactly by choice, and was contemplating going after a guy she was interested in, Joanie asked me if we could have sex again because she wanted to see if she still knew how. So I told Amy and she said fine, and we did. The encounter was okay and we were sweet with each other, but neither of us was much impressed with the fireworks compared to our beginning. But at least, she said, everything still worked.

In those days, I still had a few additional sex partners that Amy knew about, and she did, too, when she went away to St. John's College in New Mexico that year. Joanie got married again a few years later, and Amy and I got married about six years after we started living together. We married when we decided we wanted to have children to make a commitment to raise them together.

Amy loved Amos and became the greatest stepmother anyone could hope for, and Joanie and I both loved her for the way she was with him. At Amos' wedding a few years back, we all congratulated each other on what a fine job we'd done. I suppose everyone does that, true or not, when they celebrate weddings and funerals . . . but in our case it was true.

CHAPTER 44

What I learned in my first 37 years

The Aesthetics of Presence

As human beings, I think we can use our willingness to be here to maximize our enjoyment of life.

I've been around. I've traveled a lot. I've tripped a lot (on acid and the road), and I've learned a lot from my fellow travelers. One thing many of us learned together is this: Most of what you think you have control over is a delusion. But that's okay, because you don't actually need the control you think you need.

The Moral to this Story?

I hate to say it, but maybe there are some morals to this story. I don't mean *moralisms*. These morals I speak of are not *shoulds*. They're just what I think, given where I've been, what I've seen, who I've talked to, and how I've lived. I have reached some conclusions that are important to me and may be of some value to you. These are the premises that determine my promises, which I think I gleaned from growing older.

It doesn't matter most of the time *where* you are in the world. It does matter to some degree *how* you are in the world: How you feel, how you're doing, and how you *be* in the world are important matters. What counts in the best-lived life is the moment-to-moment aesthetic quality of your life, which is significantly affected by your presence to your life and by the deep conversations you have about it with other presences.

The power to have an effect on our own *affect* with regard to whatever experience comes to us is almost the only semblance of control we have in our life. We have some power to influence how our life is by facing *into* rather than *away from* what happens to us, and by looking for the golden center of our experience whether it's tough or wonderful. Fuck hoping for the silver lining, except perhaps as one of many afterthoughts.

This idea of attending to present-tense experience as more important than thinking or controlling or understanding is, I think, one of the most valuable ideas human beings have ever come up with.

Now I am seventy years old and approaching the end of writing the first volume of my autobiography and preparing to approach the end of my life. I've arranged to be frozen immediately after my heart stops beating, with the idea of being brought back to life a few years, after I die this first time, restored in health, and made young again, still being able to remember my first life. I realize the likelihood of that being done successfully is very low, and that reaching completion of this life *in this life* is the task before me now. I very much appreciate the opportunity and look forward to it.

Writing this book itself has been a part of the process of me finishing up my life and being complete with my times. I intend to forgive God in the process of transcending my little story, and I intend to forgive myself and forgive life in the process of transcending my little story. I intend to grow into God and to accept myself as I am. I have resisted self-pity all of my life, but it really hasn't been all that hard for me. Real empathic acceptance could be possible, however, if I let up a little on my self-judgment in the light of dying, I think.

The Pilgrim
by Kris Kristofferson

See him wasted on the sidewalk in his jacket and his jeans,
Wearin' yesterday's misfortunes like a smile—
Once he had a future full of money, love, and dreams,
Which he spent like they was goin' outa style—
And he keeps right on a'changin' for the better or the worse,
Searchin' for a shrine he's never found—
Never knowin' if believin' is a blessin' or a curse,
Or if the goin' up was worth the comin' down—
Chorus: *He's a poet, he's a picker—*

He's a prophet, he's a pusher—
He's a pilgrim and a preacher, and a problem when he's stoned—
He's a walkin' contradiction, partly truth and partly fiction,
Takin' ev'ry wrong direction on his lonely way back home.

He has tasted good and evil in your bedrooms and your bars,
And he's traded in tomorrow for today—
Runnin' from his devils, lord, and reachin' for the stars,
And losin' all he's loved along the way—
But if this world keeps right on turnin' for the better or the worse,
And all he ever gets is older and around—
From the rockin' of the cradle to the rollin' of the hearse,
The goin' up was worth the comin' down—

Chorus: He's a poet, he's a picker—
He's a prophet, he's a pusher—
He's a pilgrim and a preacher, and a problem when he's stoned—
He's a walkin' contradiction, partly truth and partly fiction,
Takin' ev'ry wrong direction on his lonely way back home.
There's a lotta wrong directions on that lonely way back home.

Kris says this song is about his friend Jerry Jeff Walker. It probably is. But I think it is about Kris as well. And I think it is about me, and about a lot of us less known and less heroic.

I have fucked up lots of moments in my life by being critical about how, what, when, and where I or other folks are doing things wrongly. I've also done the opposite and been open to possibility even when things didn't go as they should according to my judgmental mind, and I've had that way of being help me deal with such moments, and the ones that came after them, in a creative way.

Usually the best way to get to a new state of being is to raise hell while you are pissed off in the first state, then get over it, and get on with the creative part.

In other words, when we resist being assholes we remain assholes. When we actually *be* assholes, we can get over it. Honesty about how we are, however we are, when we are, is what allows us to be with, then get beyond all of our states of being.

Moving on is one of the most valuable things you can do, even if you're moving out of bliss into suffering. Attempting to hold on to bliss ruins the hell out of it faster than blissfully engaging its demise.

I have lived a life of great variety and of great privilege, and I've been one of the lucky ones who found out that morality, or honorable behavior toward life, is not the same thing as moralism. Belief in, and the dishonorable obedience to principles of right and wrong that most of us were brainwashed with as children, is a God-damned shame and a sham and a dead-end street. Morality speaks for itself.

You can't hide from the truth because the truth is all there is.

Moralism is a disease, a form of insanity of great hysterical and historical importance: much ado about nothing. Moral rights and wrongs make up a system to be attached to in order to avoid experiences of fear and hatred, and a few other things. Righteousness is a way of disempowering yourself with an illusion that you have power, while you merely manipulate and are manipulated by intense pretense; this is sold to you by wealthy, moralistic people to get you to control yourself enough to leave their asses alone.

To me, aesthetics is the heart of the matter. The whole range of sensate being, and the bodily sense of self, is what counts more than personality or history or class.

My memories of experiences have taught me something. I've experienced the love of parents, sister, and brothers, friends, and former enemies. I've known the bliss of having sex thousands of times with hundreds of partners, and with no partner at all. I've had love with sex, love without sex, sex without love, and more. I also have had the give and take of the love of my own children, the love of all children, the love of adults, and the love of elders, colleagues, and friends.

I've experienced the trials and ecstasies of a great range of altered states of consciousness, triggered by, or learned from meditation, physical stress, yoga, athletic performance, and drugs of many kinds.

In sum, I've experienced a wonderful variety of experiences in the world, from sunsets to Picasso, and I've mixed a lot of experiences together in various recipes for the enjoyment of combined experiences.

I have greatly enjoyed my life and I am grateful for it. I think it is wise and good and appropriate and enlightening and "making a joyful noise unto the Lord" to do all kinds of things usually tabooed by the moralism of righteousness of all the various forms of the "one true way" taught to most of us with our mother's milk.

I have done and continue to do, and recommend to you, a strong development of habits of moralistic contradiction: Have a drink of whiskey and go for a run. Smoke pot and do yoga. Masturbate and meditate. Meditate while stressed, while straight, and while under the influence of anything. Get drunk and fuck and pray.

Eat wonderful cooking, drink good wine and delicious aperitifs, smoke pot, and go for long walks at sunset—sometimes alone, sometimes with others.

Fuck and sleep, fight and fuck, don't fuck and don't fight and stay up all night. Come as quick as you can. Take as long as you possibly can to come. Don't come when you want to. Come without ejaculation. Ejaculate without coming. Come quick the first time, keep lazily teasing until you get hard again, and then fuck for a long time before you come, and get parallel with, and identify with your partner's orgasms. Spend that high bliss time afterward in great peace, or if you get sadness or depression afterwards, be in a rapture of distress and watch the extra joy of your tears turning to joy and deep sleep.

Take acid and have some wine and do yoga and fuck. Fuck yoga and do. Go on a fast and then pig out. Do a meditation retreat, and then eat one dip of everything at Baskin-Robbins. Snort, shoot, sniff, smoke, and eat every drug you can get your hands on, several times, separately and together (with a little bit of caution unless you want to have a death experience instead of just a near-death experience).

Fall in love as often as you can with as many people as you can, and over and over again with the same person as much as you can. Get your heart broken and learn to love it. Face all of your experiences of violated expectations, and don't take anything lying down. Even though you are the source of all your anger and disappointments, let everyone you get angry about, or disappointed in, know about it in no uncertain terms, and then get over it.

Learn how to get out of your mind and into your experience in relationships, and to engage and express yourself and learn how to forgive everyone no matter what. That is the only way to accomplish the relief and bliss and ecstasy of forgiveness. And forgiveness is the only way to live.

Sing and shout. Sing off key. Sing on key. Sing alone. Sing in a chorus. Play music, dance, and note the heightening and deepening of your bodily experience and the joy of sound, and play with gravity. Do all those things in all kinds of drug- and alcohol-induced adjunct states of experiential turn-on.

Talk about these experiences, write about them, and send your descriptions to me and others so we can compile a kind of Wikipedia of altered states of being. As we develop the bliss index of oft-loved experiences, experience combinations, and conversions of states of experience from low to high, we may actually get a grasp on guidelines for the openhearted laugh, love, live, and be happy life.

Abandon all hope and make a joyful noise unto the Lord. There is no right way to live, including this very preachment here. I hope this story of my early life has made you laugh and cry your ass off and fall into love. But do these things as a rule of thumb, an inclination, a guess, a leaning. Don't believe a word of it. This is what this book is about. In joy enjoy. Good luck. More power to you.

Acknowledgments

I have been very lucky and had a wonderful privileged life. So many people were kind to me and cared for me and were willing to share what they had to help me along. They were the people who taught me to love back just as they loved me. All of us need this, but many of us, most of us, didn't get quite enough of it because deprivation and scarcity has, for thousands of years, been a central element of the delusion of civilization we were born into—the Judeo-Christian tradition—a particularly poisonous, long cultural aberration about to be voted "least likely to succeed" and "most likely to assume the lion's share of credit for the demise of humankind."

Those of us who survived our dysfunctional families made it because we were lucky. We needed kind people who paid attention to us. Because of kindness of others and the luck of being hurt and being misfits in the first place, we were able to survive in the moralism-poisoned cultural context of Judeo-Christian twentieth-century America. We maladapted cultural orphans received the sustaining kindness of caring strangers with gratitude and relief, and it is we who are the memetic source of further evolution beyond that culture, if such a thing occurs. We are the only hope for survival of humankind in the new environment born out of bare survivors of civilization's poison.

And yet, from the very sustenance we received from these kind people, we and others have still been poisoned, and continue to poison our fellow passengers and our offspring on this Earth ship. Because the kind people were, by virtue of that very kindness, doing their part in maintaining a poisonous system, their help has also hurt all of us deviant survivors. None of us have survived undamaged. When good people work in poisonous systems and give life-saving help to some individuals, they do their "helpees" damage at the same time, and perpetrate damage to many others, *because they keep the system going.*

The system could not survive without us fucked up fuckups. It is a strange, damned blessing to be a bad copy of a memetic continuation of civilization itself, *the meta-cultural sickness and mental illness that is destroying the habitat within which it lives.* We are a culture of murderers hell bent on destruction for the sake of personal profit—every God-damned one of us—and the sooner most of us die the better for the future of all living beings, including what remains of us.

What this general conclusion means to me personally is that I can see that while I was busy looking for, and lucking out in finding people who were kind to me and acknowledged my abilities and enthusiasms when I very much needed it, they all did me a disservice as well. They made me a success, but at a cost. They taught me to be proud of being promoted from field nigger to house nigger, hid from me the evils of slavery (out of kindness I suppose), and made me proud to advance as a slave. I became civilized.

Thanks a hell of a lot.

These ignorant, kind teachers helped me along the way, doing the best they could in the mental and psychological circumstances of the dark ages of the human mind. This is where corporate economic slavery and antique moralism combined to create the last half of the twentieth century, so far the deadliest and cruelest of all the centuries of human history, and the first part of the twenty-first century, which so far sucks even more.

Many teachers granted me the kindness of their caring attention. Here are the ones who stand out in my memory.

When I was thirteen years old and a freshman in high school, though I was short, a year younger than the rest of my teammates, and slow, I took up basketball with serious dedication. Like many Southern boys, sports at school and the dream of being a baseball and basketball player gave me something to aim for and filled in the gaps for what was missing and what was difficult to bear in life at home. Coach Eli at Churchville High School was, I think, the first substitute for my dead father who noticed me and was kind to me. It didn't take much, as his kindness was encouraging to me.

He somehow seemed to know I was having a tough time at home, though I never told him a thing. He was Jewish and an alien among hillbillies, and I was smart and small, not too good at the game, and an alien among my peers. So we were, at least in my imagination, outsiders, but insiders together. He seemed to get that I was trying as hard as I could and doing the best I could to succeed not only in basketball, but to survive and help my brothers survive in a family that was violent, hurtful, and poisonous. He saw that I was trying to be a success in a school that was gradually teaching me the best of the ignorance and insensitivity and delusional horseshit my culture had to offer. He wasn't particularly kindly in manner, but still, to me, he seemed evenhandedly kind. He was actually businesslike, yet at the same time attentive and encouraging, and did not criticize me. During basketball practice, though I was a mediocre player and definitely only B-team material, he honored me with the quality of his attention. I was so very eager for the encouragement that came from his attention that it helped me survive my childhood.

Like many teachers in my life, Coach Eli was humane in a way that was not outstanding, yet stood out in the context of less humane communities. He stood out from the mind-bound, tradition-bound, anger-bound, moralism-bound, alcoholism-bound, conventional, secretly furious, ass-kissing, judgmental Nazi wannabes who never learned to *think* or *be* on their own. These kind of folk made up the majority of my family, teachers, and fellow students, who posed as good citizens all their lives (just as they were taught), while getting away with as much shit on the side and in secret as they possibly could. In the best tradition of the Judeo-Christian form of moralistic self- and other-poisoning, they lived as hypocrites all their lives. Luckily, I learned this at an early age and have partially escaped doing and being that way—the way of the crippled majority—and I am eternally grateful to be among the crippled deviants instead. So, here's to Coach Eli. (My son Elijah, I just realized, may be named after you. Elijah probably means "descendant of Eli.")

Thanks also to Miss Maude, my first grade teacher, who was kind and loving, and taught me to love going to school.

Thanks to Mr. Miller, my golf coach in College Station Texas in 1955, who was crippled by polio, and no longer able to play golf, but could remember what it took to play so well that we were able to learn the game from him and to value the privilege of playing it as well.

I am grateful to my sister Anno and brother-in-law, Joe Toombs, for letting me live in the barracks known as "married student's housing" at Texas A&M in 1954–5 and for being kind to me when I really needed it.

Thanks to Phil and Marge Philbrook. Phil, the minister in charge of the United Christian Fellowship House at Arlington State College, was kind, just, and a great ping-pong player; he introduced me in 1957 to ideas from great existentialists and to audiotapes of Joe Mathews, who became an important mentor to me a few years later. Marge, his wife, supported him and was kind to me; she kept an eye on both of us.

Up until I met Phil, when I was sixteen years old and starting college, I'd just luckily stumbled across my mentors and helpers, including him. After that, I participated in the luck. I started looking for, and finding people whose compassion, wisdom, and daring showed forth. I went and found them because of their writing and speaking. I acknowledge these individuals.

Thanks to Joseph Wesley Mathews, head of the Christian Faith and Life Community in Austin and the Ecumenical Institute in Chicago, for his brilliance and contactfulness, and for daring to challenge the established church and all established orders.

Thanks to John Silber, Ph.D., chairman of the Philosophy Department at the University of Texas in the early '60s, for acknowledging my writing and my spirit.

Thanks to James Bevel, ally and colleague of Reverend Martin Luther King, Jr., and a leader in the Southern Christian Leadership Conference and the anti-Vietnam War movement, for being honest with me about himself and about our whole movement.

Thanks to Abraham Maslow, the father of humanistic psychology, for one day of conversation about the real economics of life, just a few weeks before he died.

Thanks to Fritz Perls, the founder of Gestalt therapy, for seeking me out and unrelentingly expecting the best from me, and also for being so damned mean to me in order to interrupt my mind.

Thanks to Milton Erikson, a kind and gentle hypnotist, and one of the greatest in the history of therapeutic hypnotism, for being a country boy like me, and for teaching me hypnosis and showing me kindness at the same time.

Thank to Jack Stork, my sister Eleanor's second husband, for being unrelentingly curious, a lifelong learner, and a good friend.

As I list these folks who stand out in my memory, other faces appear in my mind's eye whose names I've forgotten: the woman who was my therapist for a while at the University of Texas at the end of undergraduate school and the start of graduate school; friends who were my peers in college; some of the people I worked for, and with, in all sorts of jobs over the ten years when I was working my way through college; fellow protestors in the civil rights movement and the anti-Vietnam War movement; and hundreds of hippies I met in Haight-Ashbury in San Francisco, on the road back and forth across North America, and on the trail that led onward to temporary communities all over the world.

I would like to thank my father, Howard Blanton, who I know only in my furthest back, early inner being and mind, who loved me when I was small and died when I was five. Many of the people who nurtured me later on were a replacement and substitute for him.

I also am grateful to my mother, Eileen; my sister, Eleanor, "Anno"; my brother James; and my stepbrother, Mike Hevener. They made up the family that first taught me love by example before and after my daddy died, and before my mother fell apart and the family dutifully followed. I did my best to tell our story in this book.

The people I grew up among sustained a culture and economic order that killed and damaged millions of other people, and stole and consumed a fourth of the world's resources, even as it helped me survive. I don't know what I would have done without them. Often their good graces significantly delayed me; they kept me from becoming a true revolutionary and from using my fury at human ignorance to transcend it for moments of enlightenment (or to kill some of the ignorant, God-damned bastards in charge.) Luckily, I had some other teachers, who weren't so nice, whom I shall now acknowledge as well . . .

Thanks to my teachers, sick and poisoned by civilization themselves, who did their best to hurt me. Some hurt me out of malice, unconsciousness, meanness, or ignorance. Some hurt me accidentally. Some hurt me while trying to help. Thanks to all those angry, ignorant people (like my shell-shocked stepfather, George W. Bush, and Dick Cheney) who sought, out of their much-damaged selves, to damage me, my loved ones, and many others both intentionally and by accident. I have been, and still am, sorry that I didn't kill some of you bastards.

I thank you for showing me the way as signposts of darkness. Thanks for warning me and showing me so clearly how not to be. Thanks for infuriating me by your unfairness, injustice, and incredible ignorance and malice aforethought and afterthought. Thanks for your God-damned greed. You stand out in my life and in my memory along with those who loved me, and you kept me from being seduced into the mere normalcy of the sick and poisonous religious and cultural tradition in whose context my spirit would have died without your instruction. You kept me from indulging in the patriotism, putrid sentimentality, and mush-minded, narcissistic, self-congratulatory ignorance of the majority of my pathetic fellow countrymen and countrywomen.

Along with those who cared for me, and with the full cooperation of my God-damned mind—a mine field of bullshit interpretations—we have participated together in the shuck and jive, and bullshit pretentiousness of our time. Like I said, thanks a hell of a lot. (I just spit on the floor.)

So, thanks to all of my teachers who helped and hurt, and to those who hurt and helped. I appreciate all of you. I am but a vessel, filled and emptied with the wisdom and ignorance of my time, and with a late-dawning perspective on how fucked up (and how fucked) we all are. This first life has been instructive, fulfilling, nerve racking, painful, and exciting, and a joy to live, because of all of you. I appreciate the help. I certainly hope I can come up with something better next time, if there is one. I would like a less costly and damaging life than we've been able to have together while we have slaughtered people and other species by the millions to maintain our fix.

My acknowledgments would not be complete without saying thank you to my children, Bruno, Elijah, Carsie, Amos, and Shanti, and their mothers. The most valuable, real, and independent creations of my life have been these children, whom I co-parented. I've been married five times and raised children with four of my wives, women who really did more of the raising of our children than I did.

Now I am recently divorced from, and sometimes living with, though not sleeping with, Maria Teresa Juana Sastre Kjorling. At present, Maria is starting a private practice of psychotherapy in Stockholm and working with various mental health clinics there while devoting effort to mothering our son, Jack Bruno Buddha Nadal Sastre Kjorling Blanton (four years eleven months old, as I write).

My ex-wife Amy and I lived together for twenty-three years. We separated ten years ago. She lives near me, and our son, Elijah Forest Blanton (eighteen, as I write), has stayed with both of us on an alternating basis. She has Elijah much more than I do, and she does more with his home schooling than I do, but we share in his upbringing and we both love him with all of our hearts. He is home schooled and is starting college this fall.

Our daughter, Carsie (Carson Amanda Bradley Blanton, twenty-five as I write) is on her own and becoming a star as a singer/songwriter (visit her website: CarsieBlanton.com). We are proud of her, and I cry a river the entire time she performs every time she performs. I feel grateful to have her in my life and I'm so happy Elijah and Bruno have her for a sister. I'm also glad Maria has her as a stepdaughter.

My son Amos Benjamin Richard Hanuman Warren Gautama Lightnin' Bokonon Blanton (thirty-six, as I write) lives in Boston and is married to Kara, who makes flutes and shares life and music with him. They have a little boy, Lander. Amos is trained as a therapist, and works with computer games and computer-aided instruction for kids at M.I.T. His mother, Joanie, and I lived together only a little over a year, but we stayed in touch with each other and co-parented Amos while he was growing up, living close to each other in Washington, D.C., when he was little. Amos is a kind and loving man who passes it forward in a beautiful attentive way.

My daughter, Shanti, aka Leah Galadriel Shanti Blanton (forty-three, as I write), and her husband, Seth, live in Oakland, California. They have two boys, Liam, born in June 2002, and Zolly Lachlan Corrigan, born in November 2006. Shanti has been a healing influence on me her entire life and has nurtured many other people in our whole human family and will continue to do so for as long as she is here. It seems a miracle to me that in spite of our ineptitude and accidental, pell-mell, stumblebum lives, love triumphs in the end.

My second wife, Judy, and I were together for ten years. I am grateful to her for the way she has been Shanti's mother and grandmother to Shanti's two boys.

My brother Mike (Thomas Michael Hevener, sixty-two, as I write), who was really the first child I helped raise, and the first one to help raise me, lives in Staunton, Virginia. We email and talk on the phone now and then, and visit occasionally. I still love the little boy in him that I first learned to care for and take care of.

My brother James (James Campbell Blanton, sixty-nine, as I write) lives in Northern California with a woman named Gloria Jean. His three sons, Flash, Casey, and Zeke, live near them. I feel like he knows how it was for us and what it was like at home in the story I am telling here better than anyone other than me, and, in many instances, better than me.

Until her death in 2010 at age seventy-eight, Eleanor Ann Blanton Toombs Stork, my sister, lived in Arizona with Jack Stork, my brother-in-law. They had four kids, now all over thirty-five. She always loved me. Jack (seventy-four, as I write) is still very much alive. I miss her and love her memory and though I don't believe we re-unite in the hereafter, if we did, I would dearly love to see her again like she was before she got Alzheimers and died.

This book is a byproduct of my relationships with all the people I have loved and appreciated, friend and enemy, kith and kin, who have guided me through this first life. After I get cryogenically frozen and then thawed out and brought back to life a little later in this century after I die this first time, if we all still exist then, I look forward to spending another lifetime or two. I won't have any excuses then. I won't be able to say, "If I'd 'a known then what I know now . . . ," because I will know then what I know now, and I'll have to discover new mistakes to learn from. I love all of you for the life I've had. I could not have done it without you. Thank you.

Coming up in Volume Two

(To be released at the end of 2012)

From year thirty-seven to year seventy-one is the second life I got after I didn't die at the same age my daddy did, like I expected. I had three more children. I started it off with a union that lasted twenty-two years and bore two children. Then I lived alone and with several other temporary relationships a good while, and then married again and had one more boy. I wrote a lot of books and attended and conducted a lot of workshops and trainings and learned how to use what used to use me a little bit.

I never was as nice as I acted like I was, and never was as rotten as I thought, and that turned out okay after all. There are many more activist and writing adventures and evidence that the world is turning my way, only not fast enough. A well wasted life may be the best we can do—better than a plain old wasted life, huh?

Radical Honesty Resources

www.radicalhonesty.com